JERUSALEM DIVIDED

CASS SERIES: ISRAELI HISTORY, POLITICS AND SOCIETY
Series Editor: Efraim Karsh
ISSN: 1368–4795

This series provides a multidisciplinary examination of all aspects of Israeli history, politics and society, and serves as a means of communication between the various communities interested in Israel: academics, policy-makers, practitioners, journalists and the informed public.

Jacket illustration: Jerusalem: a divided city, 1948–67.
Source: Israel Press Office (photograph); Israel State Archives (map).

Jerusalem Divided

The Armistice Regime
1947–1967

Raphael Israeli

FRANK CASS
LONDON • PORTLAND, OR

First Published in 2002 in Great Britain by
FRANK CASS & CO. LTD.
Crown House, 47 Chase Side, Southgate,
London N14 5BP, England

and in the United States of America by
FRANK CASS
c/o ISBS, 5824 N. E. Hassalo Street
Portland, Oregon, 97213-3644

British Library Cataloguing in Publication Data:

Israeli, Raphael
    Jerusalem divided: the armistice regime, 1947–1967. –
    (Cass series. Israeli history, politics and society)
    1. Armistices 2. Jerusalem – History – Partition, 1948
    3. Jerusalem – Politics and government – 20th century
    I. Title
    956.9'422'052

                    ISBN 07146-5266-0 (cloth)
                    ISBN 0 7146-8241-1 (paper)
                    ISSN 1368-4795

Library of Congress Cataloguing-in-Publication Data:

Israeli, Raphael
    Jerusalem divided: the armistice regime, 1947–1967 / Raphael Israeli.
        p.cm. – (Israeli history, politics, and society)
    Includes bibliographical references (p.) and index.
    ISBN 0-7146-5266-0 (cloth: alk. paper) – ISBN 0-7146-8241-1 (pbk.: alk.
    paper)
        1.Jerusalem–International status. 2. Israel–Arab War,
    1948–1949–Armistices. 3. Arab–Israeli conflict–1948–1967. 4. Israel–Arab
    Border Conflicts, 1949– I. Title. II. Series.
    DS109.93 .I87 2002
    320.95694'42'09045–dc21

Typeset by Frank Cass Publishers
Printed in Great Britain by MPG Books Ltd, Bodmin, Cornwall

To my wife Margalit
The true Lover of Jerusalem

Contents

Preface

The controversy surrounding the status of Jerusalem has been with us since the establishment of the State of Israel, particularly since the city was reunited following the Six Day War of 1967.

Raphael Israeli is among the senior researchers in Israel who have devoted their scholarship to the study of the Arab–Israeli dispute. At the same time, far from enclosing himself within the academic tower, he currently and frequently writes on contemporary affairs and provides insights into matters of national, regional and international interest. Due to his standing and reputation as a researcher, his opinions and analyses are widely heeded by Israeli policy-makers and decision-takers.

In the present book about Jerusalem, Professor Israeli has chosen to focus on the period between the fateful UN Partition Plan of 1947 and the 1967 Six Day War. This account, based on a wealth of documentation and on the personal experience and knowledge of the author, systematically examines the developments and major policies that resulted in a divided Jerusalem during those 20 years.

In pen strokes much more sensitive than the blunt markers which delineated the demarcation lines in the heart of Jerusalem, Professor Israeli depicts, stage after stage, the brutal nature of the reality that was imposed on Jerusalem as a result of its partition. This was a reality of stagnation, hostility and frequent outbursts of violence.

I trust that this book will find its place on the bookshelves of all those interested in Jerusalem: researchers of its past; scholars of politics and diplomacy; and statesmen and diplomats who follow the current peace process and have a stake in bringing the Israeli–Palestinian conflict to a close.

May we all, with the help of this remarkable book, carry Jerusalem to a brighter future.

EHUD OLMERT
Mayor of Jerusalem

Foreword

This book is the product of many years of research in the various Israeli state archives, both civil and military, and in the United Nations (UN) archives in New York and Jerusalem. It also sums up the author's personal involvement as an Israeli member of the Hashemite Kingdom of Jordan–Israel Mixed Armistice Commission (MAC), which ceased to play an active role following the swift and traumatic events of the 1967 Six Day War.

Before that war, and for some 20 years between the UN's November 1947 resolution on the partition of Palestine, and up until the June 1967 reunification of Jerusalem by Israel, the city was divided between Israel and Jordan; its heart was criss-crossed by barbed wire and watched over by the military outposts of both sides. Sometimes it was these troops, both Israeli and Jordanian, who by their very presence, prevented unnecessary friction between the citizens across the armistice line. At other times, soldiers on both sides of the divide initiated flare-ups, intentionally or in an innocent attempt to defend their citizens.

To avert serious bloodshed each time a minor border incident occurred, the parties relied on their MAC, based in no man's land near the famous and awe-inspiring Mandelbaum Gate, right in the middle of the dividing line. The Commission was established within the framework of an Armistice Agreement signed under UN auspices in Rhodes in 1949 at the end of a war which, for the State of Israel marked her independence, and, for the Palestinian Arabs came to be known as *al Nakba*, 'the disaster'. The MAC comprised two members from each side: a senior delegate (usually a civilian) assisted by an officer of the armed forces, with a UN Military Observer (UNMO), acceptable to both parties, as Chairman. In the nature of things, the chairman determined the course of the commission whenever the parties were not of one mind – which was more than usual.

The Armistice Regime, which had a considerable effect on life in Jerusalem for two decades, is the topic of this book. Two other cities, in other countries, were split in two concurrently with Jerusalem –

Belfast and Berlin. After Jerusalem was reunited, two more cities were split in two – Nicosia and Beirut. Often enough the same terminology was used in all four situations: no man's land, demilitarized zone, green line, UN Observers, etc. Yet the case of Jerusalem remains *sui generis*. Jerusalem attracted the attention of the world not only when it was divided, as this book will show, but perhaps even more so after its reunification by Israel in 1967. Current diplomatic wheeling and dealing concerning Jerusalem is only the most recent controversial situation as regards this sacred and universally coveted city which remains the focus of interest and intrigue for governments, churches, the UN, Jews, Arabs, Muslims, Christians, scholars, tourists, dreamers, diplomats, journalists, clerics, mystics and adventurers.

As this book is being written, there are uncertainties about the viability of the Oslo Accords between Israel and the Palestinians, according to which the question of Jerusalem is to be considered during the final phase of their implementation. Already, many interested parties have voiced their favorite solutions: the Palestinians want East Jerusalem under their sovereignty as their capital, while Israel wishes to maintain a united Jerusalem under its rule. Some Muslim groups would like to have direct control over specific locations, while others hark back to the option of internationalization that was endorsed by the UN but never implemented. It is for those who want Jerusalem redivided that this book might be useful, for it will define the pitfalls involved, based on the experience of the city's 20-year partition between 1947 and 1967.

I am immensely indebted to the many individuals and institutions which helped me to complete this research. First and foremost, to my home base at the Truman Institute for the Advancement of Peace at the Hebrew University in Jerusalem which helped finance my tireless, intelligent and creative assistants, Uri Beitan and then Leiah Elbaum, and provided the library and office facilities for our work. I also owe much to the staff of the Israel State Archives, the Zionist Archives, the Foreign Ministry Archives and the UN Truce Supervision Organization (UNTSO) Archives – all in Jerusalem – for giving me access to essential records; to the Israeli Defence Forces Archives in Ramat Gan for allowing me and my assistants to photocopy documents and maps; and to the Jerusalem Archives and the Turdjman House Archives, for permitting my team to sift through their files and glean from them many valuable findings.

But there is one person without whose help this whole enterprise would not have come to fruition. His firsthand knowledge of the relevant armistice questions, his thoroughness and balanced judgement, his incisive remarks, his advice and friendship, and especially his encouragement in all stages of the research and writing, were vitally helpful. Indeed, his imprint is felt in all the chapters of this book, and I cannot thank him enough for his contribution to this work. He is Moshe Erell, Head of the Armistice Division at the Israeli Foreign Ministry, and my mentor and supervisor as I took my first steps at the Armistice Commission in Jerusalem in the 1960s. Since then I have had the good fortune of remaining in close contact with him through the years, while he has served as the Ambassador for Israel in Nepal, Brazil, Australia and Sweden. I have had the privilege of discussing with him my plans for this book from the start, and was pleased to receive his wholehearted support, moral and practical.

I express my sincere gratitude to all these friends. But the responsibility for any errors of fact and interpretation in this work rest on my shoulders alone.

RAPHAEL ISRAELI
Paris, August 1998

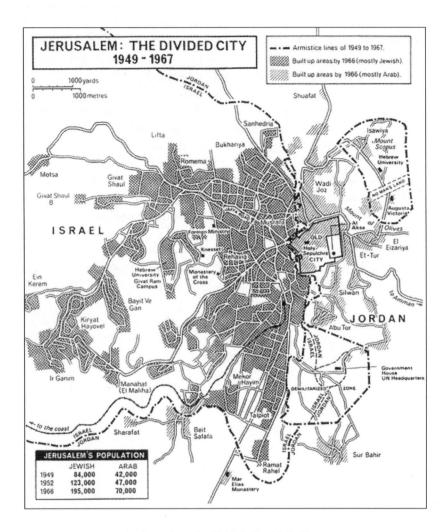

JERUSALEM: THE DIVIDED CITY 1949 - 1967

— · — Armistice lines of 1949 to 1967.

Built up areas by 1966 (mostly Jewish).

Built up areas by 1966 (mostly Arab).

JERUSALEM'S POPULATION		
	JEWISH	ARAB
1949	84,000	42,000
1952	123,000	47,000
1966	195,000	70,000

Jerusalem: the divided city, 1949–67
[courtesy of the Israel State Archives].

Introduction: Everyday Life in Divided Jerusalem

The armistice line in Jerusalem was not only an issue for local politicians and the military; it affected many aspects of everyday life in the city. The dividing line had been drawn on a map with a thick pen which blurred the exact boundary between the Israeli and Jordanian side. Some houses were cut in half by the line, and sometimes entire houses or streets were blotted out by it. Border residents had to reconcile themselves to all kinds of inconveniences. Some could not go out to their balconies, which were located in no man's land, or their children were unable to play in their yards because suddenly the armistice line had come between their homes and their yards.

Due to the danger of sniping and border incidents, slums developed along and close to the armistice line. What today is prime real estate overlooking the Old City was at that time taken over by dim apartments, with few windows in those walls facing the Jordanian-held Old City. These run-down areas – such as those in the Katamonim, Talpiot, Abu Tor and Musrara neighborhoods – included, or sometimes consisted exclusively of, *ma'abarot* (singular *ma'abara*) or transit camps for new immigrants, and were populated mostly by new immigrants from North Africa and the Middle East. The *ma'abarot* were infamous for their poor sanitation and neglect, resulting in part from the incompetence of the local authorities, but also from their sensitive border locations, especially as there was often disagreement or confusion as to whether certain buildings were in Israeli territory or in no man's land.[1] It was only with an official recognition and registration of civilian occupation of abandoned houses in no man's land that the municipal authorities were officially allowed to provide services to these areas.[2] In 1966, Jerusalem mayor Teddy Kollek called on the Israeli government to grant Jerusalem's *ma'abarot* development town status, a designation which would have entitled the city to receive aid in dealing with both large numbers of immigrants and its special problems as a frontier city. As Kollek put it himself: 'Each of the capital's immigrant quarters is at least as heavily populated with new immigrants as some of the immigrant towns which have been granted development status, only those [the Jerusalem] quarters are closer to the border and they receive less assistance.'[3]

There were many incidents of sniping in these areas; with areas close to Jordanian positions, such as Musrara and Abu Tor, particularly vulnerable. Sometimes the shootings would be explained by the Jordanian authorities, and at other times stoning or shootings of Israeli civilians living by the border would be put down to 'a crazy Jordanian' on guard duty by the line. Civilians living by the line were in constant danger while performing day-to-day tasks. On 29 June 1950, a group of immigrants standing together by a well in the Musrara quarter were fired on from Jordanian positions on the wall of the Old City. Three men, 17-year-old Avraham Nahmias, 21-year-old Yosef Rumi and 27-year-old Avner Waaknin, were wounded. Nahmias subsequently died of his wounds. The previous day another man had been wounded while drawing water from the same well.[4] In early July 1951, Jordanian soldiers stationed on the walls of the Old City stoned Musrara repeatedly over the course of several days; this culminated in the shooting of a resident of the neighborhood, 25-year-old Avraham Ben Haim, by Jordanian Legionnaires, allegedly after he crossed into no man's land. Ben Haim subsequently died of his wounds, and after Israel lodged a complaint at the MAC meeting senior Jordanian officials apologized for the fatal shooting. A week later, three men were shot and wounded inside a house in the Musrara neighborhood.[5] These shootings were later put down to confusion over whether the house was officially occupied and in Israeli territory or an abandoned house in no man's land. In a previous MAC meeting it had been agreed to recognize the occupation of houses in no man's land, and after the incident it was agreed at a subsequent MAC meeting to mark the 70 houses in no man's land which had been occupied by Israelis or Jordanians, and so reduce the risk of similar incidents.[6] While the fact that most residents remained in these border neighborhoods was frequently attributed to 'the Jerusalemite spirit', many of the poor immigrant residents had little choice. As one young woman from Musrara put it to

General Uzi Narkiss, Officer in Command (OC) Central Command: 'What can we do? We've nowhere else to go.'[7]

Perhaps the most serious sniping incident in the armistice period occurred on 31 May 1965, when Jordanian Legionnaires opened fire on civilians in Israeli Jerusalem from two different positions atop the walls of the Old City.[8] Gunfire from a sandbagged position near the Jaffa Gate injured two French volunteers working with the Sisters of Charity – 19-year-old Caroline Delassus, and 62-year-old Georgette Buhr – who were hit while standing on the roof of the St Vincent de Paul Convent. Meanwhile, in a nearby building, an Israeli woman was wounded by a Jordanian bullet while closing the window of her apartment. Shots fired from another Jordanian position killed 14-year-old schoolgirl Yaffa Binyamin, the eldest child of a large Iranian immigrant family, and wounded 35-year-old housewife Allegria Ben Arouche, both of whom had rushed out to Arouche's balcony upon hearing shots. Nearby, a Christian Arab carpenter, 29-year-old Geries Assous from Galilee, was killed by Jordanian fire while working at the Notre Dame Convent which straddled the border. The deadly accuracy of the Jordanian gunfire was attributed to the short range; the two French women, for example, were shot from a distance of only 80–100 m. The incident shocked residents of the border areas who had been enjoying a relatively calm period. Police were sent to border neighborhoods to calm frightened residents, some of whom had begun to evacuate their apartments in panic. Shortly thereafter Musrara residents gathered around the seven-storey apartment building where the Binyamin family lived; one angry tenant asked a newspaper reporter: 'Will you join me and cross into Jordan and let them have it?'

Bet Tannous, a large apartment building facing the Jaffa Gate of the Old City, was also on the edge of the Israeli side of the border and well within range of Legionnaire snipers manning Jordanian positions on the walls of the Old City. Residents became used to regular shootings. Shutters on windows facing the Jordanian lines were generally kept closed for fear of attacks by snipers. On the Israeli side, the thick line of the armistice border marker pen passed over Bet Tannous's backyard, creating tension over whether the yard was technically no man's land or Israeli territory. Each time a resident went into the yard, or the municipality came to collect the rubbish, or the gas company came to change the gas cylinders, the Jordanians would lodge a complaint to the MAC that Israel had breached the Armistice Agreement by trying to annex no man's land and expand Israeli territory.[9]

The most problematic area along the dividing line was perhaps Abu Tor, where the border split the neighborhood into Arab and Jewish halves, with sometimes only a narrow street or a yard separating the Jordanian side from the Israeli.[10] Relations between the neighbors were good, with housewives chatting over the fences and yards that marked the border. Despite the hostilities, many women in the area still traded recipes or, if they ran out of bread or flour, could rely on their neighbors across the border to lend them some.[11] Friendships were formed between neighbors on either side of the line, who could swap gossip over the fence, but who could never visit one another's houses due to the line which separated them. However, border tensions could flare up in seconds and the residents were well aware that at any moment a sniper might open fire and send them scurrying for cover.

Construction or renovation work on buildings near the line was also a sensitive issue. The Jordanians vehemently opposed any Israeli construction near the line, fearing that the Israelis would use any opportunity to push their border into Jordanian territory or no man's land. On 6 February 1950 24-year-old Yosef Friedman was shot while working on a building in Abu Tor.[12] General Uzi Narkiss recounts the story of one poor immigrant family in Abu Tor whose house was quite literally on the line. The house did not have indoor plumbing, and the outdoor lavatory was even closer to the line than the house itself, putting the lives of the family in danger when they went to the outhouse. Eventually in early 1966 the residents decided that they needed to build a new lavatory directly adjacent to their home, as trips to the outhouse had become too dangerous. The Israeli authorities would only give them a conditional building permit, fearing that the Jordanians might object and force the demolition of the new outhouse. Once construction work began, the Israeli army set up a command post nearby to prepare for a possible incident. The Israeli Army Chief of Staff (COS) kept in contact with the Prime Minister and Defense Minister, and units were placed on the alert. Jordan was quick to file a complaint with the MAC, charging illegal construction in no man's land. Israel insisted the structure was in Israeli territory. The MAC held four meetings on the subject for a total of 18 hours, eventually deciding to condemn Israel. The lavatory, however, remained in place.[13]

Proximity to the line was especially problematic for families with children. There were many cases of children accidentally crossing the line while playing near their homes, chasing a ball that landed on the other side or just straying too far. When children went missing and neither their parents nor the Israeli police could find them, the next step was to check with the Jordanians. In one incident, seven-year-old Sasson Sig from the Makor Barukh neighborhood and his friend Shlomo Givol, aged nine from Katamon, were playing together one Saturday and went missing. Their parents and the Israeli police searched for the missing boys, and eventually turned to the Jordanians for help. It turned out that the two boys had accidentally crossed over into Jordan. They were arrested upon arriving in Jordanian territory and were being held by the Jordanian police. Later it came to light that a third boy, 13-year-old Hanan Dayan of Katamon, was also being held in Jordan after he too accidentally crossed the border. His parents had waited until after the Sabbath was over to inform the police of his disappearance. All three boys were returned to Israel on Sunday.[14]

Toddlers were also regular accidental visitors to Jordan. In one case in 1954 two-and-a-half-year-old Baruch Heik wandered across the line near the Makor Haim *ma'abara*. He was found by a Jordanian policeman from Bethlehem who took him home to his wife and children, bought new clothes and shoes for the shabby dressed *ma'abara* toddler, and cared for the Israeli infant for two days until his return was negotiated through the MAC. Heik was handed back to the Israelis with great ceremony in the presence of senior officials from the UN, the Jordanian Legion, the Israeli police, and dozens of *ma'abara* residents.[15]

Also along the line were the neighborhoods of Me'a Shearim and Bet Yisrael, populated mostly by the strictly traditional ultra-orthodox Jews, many of whom were from the Old Yishuv, Jews who lived in Palestine prior to the rise of political Zionism. These ultra-orthodox Jews, who were to a large extent either non-Zionist – or in the case of sects such as the Netorei Karta, even anti-Zionist – had found their neighborhoods caught in the middle of the fighting during the battle for Jerusalem and so were forced to take up arms and participate in a struggle in which they had wished to remain neutral.[16] With the partition of Jerusalem these neighborhoods remained on the front line, and their residents were the first to suffer whenever there was tension along the armistice line.

The division of the city was especially traumatic for Jerusalem's religious inhabitants, who were separated from many of

Jerusalem's ancient holy sites. For centuries the religious Jews of Jerusalem had prayed at the Western Wall, part of the outer remaining wall surrounding the Temple Mount and the last remnant of the ancient Jewish temple which was destroyed by the Romans in AD 70. Though the Armistice Agreement provided for Jewish access to the Western Wall, Jordan consistently refused to abide by this clause.[17] Jews had no choice but to worship from afar.

According to Jewish sources the temple was destroyed on the ninth day of the Jewish month of Av, commemorated by Jews as a day of fasting and mourning. In memory of the destruction, Jerusalem's Jewish residents had developed a tradition of walking around the walls of Jerusalem's Old City on the ninth of Av, after which they flocked to pray at the Western Wall, to recite lamentations and to pray for redemption. With the partition of Jerusalem this was no longer possible. Instead, Mount Zion, the closest part of Israeli Jerusalem to the Old City and a vantage point towards the Western Wall, became the focus of the ninth of Av mourning rituals.[18] For many religious Jews the ninth of Av took on new significance, as the mourning over the destroyed temple was compounded by their banishment from even the Western Wall. Some saw this as a sign of divine displeasure requiring repentance.

Mount Zion also became a substitute pilgrimage site for the priestly blessing ceremony traditionally held next to the Western Wall on the Passover festival. Despite the tension inherent in such a large gathering close to the border with Jordan, thousands of Jews made the pilgrimage to Mount Zion to be blessed from atop the mount. From the parapet above King David's tomb on Mount Zion they were able to look over into the Old City, the closest they could come to praying at the Western Wall itself.[19] The substitution of Mount Zion for the Western Wall in these rituals reminded Jews of their enforced separation from their holiest sites, while also keeping alive traditions associated with the Old City and the Western Wall. It was especially poignant for the thousands of new immigrants, many of whom had chosen to live in Jerusalem for religious reasons and expected to be able to live close to Judaism's holiest sites. However, when they arrived during the 1950s and 1960s they discovered that the Western Wall and the Temple Mount were beyond reach.

In some respects Mount Zion acquired its own character as a site of worship beyond its role as a substitute for the Western Wall.[20] Pentecost (The Feast Of Weeks) is traditionally believed to mark both the biblical King David's birthday and the anniversary of his death. Thousands of pilgrims made their way from all over Israel to Mount Zion, the location of King David's tomb.[21] The festival was inaugurated with the lighting of 300 candles on Mount Zion, two for every chapter of the book of Psalms, traditionally ascribed to King David.[22] The Mount Zion Committee which organized Pentecost activities also gave out flowers grown on Mount Zion to the wardens of synagogues across the country as decorations for the festival. In this way Israeli Jews made maximum use of the limited piece of sacred Jerusalem in their hands.

Partition and the complexities of the armistice also affected tourism to Jerusalem as the armistice line also divided many of the city's Christian holy sites in addition to the above-mentioned Jewish sites. For example, the Church of the Holy Sepulchre was in the Jordanian-held Old City, while Mount Zion, location of the Dormition Abbey and the traditional site of the Last Supper, was in the Israeli zone. Tourists wanting to visit holy sites on both sides of the line had the hassle of going through both Jordanian and Israeli bureaucracy and border guards. In the introduction to its chapter on the Old City, a 1960 guide book to Israel notes:

> To enter the Old City you need a permit from the Israeli District Commissioner of Jerusalem who gives it in accordance with the instructions of your consul. Each permit has to be acknowledged by the Jordan authorities, who have never accorded it to anyone of the Jewish faith. The way to the Old City is through the Mandelbaum Gate.[23]

Despite the city's image as a war zone tourists continued to visit. Many were shocked at the warnings they were given by their Israeli hosts about straying too close to the border. A British summer student at the Ulpan Akiva Hebrew school in 1960, recounted how upon arrival the students were taken on a tour of the city and strictly warned not to take photos, or even take out their cameras anywhere near the border, in case a Jordanian soldier mistook the move for a hostile act and opened fire. The students were also told not to make any sudden moves or to stray too far from the group, for fear of causing a diplomatic incident.

The partition of the city also created a peculiar type of border tourism on the Israeli side. Travel articles in the Israeli press suggested walking tours around Israeli Jerusalem's western areas, but as the sightseeing trail drew closer to the line the writer would recommend which roofs and towers to climb on to for the best peek into Jordanian-controlled Jerusalem, in particular the Old City. For example, a 1965 sightseeing article advised visitors that the roof of the 'Notre Dame Convent provides a wonderful view of the Old City'; while 'from the Hebrew Union College' one might have 'a beautiful view of the Old City's Jaffa Gate and David's Tower'. It also urged walkers to 'stop at the Abu Tor observation point to look out over the Old City and the Mount of Olives. See Jordanian sentries stationed only metres away.'[24]

Even getting to and from Jerusalem could be dangerous as the routes also passed close to the border in many places. In January 1966 a 15-year-old girl from the town of Ramla was injured when a Jordanian soldier opened fire on a Jerusalem–Lydda (Lod) train. The Jordanians claimed that the soldier involved had been going through a mental breakdown and as a result the chairman of the MAC decided not to pass a resolution condemning the shooting, though the MAC did concede that it was a violation of the Armistice Agreement and that it viewed the incident with 'grave concern.'[25]

Despite the tensions in the border areas, life continued pretty much as usual in the rest of the city. Not far from the border, shops and cafés did good business on Jaffa Road, Ben Yehuda Street and King George Street in the city center. People went to work, politically active students demonstrated from time to time and new neighborhoods developed in the city's western suburbs, such as Givat Shaul. Yet, even so, people were reminded of Jerusalem's divided status. Jerusalem's flagship Hadassah Hospital and the Hebrew University's campus were isolated in the Mount Scopus enclave surrounded by Jordanian territory, accessible only by the fortnightly convoys authorized by the Armistice Agreement. Eventually a new Hadassah Hospital opened in the abandoned Arab village of Ein Kerem on the outskirts of western Jerusalem, while the university founded a substitute campus in Givat Ram on the other side of town.[26]

Independence Day military parades in the Israeli part of the city had to be coordinated with the MAC in case the Jordanians mistook the parade for a military build-up contrary to the armistice rules. Even decorating the Hadassah Hospital in the Mount Scopus enclave with an illuminated Star of David for Israel Independence Day was problematic, with the Jordanians complaining every year to the MAC that it violated the armistice.[27] For many Israelis, though, Independence Day celebrations in the capital were an important display of national pride, precisely because they signaled to the Jordanians on the other side that Israel was there to stay. As one newspaper report noted of the firework displays: 'Overheard often was the remark "Bet they can see them in Jordan".'[28]

One of the more minor inconveniences concerned international mail which ended up in the wrong Jerusalem. In 1959 Yitzhak Katz from London, UK, was a student at the Merkaz Harav Yeshiva (a religious seminary) in central Jerusalem whose students were housed in Bayit Vegan, a suburb of Jerusalem. A letter from his family in London accidentally arrived in Jordanian Jerusalem. The Jordanians sent it back to the UK stamped 'unknown address', whereupon it was sent back to Jerusalem, this time arriving on the right side of the line, complete with British, Jordanian and Israeli postmarks.[29]

So, while life in Jerusalem was tense in those days, it was also very colorful, interesting, full of surprises: the unexpected often happened, the expected was mostly overtaken by events beyond one's control. The coming pages will attempt to describe, step-by-step, how this situation came about, how the powers-that-be governed the impossibility of a divided city, and how the war of 1967 would undo all that.

NOTES

1. *Jerusalem Post*, 17 December (1954).
2. Ibid., 11 July (1951).
3. Ibid., 16 February (1966).
4. Ibid., 29 June (1950).
5. Ibid., 8 July (1951).
6. Ibid., 11 July (1951).
7. Uzi Narkiss, *The Liberation of Jerusalem* (London: Vallentine Mitchell, 1983), p. 36.
8. *Jerusalem Post*, 1 June, 2 June and 29 June (1965).
9. Narkiss, *Liberation of Jerusalem*, pp. 35–6.
10. *Jerusalem Post*, 11 July (1951).
11. Narkiss, *Liberation of Jerusalem*, p. 32.
12. *Jerusalem Post*, 6 February 1950.
13. Narkiss, *Liberation of Jerusalem*, pp. 30–4.
14. *Ha'aretz*, 15 January (1961).
15. *Jerusalem Post*, 1 June (1954).
16. Ibid., August 1948.
17. *Ha'aretz*, 10 January (1961).
18. *Jerusalem Post*, 10 August (1951).
19. Ibid., 24 April (1951).
20. Narkiss, *Liberation of Jerusalem*, p. 34.
21. *Jerusalem Post*, 4 June (1965).

22. Ibid., 3 June (1965).
23. Zev Vilnay, *Israel Guide* (Jerusalem: Central Press, 1960), p. 139.
24. 'A Walk Around Jerusalem', *Jerusalem Post Independence Day Supplement*, May (1965).
25. *Jerusalem Post*, 2 January (1966).
26. *Ha'aretz*, January (1961).
27. *Jerusalem Post*, 7 May (1965).
28. Ibid.
29. Yitzak Katz, student at Merkaz Harav religious seminary during the late 1950s. Interviewed on 5 January 1999.

1. The Armistice Between Israel and Jordan

A full understanding of the Armistice Regime and its long-term effects on Israeli–Jordan relations is not possible without a look at a brief history of Jordan and its role in the first Arab–Israeli war (1948–49) and related events in later years. Prior to 1918, the modern states of Syria, Lebanon, Jordan, Israel and the autonomous Palestinian Authority did not exist. The entire region, then part of the Ottoman Empire, was divided into administrative districts and sub-districts which bore no resemblance to present-day political frontiers. All existing frontiers and borders have been created since the dismemberment of the Ottoman Empire in the wake of the First World War. Initially, present-day Israel, Jordan, and the areas controlled by the Palestinian Authority, made up a single territorial unit named Palestine, administered by Great Britain under a League of Nations mandate. The task of the Mandatory Power was to facilitate the establishment in Palestine of a '"national home" for the Jewish people', as outlined in the 1917 Balfour Declaration.

In 1922, for reasons not directly relevant to this study, today's Jordan was separated from the mandated territory of Palestine and became the Emirate of Transjordan, ruled by the Hashemite family which had been exiled from Arabia on the creation of Saudi Arabia by the Al-Saud family. Subsequently the Emirate's status was raised to that of a kingdom and Transjordan became the 'Hashemite Kingdom of Jordan'. Throughout that period it maintained a regular army known as 'The Arab Legion', trained and, to a great extent officered, by British Army professionals. Until the mid-1950s it was commanded by a British general, Sir John Glubb.[1] At various times before the establishment of the State of Israel, units of this army were stationed west of the Jordan river, inside what remained of the original mandated territory of Palestine.

In practical terms, the story of the armistice between Israel and Jordan must begin with the 29 November 1947 UN Resolution No. 181, recommending the partition of Western Palestine between the two communities which, by then, had been contending for it for half a century: that is, the Jews, represented by the Jewish Agency for Palestine, and the Palestinian Arabs, represented by the Arab High Committee. Jerusalem was to be accorded a special international status (*corpus separatum*). The Jewish leadership promptly accepted the UN's recommendation as a major breakthrough that would allow the Jews to achieve independence and to absorb the remnants of the Jewish communities destroyed during the Holocaust. However, the Arab states, as well as the Arab High Committee in Palestine, rejected the resolution out of hand as a major blow to Palestinian nationalism. Palestinian nationalist leaders saw the Arab majority in Palestine as a crucial factor in frustrating Zionist plans and in creating an Arab state in Palestine west of the Jordan river.

The Arabs were appalled by the UN resolution. One of their representatives at the UN responded to the result of the vote, when announced by the President of the Assembly, by shouting 'the Charter of the UN is dead!' Arab words were followed by acts, and violence erupted throughout Palestine, beginning with roadside ambushes of Jewish vehicles and attacks on exposed Jewish communities launched by armed bands bolstered by volunteers and supplies from neighboring Arab countries. The small but well-organized and highly motivated Jewish community responded in kind.

With the withdrawal of all British forces and officials from Mandatory Palestine on 15 May 1948, and the concomitant expiration of Britain's mandate, the Jewish leadership proclaimed the establishment of Israel as an independent state headed by a provisional government. The parallel Arab move was to invade the fledgling state. At that stage no external force could stop the fighting. The three Jewish underground organizations fighting guerrilla-style to defend Jewish positions became the Israeli Defence Forces, the regular army of the new-born Jewish State. Local Arab armed bands were now openly backed by the invading regular armies from adjoining Arab countries, including Jordan's Arab Legion. The Arab Legion was to play a vital role both in fighting and, later, in the armistice arrangements on the entire West Bank in general, and in the Jerusalem area in particular.

The UN resolution to partition Palestine had envisaged the immediate dispatch to the area of an Implementation Commission, to set in motion the practical arrangements, including the organization of armed forces designed to ensure an orderly and peaceful transformation of the country into the two-state structure proposed for it. However, the UK announced that the Implementation Commission would not be allowed in before the termination of the Mandate on 15 May 1948; this created a power vacuum in which the Arab Legion was the only regular armed force on the scene. The Legion's British commander, General Glubb, described the delicate position of the Arab army under his command thus:

> The Arab Legion in Palestine was operating as an allied army with the British Army. The arrangement was a relic from the war, when other allied armies, Free French and Poles, for example, were also present. Since the end of the war, nobody had been so rash as to attempt any definition of what the role of the Arab Legion had become. They remained in Palestine provisionally. The British Army, however, never called upon the Arab Legion to take part in active operations, whether against Jews or Arabs. They were still guarding those accumulations of war material which had grown during the war, when Palestine was one of the main Allied supply routes to Russia.[2]

In reality, however, the Arab Legion did occasionally intervene on the Arab side, as in the incident of the Iraqi Consulate in Jerusalem reported by Glubb himself: in April 1948, Jewish forces attacked the mostly Arab neighborhood of Katamon – where the Iraqi consulate was located – and the Iraqis appealed to the government of Transjordan which promptly ordered Glubb to guard the building.[3] The presence of the Arab Legion in Palestine naturally put Transjordan in an advantageous position *vis-à-vis* the rest of the Arab world, as the Arab League began mapping a course of action proceeding from its rejection of the Partition Plan. On 7 October 1947, the Arab League declared that the Arab states would be 'taking military steps along Palestine's borders.' It also formed a military committee to coordinate further military action. It was only in April 1948, however, following Transjordan's lead, that the official Arab League decision to invade Palestine was taken. On 13 May 1948, two days before the Mandate expired and a Jewish state was declared in Palestine, the Arab League proclaimed Abdallah ibn Hussein, as the King of Transjordan, Commander in Chief of the Arab armies poised to invade Palestine.

This was not an empty gesture, for it recognized the primacy of Transjordan regarding Arab concerns in Palestine, while at the same time diverting attention from the conflicting interests and disagreements over strategy which divided the Arab camp. Transjordan's Arab partners were all agreed that a concerted attack on the main Jewish populated areas was the best way to cripple the nascent Jewish state. King Abdallah gave priority to securing those areas of Jerusalem and the highlands bordering on Transjordan which were populated by Arabs, with a view to annexing these territories to his kingdom. He intended to leave his Arab allies to pin down the main Jewish forces in the coastal plain, the Jezreel Valley and the Western Negev, while he concentrated on the strategic high ground bordering Transjordan.[4]

Several different explanations have been advanced for this divergence of views between Transjordan and the other Arab states. While they are not central to the subject of this book, a brief mention of the principal points is relevant. To begin with, there was the obvious need for Transjordan to take British advice into account, given the vital umbilical connection between the Arab Legion and Britain. King Abdallah also had powerful Arab rivals in Palestine who were likely to oppose Jordanian control of Palestinian territory west of the Jordan, in particular Jerusalem which, with its holy shrines, was highly coveted by Muslims for religious reasons and as the region's main urban center. Others have argued that committing the Arab Legion, which consisted of only three brigades, further afield would have left Transjordan without loyal troops, thus possibly jeopardizing the stability of the kingdom and the security of the entire Hashemite House. Much emphasis has also been put on the presumed long-range calculation of the king that Transjordan's long-term interests lay in peaceful co-existence with a prosperous autonomous Jewish entity in areas of Palestine, under his aegis. Abdallah held serious talks along these lines with high-ranking Jewish representatives, right up to the eve of the Arab invasion of the nascent Jewish state.

Britain's refusal to cooperate in the implementation of the

Partition Plan, and its toleration, to say the least, of the Arab Legion's presence in Palestine, coupled with its woefully unequal closure of the country to fighting men and weapons from the outside, placed the mandatory power fairly squarely on the Arab side. However, Britain obviously could not risk the odium which would be caused by her officers taking part in the destruction of the Jewish community in Palestine, should that happen after the expiration of the Mandate. In contrast, an autonomous Jewish commonwealth under the Transjordan Crown could be squared with the notion of the National Home that Britain had undertaken to cultivate under the terms of the Mandate, more easily than the bloody burial of the independent Jewish state that had been recommended by the General Assembly of the UN. In fact, the needs of propriety went so far as to require of Transjordan that the Arab Legion should evacuate Western Palestine prior to the termination of the Mandate, before it recommenced the invasion the following day.[5]

Jewish interest in keeping Transjordan partly or wholly out of the impending war could not be more obvious in view of the overwhelming superiority of the Arab camp. But foregoing full independence was out of the question, and King Abdallah's proposal for Jewish autonomy under his sovereignty was rejected emphatically by Golda Meyerson (later Golda Meir), who represented the Jewish Agency provisional government in a secret meeting with the King on 11 May 1948 at his Shuneh Palace, where she arrived in disguise. She told him that if it came to war, the Jews would fight with all their might and that whatever territory was taken would be kept.[6] The last point referred to a previous understanding, or agreement, never made public in writing – and possibly never put on paper – whereby Israel and Transjordan would abide peacefully by the Partition Plan. Apparently that agreement was no longer seen as valid by the King, as staying out of the war which had become an impending reality was not possible for Transjordan. Indeed, the deployment of Iraqi and Egyptian units to Transjordan sectors of the fighting reflected the importance attached by Transjordan's allies to the collective nature of their war against the Zionists. However, in talks between the Jordanian Prime Minister, Tawfiq abu-al-Huda, and the British Foreign Secretary, Ernest Bevin, on 7 February 1948, it was made clear that the Arab Legion would not transgress the Partition Lines 'unless the Jews invaded Arab areas,' though it would not refrain from lending support to other Arab forces operating in Jewish areas.[7]

A picture emerges of Jordan's war plans as having a rather cautious design intended to draw the maximum benefit at a minimum cost from the judicious employment of the well-trained and well-disciplined Arab Legion while avoiding unnecessary exposure to world criticism. The only high profile and widely noted Jordanian breach of the Partition Lines was the Legion's capture of the Old City of Jerusalem, including the Jewish Quarter whose residents and defenders were soundly defeated by the Legionnaires.[8] The capture of the Old City was the most significant single asset gained by Transjordan in the war. It is tempting to speculate on what the chances would have been of bringing about some form of internationalization in the Jerusalem area along the lines of the original UN Plan, had the city been kept free from all hostilities, thus leaving the door open to an international initiative. But, as we have noted, the Arabs resolutely rejected the UN Partition Plan, leading to a brutal conflict which did not spare the holy city.

Transjordan, alone of all Arab states, had military forces across its frontiers in West Palestine before the Mandate expired and consequently there was no surprise when it entered the official war. The Arab Legion was engaged in fighting as early as December 1947. Generally, though, during that period the Legion preferred to save its strength for only the most crucial of engagements, allowing irregulars to undertake less important missions. Sometimes irregulars were assigned specific roles in operations undertaken by the Legion itself. On a number of occasions, the Legion intervened to defend a position under attack by Jewish forces, or in retaliation for such attacks. In April and May 1948, the Arab Legion was at the forefront of a number of attacks against the Etzion Bloc of Jewish settlements whose strategic location allowed them to fire on the important Jerusalem–Hebron–Beersheba road south of Jerusalem. The isolated location of the Etzion Bloc, as a major Jewish outpost in the midst of a mostly Arab populated region, was important for the defence of Jewish Jerusalem. Hence, the supreme effort by the Jewish command to defend it at all costs, and the equally firm resolve of the Transjordanian government to capture it. The Etzion Bloc was finally overwhelmed on 13 May 1948, with the help of hundreds of irregulars. The Jordanian victory affected future operations in the Jerusalem area and was crucial in weakening the Zionist hold on eastern Jerusalem.

With the official Arab invasion of Palestine, the precise military objectives of Transjordan became clear. The Arab Legion continued to eliminate Jewish positions which threatened its objectives by capturing a similar enclave comprising the Dead Sea Potash Works and the Beit Haarava settlement at the northern tip of the Dead Sea. A third enclave, at the southern tip of the Dead Sea was not deemed threatening by the Legion and so was left unharmed. In the Jerusalem area, in addition to the Jewish Quarter of the Old City, the Arab Legion wiped out two small Jewish outpost settlements to the north of Jerusalem, Atarot and Neve Ya'akov, situated on the road to Ramallah and Nablus, and regained control of the commanding area of Sheikh Jarrah in northeast Jerusalem. To the west, the Arab Legion established itself in the Latrun area, effectively blocking the road leading to Jerusalem from the coastal plain, one of the main centers of Jewish settlement in Palestine. Jewish western Jerusalem, now isolated and cut off from food and water supplies, came under mortar and field artillery bombardments while the Arab Legion made a number of attempts to capture Jewish residential areas. On 11 July 1948, the Egyptian Air Force attacked Jewish areas in Jerusalem, with 100-kg bombs.[9]

In the absence of positive evidence to the contrary it is easy to come to the conclusion that King Abdallah was hoping for the surrender of West Jerusalem under the combined pressure of siege, bombardments and determined assaults by Jordanian infantry and armor. At the very least he saw no harm in trying, trusting his British officers to avoid over-risky entanglements. The Arab Legion was too precious for him, and too lightly armed to engage in a prolonged and open-ended battle against stubborn Jewish resistance in built-up areas. Even so, the Israeli Provisional Government at one point judged the threat serious enough to sanction measures against a feared large-scale flight by the beleaguered residents of the besieged city. Israeli records show a number of persistent, unsuccessful and costly attempts to break the Arab Legion lock on the Tel Aviv–Jerusalem road. Nowhere else did the Arab Legion exert itself with equal energy; it left Samaria, the hilly region north of Jerusalem, to the Iraqi expeditionary force, and it made no attempt to defend Arab towns between Latrun and Tel Aviv. Nor was it prepared, it seemed, to invest inordinate efforts to capture Mount Scopus which overlooks Jerusalem from the east, or Ramat Rachel to the south of the city; these changed hands a number of times during the fighting between Israeli and Egyptian troops in the area. The Arab Legion Command must have believed that if the siege strategy around Jerusalem were to succeed, these and other outlying areas of the city would fall like ripe figs.

The overall impression is of a war conducted by Transjordan with great caution and husbandry, which was aimed not so much at the destruction of the fledgling State of Israel – which appeared to be the passionate goal of the other Arab states – as at the transformation of Transjordan from a backwater desert kingdom into a substantial and influential modern country to be reckoned with in the Arab world. Had the more powerful Arab states been able to destroy Israel, King Abdallah would probably have taken advantage of the victory to secure an outlet to the Mediterranean Sea for his country. Due to its small army, Transjordan could only be of marginal assistance to the Arab forces in their endeavor. The Arab Legion was more useful for making substantial and fairly easy gains closer to home without squandering its forces in doubtful adventures further afield. This calculation was supported by certain political considerations: in July 1948 the Arab League decided to establish a provisional Palestinian government and administration.[10] If King Abdallah was considering a peaceful settlement with Israel after the war – should his Arab partners fail to destroy the Jewish state – it may well be that he was wary of pushing his advantages too far so that peaceful relations with the Jews would still be possible later. A similar spirit guided him during the post-war armistice negotiations with Israel. Abdallah also feared that Israel was gaining in strength, and so was reluctant to provoke his opponent too far.[11]

Facing a fairly self-confident Transjordan in the autumn of 1947, and during the next six months, the Jewish community was anxious but determined to hold out despite the very heavy cost in lives, pending the arrival from abroad of arms, equipment and volunteers that would enable it to build a proper army equipped with artillery, armor and combat aircraft. This was not possible before Britain's departure from Palestine because of the restraints placed on the Jewish community by the British Army and police. Indeed, there were some cases of direct British intervention on the side of the Arabs, particularly in the Jerusalem area.[12] In these circumstances, the Arab Legion's early appearance on Palestinian territory, and its familiarity with the terrain, placed the Jewish forces at a great disadvantage and they were consequently unable to gain as much as they did on other fronts against other Arab armies. Even so, Jewish forces achieved their main objective: the preservation of western Jerusalem and some important outposts, including a corridor linking Jerusalem to the coastal plain. By the time Israeli forces were in a position to do more, the UN Security Council had decided to actively intervene in the conflict, calling on 16 November 1948 for all states concerned to negotiate armistice agreements as an intermediate step towards permanent peace.

We will now turn to a more detailed description of the military situation in Jerusalem on the eve of the armistice negotiations which produced the cease-fire, the armistice lines, and then the Armistice Agreement, between Israel and the Hashemite Kingdom of Jordan in 1949. This Agreement and its appendices were to govern, among other things, the modalities of life in the divided city of Jerusalem. The war was fought in a hilly built-up area by forces which included many irregulars, thus reducing the scale, if not the intensity, of the fighting. The only move in the battle for Jerusalem that might be regarded as typical of a field war was the severing by the Arab Legion of the road linking western Jerusalem to the coastal plain, as already noted above. To achieve this objective the Legion chose the Latrun area where the road begins to climb into the hills. This location also served as a useful outpost facing Israel's major population centers and military installations. These circumstances meant that the fighting in the Jerusalem area led to somewhat mixed 'facts on the ground' which may be summarized as follows:

1. The Israeli salient, or corridor, through the hilly region connecting western Jerusalem to the coastal plain was blocked by the Transjordanians at the point where the road rises from the plain, yet it was still usable due to a rapidly cut rough alternative pass (the Burma Road) which circumvented the Jordanian position.
2. A double armistice demarcation line, or two armistice lines, one Jordanian and one Israeli, ran north–south through the city, at a varying distance one from another – up to about one and a half kilometers – separating western Jerusalem from Jordanian-controlled East Jerusalem. Beyond the city, the two lines met at, respectively, the northern and southern limits of the Jerusalem corridor referred to above. At the center of the Jordanian armistice line, clearly distinguishable on the map, was the roughly rectangular, walled ancient city of Jerusalem.

3. Behind the Jordanian line to the northeast was the strategically located Mount Scopus demilitarized enclave under UN protection, containing both an Israeli and a Jordanian sector with a 200-m no man's land between them. The Jordanian sector included the Augusta Victoria German Hospice and the Arab village of Issawiyya. The Israeli sector encompassed the inactive Hebrew University campus and the Hadassah Hospital.

4. To the south of the walled city, where the bulge between the armistice lines was the widest, was another UN-protected demilitarized area, made up of three small zones: Israeli, Jordanian and UN. The latter contained the former residence, called Government House, of the British High Commissioner who headed the Mandate administration in Palestine. Government House served – and continues to serve – as the headquarters of the UNTSO, and the residence of its Chief of Staff (COS). The area as a whole forms a strategic location which commands the southern flank of the walled city and offers a most beautiful view of it, as well as of adjoining biblically significant valleys. It also commands the approaches to Bethlehem.

The strategic Mount Scopus area was demilitarized following an agreement signed under UN auspices on 7 July 1948, the day on which the Security Council called for a prolongation of the truce which had come into full effect on 11 June 1948 and was to last for four weeks. The number of maintenance personnel and police allowed in each sector was set in the agreement which also provided for visits by accredited individuals, and the replenishment of necessary supplies. On 30 November 1948, in conjunction with a general cease-fire agreement between Israeli and Transjordanian military commanders in the Jerusalem area, a supplementary Mount Scopus Agreement was signed by the two commanders, stipulating that relief of personnel (50 percent in each round) in the Israeli sector and provision of fresh supplies would occur on the first and third week of each month (see text in Appendix 2).

The demilitarization of the Government House area had resulted from the circumstances of the British evacuation of Jerusalem at the end of the Mandate. The British handed over this area to the Red Cross to serve as a temporary safe haven under Red Cross immunity for persons fleeing the fighting in Jerusalem. The

UN simply 'inherited' it from the Red Cross, with British approval, when it assumed a leading role in efforts to contain the crisis. The cease-fire agreement of 30 November 1948 froze the area's demilitarized status, and recognized its new function and its internal structure of zones.[13]

The situation on the ground on the eve of the armistice negotiations also reflected other changes created by the conflict:

1. Almost all Arab residents in the Jerusalem area behind the Israeli armistice line had been gradually evacuated during the intermittent fighting in the city, which had begun three days after the UN's adoption of the Partition Plan with an Arab mob attack on a Jewish commercial area situated about 500 m north of the famous King David Hotel and the equally famous YMCA building opposite.

2. The residents of the Jewish Quarter in the walled city, and any other Jewish residents behind the Jordanian armistice line, such as in the Sheikh Jarrah neighborhood, had been evacuated.

3. The water supply pipeline to Jewish Jerusalem from the coastal plain had been cut, like the road mentioned above; and, like the road, a new connection had been built circumventing the old pipeline.

4. Electricity for eastern Jerusalem, which had been supplied from a generating plant in western Jerusalem, was no longer available due to the division of the city between Israeli and Jordanian forces.

5. All no man's land between the lines was forbidden to both parties for whatever purpose, except by mutual agreement. The demilitarized zone around Government House, including the entire area used by the UN, was designated as the Area Between the Lines, which was considered to be jointly Israeli and Jordanian pending final agreements on the issue.

6. A railway line linking western Jerusalem with the Mediterranean coast was blocked; portions of it on the approaches to Jerusalem, southwest of the city, ran through no man's land.

7. A road artery linking eastern Jerusalem with Bethlehem and Hebron to the south, ran partly behind the Israeli armistice line and was thus blocked to Arab traffic.

The overall picture reflected local military realities as of 30 November 1948 when the respective Israeli and Transjordanian commanders for the Jerusalem area reached a final 'complete and sincere cease-fire' agreement. That agreement was later cited in the general Israel–Jordan Armistice Agreement, signed on 3 April 1949. A more detailed examination of the lines agreed four months before the conclusion of the Armistice Agreement, and given a formal binding status as a result, reveals a considerable inventory of losses caused by the division of what had been until then a single Arab–Jewish metropolitan area clustered around a nucleus of holy shrines in the Old City, which made the city the focus of followers of three major religions around the world.

The list of difficulties and anomalies created by the new situation is long, but it may be summed up briefly as follows, without necessarily attempting to grade the various issues in any order of importance from any point of view. Only later, when the city was reunited again in 1967, was it possible in retrospect to assess the damage caused by partition and the gains likely to emerge from reunification.

1. One immediate source of friction was the difficulty in extrapolating the actual position of the armistice lines on the ground from the thick marker lines which had been drawn on the map. Due to the thickness of the pen used on the map, the space the lines covered on the map was equivalent to a strip of land up to 60 m wide. In a built-up area the implications of this could be serious, quite apart from the obvious potential for mischief inherent in determining the exact middle of the line at specific points on the map. What was often at stake was the fate of a house, or parts of it; a military position for which there was no alternative location; a strategic road; a road junction; a source of water; or a site holy for one of the city's three faiths.

2. The proximity of residential areas to the guns of armed soldiers across the line, endangered the lives of civilians living in these areas. In a number of sectors of western Jerusalem high concrete walls were constructed to shield passers-by and residents from Jordanian fire. One of those walls was erected across the road of an important commercial center while another ran along a section of King George V Street at the heart of modern, Jewish-populated Jerusalem. A third wall protected the Jerusalem Municipality Building and important roads

leading to it, due to its location at point-blank rifle range from an Arab Legion position atop the wall of the Old City. Other barricades and barbed wire disfigured the divided city, becoming a topic of gloomy comment in Jerusalem and elsewhere.

3. Unfortunately for the residents of western Jerusalem, the walls surrounding the Old City provided many more opportunities for the Arab Legionnaires posted on them to snipe into western Jerusalem from comfortable positions, either on the battlements or behind the narrow firing slits located all around. It was not possible to try to screen every potential target area. Thus, the citizens of West Jerusalem, while going about their daily affairs, became used to being at the mercy of the Jordanian snipers.

4. A great loss to Israel was the complete paralysis of the Hebrew University campus on Mount Scopus with its great library, up-to-date research facilities, the modern Hadassah Hospital, and the many buildings for study, administration and dormitories purpose-built over the years. Instead, Israel had to rebuild its single university from scratch on an alternative site, expending much time and money in the process.[14]

5. An even greater loss to Israel was a complete closure by Jordan to all Israelis – Jews and Arabs alike – of its newly captured Palestinian territories, including holy and historical sites. The single exception made allowed Christians to participate in the annual Christmas celebrations in Bethlehem. This was a harsh blow for Jews everywhere, as Judaism's holiest sites, the Western Wall and the Temple Mount, were both located in the Jordanian-occupied Old City. For Israeli Muslims the Jordanian occupation of the Old City meant that they were denied access to Islam's third holiest shrine, the Al-Aqsa Mosque and the Dome of the Rock, also in the Old City. Jordan also denied Jordanian–Palestinian Arabs permission to visit Israel.

6. Western Jerusalem was denied use of the Jerusalem area's only airport, located at Atarot (Qalandia), a short distance north of the city. No suitable terrain for a reasonable alternative could be found in the vicinity within Israeli lines, due to the hilly nature of the terrain, though over the years unsuccessful attempts were made to build alternative airfields in the Jerusalem suburbs of Givat Shaul and Yefe Nof.

7. Tourism, especially pilgrimage to the holy places, which was the chief attraction of the Holy Land for foreigners, was severely

curtailed on both sides of the armistice lines, when the Old City–Bethlehem complex was cut off from other sites in Israel. The Jordanians were adamant in refusing to allow tourists more than a single crossing, either from east to west or vice versa. As every tourist knows, free and easy travel at will is an essential ingredient of mass tourism.

8. Israeli study and research of Holy Land history and archaeology was seriously stifled. Excavation work was completely out of the question for Israelis across the armistice line, as was all access to sites and museums in the territory controlled by Jordan. The acquisition by Israel of the Dead Sea Scrolls was a unique feat made possible by extraordinary circumstances.

9. The destruction by the Jordanians of the Jewish Quarter and its many synagogues, including the beautiful ancient synagogue of the Old City known as Khurvat Rabbi Yehuda Hehasid, went a long way to de-Judaize much of the millennia-old Jewish holdings in Jerusalem; just as the takeover of abandoned Arab neighborhoods in West Jerusalem (half of Abu Tor, Katamon, Talbiyya, the German Colony, Bak'a, Malha, Deir Yassin and Sheikh Badr) led to their de-Arabization.

10. Large-scale desecration of graves at the sacred Jewish cemetery on the Mount of Olives in eastern Jerusalem, and denial of any further use of it or access to it for memorial services, remained an open wound not only for the Jews of western Jerusalem, but also for Jews around the world whose dying wish had been to be buried on the mount, so that they might be among the first to be resurrected at the coming of the Messiah. The vast Muslim cemetery in the Mamillah area in West Jerusalem also fell into disuse and neglect, though no intentional or systematic desecration of it is known to have occurred.

But, before we examine the practical problems of the Armistice Regime in Jerusalem, let us trace the stages of UN intervention which brought about the negotiations over the Armistice Agreement. Ultimately, the fate of the Agreement and, indeed, everyday life in Jerusalem under the armistice, would depend on the details of its implementation. However, the vagueness of the Agreement left room for substantial differences of interpretation. As crisis arose between the parties in the course of implementation, the UN was to play a growing role as mediator.

NOTES

1. Also known as Glubb Pasha.
2. John Bagot Glubb, *A Soldier with Arabs* (London: Hodder and Stoughton, 1957), p. 71.
3. Ibid.
4. Aryeh Itzhaki, *Latrun: The Battle for the Road to Jerusalem* (Jerusalem: Cana Publishers, 1982), pp. 139–40. [Hebrew]
5. Avi Shlaim, *Collusion Across the Jordan* (Oxford: Clarendon Press, 1988), pp. 137–8.
6. Dan Shueftan, *The Jordanian Option* (Yad Tabenkin, 1987), pp. 57–8. [Hebrew]
7. Ibid., pp. 135, 137–8.
8. For details, see Larry Collins and Dominique Lapierre, *O Jerusalem* (London: Grafton Books, 1984), especially Chs 19, 29 and 35; also, Martin Gilbert, *Jerusalem in the Twentieth Century* (London: Pimlico, 1996), especially Chs 12–15.
9. For a poignant description of the details of these attacks, see Collins and Lapierre, *O Jerusalem*. See also Netan'el Lorch, *The Edge of the Sword* (London: Putnam and Co., 1961), p. 253.
10. See Shueftan, *Jordanian Option*, pp. 70–2; and Lorch, *Edge of Sword*, pp. 401–2.
11. A high-ranking Israeli official who took part in the armistice negotiations with King Abdallah (see Chapter 2), related to M. Erell (see Foreword) how easy it had been to obtain a certain important concession from the King who then asked the official to convey to his superiors the King's hope that the Israeli Army would help him establish himself as ruler of Syria. The King's ambitions in that direction were no secret in themselves, for Syria had been initially part of the Hashemite patrimony at the end of the First World War.
12. See Lorch, *Edge of Sword*, p. 121.
13. For details, see Count Folke Bernadotte, *To Jerusalem* (London: Hodder and Stoughton, 1951).
14. The other university, the Technion, in the northern city of Haifa, was only for technological subjects.

2. The Armistice Negotiations and their Outcome

During the 1948 war, Transjordan unilaterally annexed territories it had occupied west of the Jordan River, renaming itself the Hashemite Kingdom of Jordan. Legitimacy for the annexation was claimed on the basis of a conference in Jericho on 1 December 1948 between the King and Palestinian notables from the West Bank who, following an old Arab tradition, pronounced the *bai'a*, the oath of allegiance, to the King. Except for Great Britain and Pakistan, no country recognized the enlargement of Transjordan's territory. Nevertheless, the annexation posed no obstacle to Israel in negotiating an armistice with the government in Amman, just as it negotiated with the other adjoining Arab powers which had invaded Western Palestine the day the Jewish state was declared.

Yet, whereas Egypt, Lebanon and Syria negotiated and signed respective armistice agreements with Israel through accredited representatives meeting in formal conferences under UN chairmanship, Israel and Jordan negotiated their armistice in secret meetings with King Abdallah in Shuneh, east of the River Jordan. The results of these negotiations, embodied in agreements signed on 21 and 31 March 1949, were later incorporated almost verbatim in a formal armistice agreement signed on the Greek island of Rhodes on 3 April 1949, at the conclusion of an essentially ceremonial conference, also under UN chairmanship.[1]

Unlike Egypt and Syria, which were reluctant to engage in armistice commitments – presumably because they had not accomplished much in the war – and Lebanon, which had been an unenthusiastic participant from the beginning, Jordan was quite willing, even possibly eager. Its gains were considerable, and provoked hostility amongst the other Arab states which responded by joining forces to establish an 'All-Palestine Government' in Gaza in October 1948 and challenging Jordan's profitable territorial conquests in the former Mandated Palestine. They feared that a UN-sponsored armistice would grant international recognition to the territorial *status quo* pending a permanent settlement and so strengthen King Abdallah's hand against his less fortunate allies.

An eager negotiator is an accommodating one and, as was mentioned in Chapter 1 several factors may have motivated the King of Jordan to be flexible in his dealings with Israel. In fact, Jordan ceded control to Israel of important pieces of territory to facilitate communications within Israel. In addition, Jordan undertook commitments to meet other major Israeli concerns over facilities and holy sites in various locations on the Jordanian side of the line, including parts of Jerusalem, or in areas outside the control of either party. In the event, only some of the Jordanian commitments were honored, which reinforces the view that Jordan was indeed interested in a speedy formal armistice as a shield behind which to consolidate its gains. To further that end the Jordanians were ready to make promises which might not be kept when circumstances changed.

Unlike traditional wars, in which hostilities would run their course until a conclusion was reached, the Arab–Israeli War of 1948–49 was followed closely from the outset by the UN, which undertook to limit the hostilities and bring them to a mediated conclusion. Even before the war, at the time of the Partition Resolution itself, the UN Security Council was warned that Arab hostility to partition and to the establishment of a Jewish state in Palestine might warrant its intervention. The General Assembly, in Resolution No. 181 II, requested that the Security Council: 'consider, if circumstances during the transition period require such consideration, whether the situation in Palestine constitutes a threat to the peace ...'. It should be recalled that the two superpowers of the period, the United States and the Soviet Union, were united in opposition to Arab intervention in Palestine and the use of force to scuttle the Partition Plan. Hence, the Security Council could act more or less consistently to stem the tide of violence in Palestine. It is not within the scope of this study to examine the Council's effectiveness and determination in confronting the Arab invasion. Those were early days in the experience of the young UN; in years to come, it would act more forcefully in facing aggression.

The Security Council first took up the issue of Palestine on 24

February 1948, though it was not until April that it adopted its first resolution, calling upon 'Arab and Jewish armed groups in Palestine to cease acts of violence immediately' and inviting the Jewish Agency and the Higher Arab Committee 'to make available representatives to the Security Council for the purpose of arranging a truce ...'. A second resolution of the Council adopted the same day called for the convening of a special session of the General Assembly, to consider further the 'future government of Palestine.'[2] The recommended session was held and on 14 May 1948 it resolved that a UN mediator for Palestine be appointed, a position that was to play an essential role in shaping the Armistice Regime.

In the meantime the violence in Palestine only increased, prompting the Security Council to adopt two additional resolutions in rapid succession. On 23 April 1948, the Council established the UN's first representation in the conflict area, the Truce Commission for Palestine, composed of representatives of Council members maintaining regular consular missions in Jerusalem.[3] As Syria declined to serve on this commission, its membership consisted of representatives from the USA, France and Belgium; these had the task of enforcing the truce between the 'informally' warring parties, even before the declared hostilities broke out upon the invasion of Palestine when the British Mandate expired and the state of Israel was born.[4]

The Truce Commission could not stop the impending war and, with the termination of the British Mandate, Palestine was invaded by seven regular Arab armies. Additional Security Council admonishments eventually produced a cease-fire in this new situation. On 22 May 1948 the Council urged a cease-fire within 36 hours and required the Truce Commission to give the highest priority to establishing a truce in Jerusalem. This was the first UN emphasis on Jerusalem in the context of the war.[5] The 22 May resolution had no effect; the record of discussions by the Security Council on 26 May shows that the Arab governments refused to carry it out. The Council then adopted a further resolution, on 29 May 1948, which threatened enforcement action under Chapter VII of the UN Charter unless compliance was obtained. The cease-fire called for this time was to last four weeks. It took effect finally on 11 June 1948.[6]

This important resolution led the UN to increase its involvement in the conflict:

- First, Jerusalem was singled out once again, even more emphatically, as a special concern of the community of nations by virtue of the city's holy places and the need to protect them and ensure free access to them. In addition, the fact that the UN representatives, including the members of the Truce Commission, operated from Jerusalem, made it necessary that they be protected while fulfilling their duties.
- Second, the UN Mediator was instructed to supervise the observance of the cease-fire and other accompanying requirements.
- Third, the Mediator was to be provided with military observers to help establish and monitor the cease-fire.
- Fourth, the Mediator was instructed to take up his position as defined by the General Assembly.
- And fifth, the Mediator was instructed to report weekly to the Security Council during the cease-fire.[7]

The office of the Mediator, and the UNTSO, the body of military observers created by the Security Council in its resolution of 29 May 1948, eventually formed the machinery which guided the crafting and maintenance of the Armistice Regime. Its formal introduction into subsequent phases of the Palestine crisis was made by the Security Council in its resolution of 15 July 1948, another signpost on the tortuous road to armistice.[8]

In the course of the four-week cease-fire, which was ordered by the Security Council on 28 May and came into force on 11 June 1948, the UN Mediator tried but failed to obtain a prolongation of the truce, which occasioned further action by the Security Council. In its resolution of 15 July, following a resumption of the fighting, it put the blame on Arab countries for rejecting the efforts of the Mediator to prolong the truce, and ordered a fresh one to take effect within three days, on pain of stern coercive measures under Chapter VII of the UN Charter. This order was obeyed. The resolution further provided that the truce 'shall remain in force ... until a peaceful adjustment of the future situation in Palestine is reached.' The Council also requested that the Mediator establish procedures for dealing with breaches of the truce, and to regularly update the Security Council on the status of the truce. To this end, the Secretary General of the UN was requested to provide the Mediator with appropriate staff and facilities.

The UN Mediator was chosen by a committee of the five

permanent members of the Security Council acting under the authority of the General Assembly. The first appointee was Count Folke Bernadotte of Sweden, and the first Chief of Staff of UNTSO was Major General Lundstrom of the Swedish Air Force. Three hundred officers, and an equal number of enlisted men from various armies, plus their equipment, were provided to help carry out the Mediator's mission and the supervision of the truce. Count Bernadotte was assassinated on 17 September 1948, by Jewish extremists opposed to what they considered a sell-out of Jewish interests in Jerusalem. Bernadotte's task devolved on his American deputy, Dr Ralph Bunche, an official of the UN Secretariat, in the capacity of Acting Mediator. With the subsequent resignation of General Lundstrom, his duties as COS for UNTSO were taken over by Lieutenant-General William Riley of the US Marine Corps. It was Bunche and Reilly who shaped the Armistice Regime.

Importantly, the truce called for by the Security Council was a long-term one, as was the mandate for the UNTSO. Only definitive peace settlements between all the signatories of the Armistice Agreements could allow the truce and its supervision to be wound down. Israel held the view that the formal armistice superseded the truce, and that UNTSO's role under the armistice therefore superseded its original role under the truce. However, the UN did not accept the Israeli position. With the assumption by UNTSO of its functions under the Armistice Agreement, it effectively began wearing two hats. UNTSO's double mandate and its consequent longevity have allowed the UN, through the Security Council, to continue to play a role in the Arab–Israeli situation. Though mostly dormant, it has retained its potential for operational significance should events warrant it.

Truce notwithstanding, fighting continued for a long time, though not so much in the Jerusalem area, until the situation was ripe for a move from truce to armistice. The aim of the truce had been only to freeze hostilities; the Security Council emphasized that cease-fires and truces did not prejudice the rights, claims or positions of the parties regarding other aspects of the conflict. The armistice agreements went one step further, as the parties to them committed themselves to averting any further violence in the context of the Palestinian conflict. Transition from truce to armistice became possible when the military balance in the war swung in favor of Israel as it managed, at great human sacrifice, to survive the first Arab onslaughts. Naturally, outside mediation such as that offered by the UN was less likely to succeed so long as a military option seemed viable to the parties that had gone to war to prevent the establishment of Israel. King Abdallah of Jordan was the first to understand this, which is why he was the first Arab leader to adopt a more accommodating approach.

On 16 November 1948, the Security Council came to the same conclusion, calling on the parties to negotiate an armistice which would include the 'delineation of permanent armistice demarcation lines,' to facilitate the transition from truce to 'permanent peace in Palestine.' Yet, until Israel gained the upper hand in the fighting, the Arab states remained reluctant to join in armistice talks. Only when the leading belligerent, Egypt, suffered reverses which threatened the decimation of its forces that were besieged in the Negev desert, did it take the plunge on 12 January 1949. The other Arab countries then followed, and King Abdallah seized the moment to gain legitimacy for the practical arrangements he had been seeking with Israel.[9]

Some general observations about armistice agreements are valuable here. Generally speaking, armistice results when the stronger of the belligerents is prepared to stop fighting under stipulated conditions. If these are seriously violated by one party, the other is entitled to resume hostilities. A recent example was the armistice arrangements between Iraq and the UN which ended the Second Gulf War (1991). When Iraq failed to cooperate with the UN in the dismantling of arms of mass destruction, as required under the terms of the armistice, the UN command threatened military action. Under the regulations attached to the Fourth Hague Convention of 1907, if the duration of an armistice is not defined, the belligerents may resume operations at any time after giving due warning in accordance with the agreed terms. However, armistice violations by private persons acting on their own initiative do not entitle the aggrieved party to resume hostilities.[10]

The armistice agreements signed by Israel and its four Arab neighbors differed from most other such agreements in that the renunciation of force stipulated in them was indefinite and irrevocable.[11] The agreements did not end the conflict; neither did they constitute a permanent settlement, bring about mutual recognition by their signatories, or preclude the insistence of the Arab states that they continued to be in a state of war with Israel. However, a Security Council resolution of 1 September 1951, related to Egypt's refusal to let Israeli ships use the Suez Canal, affirmed that in view of the Armistice Agreement between Egypt and Israel, which 'is of a permanent character, neither party can reasonably assert that it is actively a belligerent.' Perhaps this formulation points to a difference between being in a state of war and being an active belligerent. In practical terms the agreements provided their signatories with a framework for coexistence pending a peaceful resolution of their conflict. Even on this count they failed, as evidenced by the many major wars fought between Arabs and Israelis in the following years.

The record available seems to indicate that UN and Israeli officials alike felt fairly confident that the armistice was indeed a prelude to an early peace. In a resolution adopted on 11 December 1948, the General Assembly of the UN requested that the parties concerned extend the scope of the armistice negotiations and seek an agreement on a final settlement of all the disagreements outstanding between them. The Security Council endorsed this request at its 437th meeting.[12] To assist the parties in the quest for peace, the Assembly established a Conciliation Commission. Only one senior Israeli public figure, the late General Yigal Allon who commanded operations on the Egyptian front, held that it should be possible, given Israel's military advantage at the time, to persuade the Arab states to move directly from truce to peace.[13]

The initial expectation that peace would follow quickly in the wake of the armistice encouraged the armistice negotiators, at least on the Israeli side, to accept arrangements whose potential for conflict seems obvious in retrospect. Shabtai Rosenne, the Adviser for Legal Affairs at the Israeli Foreign Ministry and a negotiator at the Rhodes talks, who had praised Dr Bunche for initiating the armistice agreements which earned him the Nobel Prize, later remarked: '… Bunche's famous statement to the Security Council in August 1949, that the armistice regime would sweep away all vestiges of the war, seems to have been wishful thinking on his part.'[14] However, as stated earlier, the armistice negotiations between Israel and Jordan, uniquely as we shall see below, went a considerable distance in an attempt to deal with certain complexities atypical of armistice issues. Nevertheless, the pitfalls that remained in the agreement, especially in regards to Jerusalem, fell far short of the hopes that had been pinned on armistice as a panacea for resolving the outstanding issues between the parties.

NOTES

1. Benjamin Rivlin (ed.), *Ralph Bunche: The Man and his Time* (New York: Holmes and Meir, 1990), especially Ch. 10, Shabtai Rosenne, 'Bunche at Rhodes: Diplomatic Neighbour, pp. 181–2. See also, Moshe Dayan, *Mile Stones* (Tel Aviv: Dvir Publishers, 1976), p. 86 [Hebrew].
2. United Nations (UN) Document No. S/714.
3. The term 'truce' was first used by the Security Council when it established the Truce Commission in its attempts to bring about a cessation of hostilities in Palestine.
4. UN Document No. S/727.
5. UN Document No. S/773.
6. UN Document No. S/801.
7. Ibid.
8. UN Document No. S/902.
9. See UN Document No. S/1070.
10. For details on these issues, as regards the armistice agreements between Israel and its neighbors, see Shabtai Rosenne, *Israel's Armistice Agreements with the Arab States* (Tel Aviv: Blumstein Bookstores, 1951), pp. 24–8.
11. The three other Arab states involved in the war – Iraq, Saudia Arabia and Yemen – withdrew their forces but did not conclude any armistice or other agreements with Israel.
12. UN Document No. S/1376. Incidentally, this resolution also relieved the Acting Mediator of any further functions under his authority.
13. I. Rabinovitch, *The Road Not Taken* (Jerusalem: Keter Publishers, 1991), p. 56 [Hebrew].
14. Rosenne, in Rivlin, *Ralph Bunche*, p. 184.

3. An Analysis of the Armistice Agreement

Before addressing the implementation of the armistice in Jerusalem, it is worth analysing in detail the provisions of the Armistice Agreement between Israel and Jordan, especially those which had a direct or indirect bearing on Jerusalem. As a framework for an uncomfortable coexistence, the Agreement had its strengths and weaknesses as we shall see below. Ultimately, it turned out to be a double failure. First, though it was conceived as a necessary interim step towards peace, a goal which was written into the text, peace never followed. Second, it was thoroughly breached, even shattered, by a second Jordanian assault on Israel which began in the Jerusalem area on 6 June 1967.

Following a solemn preamble, identical in all armistice agreements signed between Israel and the Arabs,[1] which emphasized their provisional nature as a transition to a permanent peace, came the operational 12 articles of the Agreement. Even this preamble was not free from pitfalls. First, it emphasized that the parties were ordered by the Security Council to negotiate an armistice, implying that one or both parties were doing so against their will. The far from successful Arab belligerents may well have felt that way, anxious as they were to avoid the slightest implication that they viewed Israel as a legitimate state and recognized it as such. Second, the reference to Article 40 of the UN Charter emphasized, again in line with Arab positions, that the agreement was made 'without prejudice to the rights, claims, or positions of the parties concerned.' On the other hand, the statement that the agreement was meant to facilitate peace, echoing the wish of the international community to bring the conflict to an end, suited Israel, not the Arabs. This divergence in interpretation, and expectations, of the Armistice Agreement was to impinge on every step of its implementation, along the Israel–Jordan border in general and in Jerusalem in particular.

Another provision of the preamble, that the negotiations took place under UN auspices, was to haunt the Armistice Regime for decades to come. The Arab governments clung steadfastly to the UN's apron, so to speak, as a refuge from direct dealings with Israel, except when a vital interest necessitated direct contact, which invariably took place in secret. The Arab states refused to deal with, or even recognize, the government of the State of Israel officially; however, for pragmatic reasons, they were willing to engage in secret, informal contacts to resolve important issues. This ambivalence would take its toll on the daily application of the Israel–Jordan armistice as we shall observe below.

The formal obligations of the parties were summed up in 12 articles, several of them specifically referring to Jerusalem:

1. The parties undertook to adhere to the following principles:
    • An absolute and open-ended commitment not to resort to military force.
    • No aggressive action by the armed forces of either party would be taken, planned or threatened against the citizens or the armed forces of the other. The problem which would embitter the Armistice Regime, especially in Jerusalem as we will have ample opportunity to show, was the permanent suspicion arising from the practical impossibility of monitoring the military planning of the other party. It stands to reason that the UN Mediator had in mind actual preparations for hostilities other than mere planning, because certain aspects of practical preparations were always observable. This well-intentioned provision became a source of much friction between the parties along the demarcation lines, particularly in the Jerusalem area, each time one of them suspected that the other was preparing or 'planning' a breach of the armistice.
    • Each party's right to security and freedom from fear of attack was recognized, in the spirit of the UN Charter.[2] One has to note, however, that while the Charter commits UN members to 'refrain from the threat or use of force' in their international relations, it also stipulates that the UN 'shall ensure that states which are not members … act in

accordance with these principles so far as it may be necessary for the maintenance of international peace and security.' Since neither Israel nor Jordan were members of the UN when the armistice was negotiated, one can only deduce that the UN Mediator who formulated the Israel–Jordan armistice agreement, was seeking to bind its signatories to the conduct prescribed for members of the organization.[3]

• The establishment of an armistice between the armed forces of the parties was also prescribed as a step towards ending the armed conflict in Palestine.

2.   Article II specified two principles which were problematic in their application to Jerusalem:

• No party should gain any political or military advantage under the truce. Presumably the intention here was to rule out any unilateral alteration of the imperfectly policed cease-fire lines before the permanent armistice lines were set. But since the truce remained in force after the armistice took effect under UNTSO's policing, one could expand the application of this provision so as to forbid any political or military alliance that either party might wish to form while the armistice was in force.

• It was recognized that the agreement should not prejudice the rights, claims or positions of either side in the ultimate settlement of the Palestinian issue, since its terms were dictated by military considerations only. This undoubtedly was yet another expression of Arab anxiety lest any wording or provision over their signature might be interpreted as implying recognition of Israel in any political sense, let alone as a state.

3.   Article III committed the parties to refrain from any act of hostility by military or paramilitary forces, including irregular forces, against the territory, population or armed forces of the other party, and to prevent crossing of the lines for any purpose to the other side. This injunction left open the issue of defensive versus offensive war-like acts, and by-passed the question of who might define them under what circumstances. The right of self-defence is recognized in Article 51 of the UN Charter in case 'an armed attack occurs ... until the Security Council has taken measures ...'. However, while large-scale

attacks proclaim themselves clearly, who can determine how, when and under what circumstances border skirmishes had flared up? The problem is all the more acute along the border of a divided city like Jerusalem, where hostilities and acts of self-defence could occur at a rate that would defy any sure determination of guilt.

4. Article IV – which determined that the Cease-fire Demarcation Lines referred to in the next article would be designated as the Armistice Demarcation Lines – also referred to Security Council Resolution of 16 November 1948, whose language made it clear that the ultimate purpose was 'to eliminate the threat to peace in Palestine and to facilitate the transition from the present truce to permanent peace in Palestine ...'. This article also obligated the armed forces of both parties to continue to enforce all the prevailing rules and regulations prohibiting civilians of either side from crossing the demarcation lines to the other side, or into no man's land between the lines. This provision was particularly relevant to Jerusalem where, as we have noted in the Introduction, the double demarcation lines which resulted from the military situation on the ground at the termination of hostilities had enclosed numerous tracts of land between them, practically all along the line, dividing the city in two.

5. Article V recognized the demarcation lines as being identical with the truce lines certified by the UN, except for the area in the north of Israel where the Iraqi forces had taken position. Most importantly for our subject, the demarcation line for Jerusalem was confirmed as following the truce lines agreed upon in the 30 November 1948 cease-fire agreement. The citation of this agreement is noteworthy for the fact that it was negotiated in a spirit of accommodation between Israeli and Jordanian military commanders, under UN auspices, and it was the first expression since the war of a common search for mutual goodwill in practical matters. This article also determined the demarcation lines in the Hebron area and south of the Dead Sea down to Eilat, again along 'existing military positions.' This was a fiction, since there was no fighting south of the Dead Sea, and it was desired by Jordan for two reasons:

- To mask its inactivity in that sector throughout the war.
- To avoid any suggestion that Israel was inheriting a legitimate international frontier, which was identical with the old border between Transjordan and Mandated Palestine. There was fear that such an implication might give a measure of legitimacy to Israel as a state, and King Abdallah was in no mood to confront the rest of the Arabs on that issue.

6. Article VI provided that Jordanian forces would replace the Iraqis in the north, and Iraq could therefore withdraw without committing itself to an armistice with Israel, and instead hand over that responsibility to the Hashemite Kingdom of Jordan. In any case, the Iraqis had not distinguished themselves in the fighting, and they seemed more like an auxiliary force of the much more effective Arab Legion. The rulers of Jordan and Iraq were cousins and so their cooperation seemed natural. It is noteworthy, however, that the area of Wadi 'Ara in northern Israel, which had been occupied by the Iraqis, was ceded by Jordan to Israel in the pre-armistice secret negotiations in Shuneh. In addition to settling the Iraqi issue, this article dealt with other important issues:

    - Paragraphs of this article dealt with Israeli compensatory gestures, and related implications of the Jordanian concessions in question. The Israeli counter-concessions were relatively insignificant, but they were magnified in the text of the Armistice Agreement so that the King could save face *vis-à-vis* the other Arab states when his secret deals with Israel became public. This was an important consideration in light of the fact that the armistice lines ended up as being more favorable to Israel than the boundaries proposed by the Partition Plan, and Abdallah could not be seen as contributing to that favoritism.
    - Paragraphs 8 and 9 also repeated the stipulation that the demarcation lines in general were agreed upon 'without prejudice to future territorial settlements or boundary lines, or to claims of either party relating thereto.' This was done at the insistence of the Arabs, lest the temporary lines became recognized as the permanent borders of Israel, for they were confident that in the long run the Arabs could nullify the status quo. But the phrasing of this stipulation, avoiding the mentioning of the Arab-rejected Partition Plan, made it a

two-way affair that abrogated even the moral validity of the boundaries recommended in that plan, thus rendering the territorial question between Israel and the Arabs completely open. The gains made by Israel during the 1948 war were only a first hint of what was to become the price the Arabs would have to pay for rejecting Israel's initial pleas to have the armistice lines recognized as permanent borders.

• It is significant that paragraph 11 of Article VI left the door open for 'such rectifications as may be agreed upon by the parties ... and all such rectifications shall have the same effect as if they had been incorporated in full in this armistice agreement.' This meant that such rectifications were envisaged which added to the provisional nature of the armistice boundaries. But it was only when peace was signed between Israel and Jordan in 1994, that such corrections could take place amicably, by agreement. The more important rectifications were the result of the 1967 war, when King Hussein, King Abdallah's grandson, acted less wisely than his ancestor and joined the war against Israel when he thought he could alter the boundaries in his favor.

7. Article VII comprised three paragraphs limiting the military forces of the parties within ten kilometers from the demarcation lines, except where geographical considerations made this impractical. For each sector, the permissible forces were defined in Annex II of the agreement, and their reduction to defensive strength was to be completed within ten days of the establishment of the demarcation lines. It also stipulated that the removal of mines from roads and areas evacuated by either party, and the exchange of plans showing the location of such minefields to the other party, should be completed within the same time frame. This article also envisaged a periodical review of the forces maintained by the parties with a view toward reduction of such forces by mutual agreement in the future. As can be seen at once, this article addressed itself to what has since become popularly known as confidence-building measures. Agreements between local commanders on both sides of the line, and direct telephone lines between designated commanders to make the rapid defusing of tension possible, were other measures exhibiting good logic and sometimes goodwill of the diplomats and officers concerned.

But, even if strictly adhered to, they could not substitute for fundamental policies, they could only bolster them. The reference here to the impracticality of reduction in forces in some areas, due to Israel's narrow waist which often did not exceed the ten-kilometer defensive zone limit, was to become a major issue in managing the armistice in the Jerusalem area.

8.   Article VIII, which touched directly on the sensitive issues concerning Jerusalem, deserves to be cited in full. It included three paragraphs:

• A Special Committee, composed of two representatives of each party designated by the respective governments, shall be established for the purpose of formulating agreed plans and arrangements designed to enlarge the scope of this agreement and to effect improvements in its application.

• The Special Committee shall be organized immediately following the coming into effect of this agreement, and shall direct its attention to the formulation of agreed plans and arrangements for such matters as either party may submit to it, which, in any case, shall include the following, on which agreement in principle already exists: free movement of traffic on vital roads, including the Bethlehem and Latrun–Jerusalem roads; resumption of the normal functioning of the cultural and humanitarian institutions on Mount Scopus and free access thereto; free access to the holy places and cultural institutions, and use of the cemetery of the Mount of Olives; resumption of operation of the Latrun pumping station; provision of electricity to the Old City; and resumption of the operation of the railroad to Jerusalem.

• The Special Committee shall have exclusive competence over such matters as may be referred to it. Agreed plans and arrangements formulated by it may provide for the exercise of supervisory functions by the MAC established under Article XI.

In one sense, this article ought to be viewed as an extension of the Article VI that was discussed above, in that both of them, each in its own way, deviated from the norms applied in regard to the armistice lines: Article VI established, in fact, certain armistice lines which differed from those representing the military positions of the parties, frozen by truce or cease-fire; while Article VIII under discussion here, allowed for certain important civilian activities across the lines, contrary to the general rule, encompassed in Article IV above, which prohibited civilians from crossing the armistice lines for any purpose. In both cases, Israel elicited important concessions from Jordan, intended to remedy serious dislocations suffered as a result of Jordanian gains in the war, which blocked Israeli access to communications' arteries, a university campus, library and hospital, a hallowed cemetery and, most unhappily, to the most sacred Jewish shrine – the Wailing Wall in Old Jerusalem.

The adjustments provided for by Articles VI and VIII were measures whose implementation could be expected to enhance normalcy, and hence stability in the new situation generated by the war and its aftermath. But, as it is readily obvious, the issues dealt with in the two articles were very dissimilar politically and practically. The stipulations in Article VI could be implemented in one move, and so they were, thus putting a seal of finality and irreversibility on their implementation. By contrast, most of those in Article VIII involved a continuous process which translated into to-and-fro crossings into or through Jordanian territory on a daily and routine basis; and those activities, which required complex arrangements, implied a high visibility and public transparency which could not escape Arab scrutiny, or even hostile acts by interested parties. Besides, this arrangement would have been constantly affected by the whims of the Jordanians and taken hostage every time something went amiss in the relations between the parties.

The Special Committee designed for this task – which was very important by virtue of its various assignments – had the special distinction of being an exclusively Israeli–Jordanian affair which could pursue the intimate style of dealing with mutual problems, so fruitful in Shuneh, where the real, though informal, armistice negotiations had taken place. Israel always favored such direct contacts with the Arab states, not only as the antithesis of Arab non-recognition, but also as the most effective way of discovering common ground. As we shall see, the promising Special Committee proved to be stillborn for all intents and purposes. Jordan soon changed its mind about it, apparently for the reasons of transparency listed above; or it may not have intended from the outset to allow the Committee to operate but had been forced by Israeli insistence to comply in order to achieve an armistice. So, the absence of the UN or another third party from the Committee, proved double-edged: it could have enabled the parties to work intimately, without foreign interference, if it had worked; but failing that, it meant that each party – in the event Jordan – could more easily stonewall its very functioning and deal it the death blow. The direct result of that development was that not only did the problems of Jerusalem become vastly more difficult to resolve, but the UN strengthened its grip on the machinations of the Armistice Regime.

9. Article IX provided that future agreements between the parties relating to reduction of forces, adjustment of demarcation lines or arrangements devised by the Special Committee, should have the force of the Armistice Agreement itself.

10. Article X regulated the exchange of prisoners of war beyond the main one effected already prior to the signing of this agreement, and referred principally to those missing in combat whose fate might still be clarified in the future.

11. Article XI is possibly one of the most important in the document, for it set the organizational framework for the supervision and the application of the armistice provisions. Its 11 paragraphs stipulate, in detail, that:
    • The execution of this agreement, with the exception of those matters falling within the exclusive competence of the Special Committee mentioned in Article VIII, should be supervised by an MAC, composed of five members, of whom each party would designate two and whose Chairman should be the COS of UNTSO, or an officer from the corps of military observers, following consultations with both parties. The Special Committee, whose authority was recognized by the parties to deal with such issues as Jerusalem, was confirmed here as acting outside the competence of the UN-sponsored armistice arrangements.
    a. The MAC should maintain its headquarters in Jerusalem, but could hold its meetings anywhere the parties deemed effective.
    b. This turned Jerusalem into the pivotal venue of the

Israeli–Jordan dealings in the coming years, though the right to meet elsewhere was recognized if the parties so decided.

- The MAC would be convened for its first meeting by the COS, within one week of the signing of the agreement.
- While it was considered desirable to adopt decisions unanimously, a majority vote would be sufficient. This provision amounted, in practice, to compulsory arbitration of the UN in all matters where the parties could not agree. It is fair to assume that the reasoning behind this course of thought was that, due to the inexperience of the parties on the one hand, and the impressive role of the UN Mediator in the negotiations on the other, it was essential not to leave it to the paralyzing recalcitrance of the parties to scuttle or delay effective action by the Armistice Commission. Be that as it may, the fact that the fifth deciding vote of the Chairman could always be cast in favor of one of the parties, tremendously increased the role of the UN, not as a mediator but as a decisive voice in conflicts to come. This, in turn, also enhanced the dependence of the parties on the goodwill, sometimes on the whims, and sometimes on obscure and outside considerations, which filtered down from the headquarters of the UN in New York.
- The MAC would formulate its own rules of procedure, meetings would be held after due notice to the parties, and the presence of the majority of the members would constitute a quorum. This further strengthened the UN position, because it sufficed that the Chairman convinced one of the parties to convene a meeting, and the legal quorum was assured, even in the absence of the second party. Again, this reasoning had probably emanated from UN reluctance to let one of the parties boycott the work of the MAC, but the end result was to strengthen the hand of the UN all the same.
- The MAC could employ military observers to fulfill its duties, either from UN personnel or from the military organizations of the parties. But all UN personnel so employed would remain under the exclusive command of the COS of UNTSO or his designated representative. Never were the parties trustful enough of each other to recruit military observers from their respective armed forces; and so, the UN again

strengthened its hand as the only source of military observers. Furthermore, since all observers remained under UN command, the MAC was helpless, even by majority vote, to entrust them with any task which was not to the UN liking.

• The Commission was empowered to investigate and make appropriate decisions when one of the parties complained against the other's breach of the Armistice Agreement via the Chairman of the Commission. This stipulation, by the very terms it used (claims, complaints, investigation, equitable settlement, and the like), in fact predicted a much longer life for the Armistice Regime than many would admit at the time. Since it would be UN Observers who received the complaints, investigated them and reported on their findings, the UN – which formed only one-fifth of the membership – in fact became the sole arbitrator in each case. This turned the entire machinery of the MAC, which was intended to operate in a spirit of cooperative deliberation, into a forum for each party to raise grievances against the other, not unlike a court of law; while the UN Chairman often, as in a court of summary trial where decisions are made or dictated from above, delivered the final verdict.

• Sole power to interpret the provisions of the Agreement was given to the Commission, namely to its UN Chairman, once the stipulations became a bone of contention between the signatories. The Commission was also encouraged to recommend to the parties modifications and revisions of the terms of armistice, as the need arose. These provisions seem too simple – in view of the vital nature of the armistice and the importance of the interests involved – to leave to a UN Military Observer (UNMO) who chaired the Commission to sway decisions on disputes one way or the other. Fortunately, Articles I and III of the Agreement were excluded from the competence of the MAC in the context of this paragraph, which meant that future revisions or current interpretations could only be made by the much wider political and diplomatic body of the Security Council.

• The MAC undertook to submit to the parties reports of its activities, as well as to the Secretary General of the UN for transmission to other UN agencies. In due course, the Secretary General became much involved in the affairs of the armistice. This shows, once again, that the expectation that the armistice would be short-lived and soon replaced by permanent peace was less realistic than the UN estimate to the contrary.

   a. Members of the Commission and its observers would be given freedom of movement and access to the area under the jurisdiction of the agreement, provided that when the decisions were not unanimous, only UN observers would be employed. That this provision met the practical need to deny military personnel of either party observation of restricted areas or facilities of the other party, is reasonable and fair. But, there is more to it than that: the phrase 'members of the Commission and its observers' covers up the fact that the Commission as such had no observers, because all were under the command of the UN, and no task could be assigned to them that was not scrutinized and approved by the UN. This interpretation is strengthened by the other provision in this paragraph which required unanimity in order to dispatch other than UN Observers to fulfill tasks assigned to them by the Commission. Presumably the UN could also employ its investigators as it saw fit, disregarding the wishes of the parties concerned.

- The expenses of the Commission were to be apportioned between the parties, except for those relating to the UN personnel. The idea was, of course, to preserve UN neutrality and independence by not resorting to the generosity or otherwise of the parties. In practice, the UN could thereby also decide on its course of action, often independently of the will of the parties or the terms of reference of the Commission; this ability could have been seriously hampered if all UN activities were scrutinized and restricted by those who held the purse strings.

12. Article XII, which comprised five paragraphs, is of a general declaratory nature and strengthens some of the previous stipulations:
    - The agreement would come into force immediately and did not require ratification by either party. The reason assuredly was that ratification would have involved endless opportunities for delay and worse, given the traumatic

emotions generated first by the Partition Plan and then by the war and its aftermath, on both sides. And this was quite apart from the acuteness of some problems that had been left unsettled by the armistice, chief among which was Jerusalem. As it was, some sharp debating did take place in the Israeli Knesset after the Agreement was signed, and there is no telling where things would have ended had this debate preceded the completion and signing of the document.

• The agreement would remain in force until a peaceful settlement in Palestine was reached. As has been mentioned above, the Armistice Agreement deviated from the norms of the Fourth Hague Convention (para. 36), which had set limits on armistice and in fact allowed the parties to remain in perpetual armistice as long as it was not superseded by a peace settlement. Even Security Council Resolution No. 242 – adopted on 22 November 1967 following the Six Day War – which sanctioned the obsolescence of a good many provisions of the armistice, did not go so far as to invalidate them. But, in the real world, after Israel's declaration that the armistice had died and was buried, in the aftermath of the 1967 war, a series of cease-fire arrangements governed the relations between Israel and the Arab world, until the peace treaties between Israel and Egypt (1979) and Israel and Jordan (1994) superseded them. As regards the rest of Israel's Arab neighbors (Syria, Lebanon and the Palestinian Autonomy), some practical arrangements have replaced the Armistice Regime, mostly also with UN involvement.

• The parties could revise the agreement by mutual consent, and one year after its signature either party could request the Secretary General of the UN to convene a meeting for a review. This should, again, exclude Articles I and III, but participation in such a meeting would be obligatory. This paragraph reinforced the previous one in that it conferred immutability on the two articles which represented the essence of the armistice; namely, the parties could not change what had been ordered by the Security Council even if they wanted to, since they had left themselves absolutely no way of weakening the binding force of these provisions. Furthermore, with regard to the other provisions of the paragraph, the parties left themselves no way of refusing to discuss changes, if either of them wished to do so. All this apparent impregnability of any commitments made was to prove illusory, as we shall see in the coming chapters which will trace the principal ways in which the Agreement and the Armistice Regime gradually lost their effectiveness.

- Paragraph 4 also affirmed the grip of the Security Council on the armistice, as it stipulated that should the above mentioned review meeting fail, either party would be free to raise the issue before the Council. It seems that this paragraph, like the precedent one, was intended to provide ample reserves of life-sustaining devices for a regime whose duration was uncertain, and which should be conducive to peace in any case. It was foreseen, nevertheless, that in case the regime lasted for years, any needs and situations which arose would call for adjustments and revisions. There must have been those among the personalities involved in the crafting of the Armistice Regime who were not sanguine about the prospects of an early peace.
- The Agreement was signed in quintuplicate by the parties: one was retained by each party; two were sent to the Secretary General for submission to the Security Council and to the Conciliation Commission; and one was given to the UN Mediator.

This last article, like several of the others, indicated the new direction chartered for the crisis in Palestine. As early as 11 December 1948, well before the Armistice Agreement was even negotiated, the General Assembly turned its attention to life after the armistice, appointing a Conciliation Commission on Palestine to help the parties along the road to a permanent settlement. But it seems that the primary goal of the governments concerned was to set in motion, as soon as possible, an international initiative on the future of Jerusalem, lest Israel and Jordan made their own arrangements to lend permanence to the partition of the city or to resume fighting to break the stalemate. Among the tasks of the Conciliation Commission was to present the General Assembly with detailed proposals for a permanent international regime in Jerusalem. On 11 August 1949, after the conclusion of the armistice on all fronts, the Security Council approved the completed work of the Mediator, noting with satisfaction the four armistice agreements concluded between the parties to the conflict.

NOTES

1. Regarding the slight differences in the phrasing of the parallel paragraph in the agreement with Egypt, although both were based on the same draft prepared by the Acting Mediator, see Rosenne, *Israel's Armistice Agreements*.
2. Shabtai Rosenne (see also below) felt that mutual commitments of this kind might well imply mutual recognition by the signatories of the armistice agreements (see p. 41 of his book, *Israel's Armistice Agreements*). It is also of importance to note that the right of the parties to 'freedom from fear of attack' affirmed in this paragraph, was to be later echoed in Security Council Resolution 242 of 20 November 1967, which is the agreed 'recipe' for peace between Israel and her neighbors: the envisaged peace is indeed to include acknowledgement of the parties' 'right to live in peace … free from threats or acts of force'.
3. The eminent expert in international law, Shabtai Rosenne felt that mutual commitments of this kind might well imply mutual recognition by the signatories of the Armistice Agreement (see, *Israel's Armistice Agreements*, p. 42).

4. The Birthpangs of the Armistice Regime in Jerusalem

It is a truism that agreements are made when it is in the interest of their signatories, for whatever reason, to make them; and are honored when it is in the interest of the parties, for whatever reason, to honor them. Still, there are always those who will ascribe noble motives to pragmatic decisions. Following the conclusion of the first armistice agreement between Israel and its neighbors – the one with Egypt – the then Chairman of the UN Security Council took the first opportunity, on 3 March 1949, to express his congratulations:

> I am sure the Security Council will want to express its deep satisfaction at the happy conclusion of the armistice negotiations between Egypt and Israel, and at the lofty outlook, spirit of conciliation and idea of international solidarity shown by both parties.[1]

Despite this grand UN rhetoric, the record of events shows amply that Arabs and Israelis – particularly those Arabs whose record on the battlefield would not have justified it otherwise – had good pragmatic reasons for negotiating an end to the fighting between them, if only to heed the order of the Security Council, which none of them could afford to disregard. The Acting Mediator, Dr Ralph Bunche, addressed himself more to the point in the report he submitted to the Security Council on 20 July 1949, after all four armistice agreements had been signed and sealed. He wrote: 'These are agreements voluntarily entered into by the parties, and any breach of their terms would involve a most serious act of bad faith.'[2] Logically, the second half of this sentence sat rather uncomfortably with the first, especially in a formal presentation of the results of a peace mission just accomplished. The architect and midwife of the Armistice Regime evidently felt that peace was not at hand, the efforts of the Palestine Conciliation Commission notwithstanding.

Israel had strong misgivings concerning the readiness of her Arab neighbors to accept her as an equal and to live in peace with her. The Security Council discussion of Dr Bunche's report was intended, among other things, to open the way for renewing arms supplies to the countries involved in the 1948–49 war; the Security Council had interdicted this trade as part of the truce ordered by it in that year. The interdiction was repealed by a resolution of the Council of 11 August 1949, to Israel's consternation,[3] and in spite of her diplomatic efforts to mobilize support for the continuation of the embargo.[4] In fact, rearmament soon gathered pace among the Arabs, forcing Israel to follow suit in due course. Thus, from the outset, the Armistice Regime was to be tested and implemented in a mixed atmosphere of hope, fear and suspicion.

In retrospect, it seems that the source of the difficulty was a profound difference of outlook between Arabs and Israelis regarding the war and its implications. The Israelis viewed the rights and wrongs of the situation, to say the least, as the Allied Powers had seen the position created by their war against the Axis powers which had ended only four years previously. The Israelis saw the Arabs as the defeated aggressors whose victory would have amounted to Israel's destruction, while they had been saved by the skin of their teeth from imminent disaster at the tremendous cost of 7,000 killed out of a population of 700,000. Like the victorious Allies, Israel naturally took the position that one does not reward defeated aggressors with territorial gifts, and that hostile populations that had made common cause with the aggressors should not be treated as innocent victims of misfortune. These positions found support in two relevant UN resolutions and in the views of UN Secretary General Trygve Lie, who branded the Arab invasion of Palestine 'the first armed aggression which the world had seen since the end of the war.'[5]

The Arab states took a very different view of the rights and wrongs of the post-armistice situation, refusing to take either blame or responsibility for the consequences of their rejection of the Partition Plan and their decision to make war on Israel. Also, they found it hard to accept that their defeat in war at the hands of tiny and resourceless Israel – still tiny and resourceless in spite of the territorial gains represented by the armistice lines – reflected an enduring and objective military situation. They continued to view the establishment of the Jewish State as a travesty of justice and a fleeting episode, bound to disappear into oblivion in the course of history. Thus, reconciliation and reaching a peaceful settlement with Israel was out of the question for them. Quite the contrary: as peace became increasingly elusive, and in the wake of the new arms race, talk began in the Arab world of a 'second round.'[6]

The inability of Israel and Jordan to move on from the armistice to a permanent peace was disappointing for a number of reasons. First, the two countries enjoyed a unique intimacy of dialogue, going back to the meeting between King Abdallah and Mrs Golda Meyerson (Meir) before the war. While Arab and Israeli representatives were exploring peace prospects with the Conciliation Commission at Lausanne, not facing one another in direct talks, high-ranking Israelis held meetings close to home – mostly in Shuneh, Jordan – with King Abdallah and his ministers, in a businesslike manner. Second, on key issues relating to Jerusalem, the two sides still needed each other to resist the *corpus separatum* model envisaged in the Partition Plan. Moreover, they already had a solution in principle – under Article VIII of the Armistice Agreement outlined above – for specific issues regarding their peaceful coexistence within the area threatened by internationalization. Finally, King Abdallah continued to hope for Israeli aid, passive at least, which would help him realize his designs on Syria.[7]

The failure of Israel and Jordan to maintain the cordiality of their secret armistice talks can be assessed in consideration of the following specific difficulties:

- While Israel was anxious to implement the provisions of Article VIII as soon as possible, Jordan was eager to discuss territorial reversion to the Partition boundaries and a sovereign corridor for itself to the Mediterranean at Gaza, across the Israeli Negev, as a basis for peace negotiations. The question of the Palestinian refugees, who had settled in refugee camps on the West Bank, now under Jordanian rule, or even in Transjordan itself, likewise featured among Jordanian concerns and demands, though with a somewhat lesser emphasis.[8]
- There was great uncertainty as to Jordan's ability to strike a separate deal with Israel, if it wanted to. It had many disagreements with other Arab states, quite apart from the

natural reservations to be expected over any Jordanian breach of Arab solidarity.[9]

- There was growing Israeli despair regarding Jordanian willingness – and perhaps political strength – to honor its commitment in Article VIII to permit the reopening of the Israeli university and hospital on Mount Scopus, and free access for Israelis to the holy places in eastern Jerusalem.[10]

- There were also doubts concerning the usefulness of a political settlement with King Abdallah and his unstable and possibly transient kingdom. Israeli Prime Minister David Ben-Gurion felt that such a settlement would hardly bring meaningful political and economic benefits for Israel; rather, it was most likely to displease the durable and more formidable Egypt, the key country in the Arab world, and delay the more promising settlement with her.[11]

Receding expectations of a good Israeli–Jordanian relationship, coupled with the lack of progress by the Palestine Conciliation Commission and mounting friction with Israel's other neighbors along the armistice lines, inevitably had a detrimental effect on the functioning of the Armistice Regime between Israel and Jordan in general and in truncated Jerusalem in particular. Before delving into the specific issues which plagued the two sides in Jerusalem, it is useful to recapitulate the relevant elements of the armistice machinery which was to deal with these problems. Three factors were expected to interact: the MAC, the armistice lines themselves, and the Special Committee analyzed above. The Armistice Regime was put into place fairly quickly by the MAC. With the preliminary delineation of the armistice lines on the ground, the armed forces of both sides took up their new positions and were reduced in the prescribed defence zones, as agreed in Article VII. Any movement or shooting across the lines was strictly forbidden.[12] The Special Committee was established so that it could address itself to the implementation of Article VIII described above.

To these essentials must be added some important details of the *modus operandi* of the MAC, which may be seen as the policeman and court of first instance of the Armistice Regime. Its Chairman was the COS of UNTSO, an appointee of the Secretary General of the UN or his representative. Normally, the COS appointed a permanent Chairman of the Commission from among his corps of military observers, and the two parties appointed a Senior and a

Junior Delegate from among their armed forces. Unless the two sides decided to unite against the Chairman, he determined the outcome of discussions and voting in the MAC, and it was his prerogative to call meetings of the MAC, which could be formal or informal, urgent or regular. For investigations of alleged breaches of the armistice, the MAC used the services of the UNMOs. The MAC could establish subcommittees, usually *ad hoc*, to deal with current issues when the plenary of the MAC was able to meet only in emergency sessions. The subcommittees were usually manned by the Junior Delegates of the parties and chaired by the Operations Officer of the MAC, appointed by the Chairman from among his military observers. Under the umbrella of the MAC, the parties could reach a variety of practical agreements on minor issues. They could also institute procedures for quick and direct contact between local commanders and all sorts of technical experts (for example, for health and sanitation, animal husbandry, veterinary medicine, agriculture, cartography, land surveying, water and sewerage, mine removal, and the like), so that emergencies could be handled immediately to avoid mutual undesirable developments.

By virtue of his position as overall supervisor of the truce and commander of all UNMOs, the COS of UNTSO was in practice the overseer of the various armistice commissions and the intermediary between the MAC and the Security Council, which was effectively the court of appeal for the MAC. It became customary for the MAC, and especially its subcommittees, to deal with current matters; while issues of political or diplomatic importance were handled at the level of the COS of UNTSO. In response, Israel established a Division for Armistice Affairs in its Foreign Ministry, headed by a senior diplomat who was assisted by a senior military officer. The two also served as the political and military supervisors respectively of the Israeli representatives to the various MACs, and as liaison officers to the Israeli political and military establishments. The Jordanians appointed a senior officer to head their delegation to the MAC who usually handled all dealings with the UN, aided by senior Jordanian Foreign Ministry officials when necessary.

In concluding this outline of the armistice apparatus, it is pertinent to cite an opinion of UNTSO COS General Riley about the nature of the MACs, which he expressed during a Security Council debate on 30 October 1950 which arose from complaints by the parties to the armistice agreements. Riley suggested that the MACs had by then outlived their usefulness regarding the military portions of the armistice agreements, as only three or four military violations of the armistice had been reported. On the other hand, there were about 200 'police' complaints 'particularly involving the stealing of cattle, sheep, goats and water pipes' which were not of the kind that the MAC should handle, unless the parties concerned agreed to use that common meeting ground to settle those problems.[13]

General Riley seems to have been oblivious to the fact that theft, and for that matter infiltration across the demarcation line – mostly from Jordan into Israel – reflected an attitude whose implications could be dangerous; as indeed they proved to be. For while on the human level, one could understand the plight of an Arab who was displaced from his land during the war and could not resist the temptation to sneak across the border and steal what he could find on his way, the scale of such incidents soon became alarming, with infiltrations for 'economic' purposes soon followed by infiltrations for harassment and murder. The new political situation to which the parties had committed themselves required their vigilance lest acts of this sort poisoned their precarious relationship. In time it became clear that the Arab countries had not come to terms with coexisting peacefully with the neighbor whose life they had attempted to extinguish at birth. Six weeks after the General's statement at the Security Council, the situation along the Israeli–Jordanian line assumed a distinctly threatening character with the killing, on 16 December 1950, of an Israeli civilian by rifle fire from the wall of the Old City in Jerusalem. On 25 January 1951, another Israeli civilian was shot dead in the Jerusalem area. By the middle of February 1951, a total of 16 serious complaints were submitted by Israel and Jordan to the MAC alleging grave armistice violations and requesting emergency meetings of the Commission. On 12 March 1951, General Riley submitted a comprehensive report to the Security Council about these events and the ensuing developments. Some excerpts from this report illustrate the practical functioning of the Armistice Regime between Israel and Jordan and convey the flavor peculiar to the formal characteristics of the armistice machinery.[14]

After listing the 16 complaints, the report informed the Security Council that:

An emergency meeting of the Commission on 12 February 1951 was called to deal with these complaints alleging border incidents and ended in deadlock with the delegations disagreeing on the order in which the complaints were to be considered. The Jordanian delegation insisted that priority should be given to its complaint of 7 February, in which it alleged that an Israeli armed band had blown up two houses in the village of Sharafat, just south of the Jordanian-controlled part of Jerusalem, killing ten Arabs and wounding eight. The Israeli delegation, however, took the view that the complaints regarding which emergency meetings had been requested should be dealt with in chronological order.

The report then stated:

On 14 February 1951, following several informal discussions, the Hashemite Kingdom–Israel Mixed Armistice Commission adopted the following decision unanimously:
• The HJK [Hashemite Jordan Kingdom]–Israel MAC condemns the wanton killing and murder that have taken place in the past few weeks in the border areas, and deplores the incidents which have recently taken a turn for the worse.
• The MAC draws attention to the imperative need of preventing a recurrence of such acts which have led to complaints referring to the killing of innocent people, the blowing up of homes, murder and rape.
• In view of the fact that high-ranking officers, representing HJK and Israel, will meet shortly to discuss steps to be taken to prevent in future all such incidents, the MAC decides that the above-mentioned complaints be considered as having been acted upon.

The Commission also made the following unanimous decision concerning the powers of its Chairman:

• The Chairman shall … as from 15 February 1951, have the sole right to decide whether a future complaint … calls for an emergency meeting or not.
• If the Chairman accepts a complaint as necessitating an emergency meeting, he will call a meeting … within 24 hours of the submission of the complaint to him, attendance at which will be compulsory.

- In case more than one emergency complaint is accepted by the Chairman at the same time, he will have the right to decide which of the complaints is to be discussed first, provided all such complaints are discussed within 24 hours of their receipt.

Following the emergency meeting held by the MAC on 14 February, the Israeli and Jordanian delegations held more discussions, on 15 and 16 February, as a result of which they decided to strike off the agenda 100 additional complaints which had been on the agenda for some time (52 from Jordan and 48 from Israel). These incidents, which exposed the fragility of the armistice arrangement and, contrary to Riley's initial assessment, dangerously pushed the parties towards a spiral of violence and reprisals, generated a series of long-term conclusions which emerge from the General's report of 12 March 1951:

- The two serious Israeli complaints heading the 16 listed in the report to the Security Council, alleging the killing of civilians by Jordanians, were not acted upon by the MAC because either the Chairman or, more likely, the Jordanians, would not let the Commission meet, on one pretext or another.
- The two serious Israeli complaints were followed by four Jordanian and one Israeli complaint, none of which alleged loss of life or injuries to persons. Still the MAC remained inactive. Then, from 5 to 9 February, a number of serious incidents occurred. These involved loss of life, injury and the rape of an Israeli woman, and included the serious Israeli action which took place on 7 February in the village of Sharafat, which resulted in the death of ten Arabs, the wounding of eight and the destruction of two houses. Only after 9 February did the MAC finally meet in emergency session, at which Jordan was anxious to have the Sharafat raid discussed ahead of all the others. It is difficult to dismiss the thought that had the MAC acted immediately after the Israeli complaint of 16 December 1950, the ensuing unfortunate chain of incidents might have been avoided.
- From the language used by the MAC – particularly the details linking the condemnation to specific complaints submitted to it – one can conclude with certainty that the murder and rape attributed to Jordanians, and the raid on Sharafat attributed to Israel, were acknowledged by the respective delegations of both

sides. Thus, the Israeli raid was noted as an act of retaliation signaling a new Israeli policy in the face of the deterioration of the Armistice Regime. Henceforth, Israel would use punishment in an effort to discourage and deter attacks from Jordanian territory.

- Whatever the nature and logic of the tactics employed to block immediate MAC investigation and discussion of the first Israeli complaint, retaliation eventually forced the issue. Moreover, it persuaded the MAC to adopt rules guaranteeing that similar paralysis did not occur again.
- The wholesale mutual cancellation of complaints of 14 February, after disposal of the 16 incidents listed in General Riley's report, suggests early abuse of the armistice system, either through irresponsible flooding of the registers of the MAC with trumped-up complaints, or through a routine flouting of the regulations prohibiting any crossing of the armistice line, or – worse – through a more or less systematic policy of harassment.
- General Riley told the Security Council on 30 October 1950, that during the previous 12 or 14 months – that is, within five months of the signing of the Armistice between Israel and Jordan – the MAC had received hundreds of complaints about theft of cattle, sheep, goats, and water pipes, but only four complaints of a military nature. This meant that: (1) after five months of respecting the armistice lines, people realized there were no penalties for flouting them; and (2) stolen animals and irrigation pipes were moving from Israel into Jordan, not vice versa. Thus, the way was open to more harmful and dangerous activities.

Political developments regarding the armistice were no more reassuring in that initial period. In fact, General Riley's appearance before the Security Council on 30 October 1950, was occasioned by an Israeli complaint to the Council over the almost total lack of progress in implementing the provisions of Article VIII. These provisions were crucial to a reasonable Israeli–Jordanian coexistence. Had Israelis been enabled to cross over into the Old City to visit holy places freely, and to move freely through Jordanian-held territory in and out of the Hebrew University and Hadassah Hospital on Mount Scopus, the psychological impulses leading to active hostility between Israelis and Jordanians could have been mitigated. At the 517th meeting of the Security Council, on 30 October 1950, the representative of Israel, Mr Abba Eban, spoke of 19 months of paralysis in the Special Committee formed under Article VIII.[15]

While Israeli was convinced that Jordan's commitments in that Article were incontestable and that Jordanian stonewalling was obvious, the Security Council was not prepared to go beyond noting that the Special Committee had been formed and expressing the hope that the Committee would proceed expeditiously to carry out its various functions.[16] In a resolution of 17 November 1950, the Security Council obliged Jordan to resume discussions in the Special Committee, but there was no progress. In a meeting with a senior Israeli representative, Mr Reuven Shiloah, on 23 February 1951, Jordanian Prime Minister Samir al-Rifa'i explained candidly why his country did not intend to implement Article VIII. He said that there were no longer any prospective gains for his country in that context, since Jordan had reconstructed its own road to Bethlehem and had arranged for its own separate power supply for eastern Jerusalem. Israel could note with satisfaction, he added, that Jordan had cooperated with her in making it possible to put the Jerusalem–Tel Aviv railway line back into service, and that was that.[17]

Article VIII did not offer any additional benefits for Jordan in return for Israeli access to the holy places and the reopening of the university and hospital on Mount Scopus, or renewed use of the Jewish cemetery on the Mount of Olives. Israel's road links and water supply to Jerusalem were already secured independently.[18] The Special Committee was officially laid to rest, it seems, by a report dated 4 November 1952 from the COS of UNTSO to the Security Council, stating that: 'Jordan has declined thus far to meet in the Special Committee.'[19] And so the glorious Article VIII that was to make life in Jerusalem liveable was lost forever. *Sic transit gloria mundi.*

A further considerable disappointment was handed by Jordan to Israel in relation to Article XII(3) of the Armistice Agreement. That article allowed either of the parties to call on the Secretary General of the UN to convoke an Israeli–Jordanian conference for the purpose of reviewing, revising or suspending provisions of the Armistice Agreement, other than Articles I and III. Participation in such a conference was to be compulsory. Israel requested that the Secretary General activate this provision, but Jordan refused to accept his invitation to attend, and that was the end of the matter. Another hope had been dashed.[20]

By that time, the Armistice Regime had become an uncomfortable structure of relationships devoid of prospects of a better accommodation in the near future, or peace in a foreseeable one. As early as 1951 the Jordanian delegate to the MAC told the Israeli delegate to the Special Committee, that it was widely believed among Arabs that an Arab victory over Israel would have been achieved in the 1948–49 war but for the UN intervention to stop the fighting, and that the Arab world was watching for an opportunity to launch a second round of war. Consequently, the Jordanian delegate concluded, no settlement of any kind could be expected unless the Powers were to impose one.[21]

In July 1952, one year to the month after the murder of King Abdallah in Jerusalem, which damped prospects of Israeli–Jordanian cooperation, a military coup in Egypt brought the Young Officers to power, among them Gamal Abdul Nasser who had been humiliated on the Egyptian front in the 1948–49 war. Nasser, who was to become the hero of Arab nationalism and set his country on a course of adventurism characterized by strident hostility to Israel, added fuel to the armistice fires practically everywhere by initiating border incidents along the armistice boundaries with Israel. The Jerusalem front was not spared by these events and so all concerned, including UNTSO, were affected by mistrust and suspicion, accompanied by paramount and inordinately vigilant concern for their own respective interests, as we shall explain below.

Nowhere in the Jerusalem area would this general decay of the Armistice Regime become as acute as in the two zones of Mount Scopus and Government House, which should have come under the jurisdiction of the still-born Special Committee. This will be the concern of the next chapter.

NOTES

1. Security Council Official Records, Fourth Year, No. 16, p. 2.
2. UN Document No. S/1357.
3. It was the Arabs who stood to gain more land than Israel from the beginning of the arms race, and Israel who was exhausted from the war and was busy absorbing the incoming vast numbers of new immigrants, and feared the renewal of hostilities. See also, Note 6 below.
4. See UN Documents Nos S/1376, 70 (10 June 1949) and 220 (17 August 1949): Foreign Policy Documents, Israel State Archives (ISA), Jerusalem.
5. See Trygve Lie, *In the Cause of Peace* (New York: Macmillan, 1954), p. 174. See also, the General Assembly recommendation of 11 December 1948, and the Security Council Resolution of 11 August 1949, both of which called for 'agreement by negotiation' on

'all questions outstanding' between the parties; thus leaving open territorial questions and repatriation of Arab refugees. Only the first of them referred to the refugees, in a formula which included resettlement and tied any eventual return to 'willingness to live at peace with neighbors.'

6. Concerning rearmament in preparation for the second round, see the Israeli Government press release of 25 January 1950 (Foreign Policy Documents, ISA). As to the threats of a second round, made officially and publicly by the Arabs in violation of the respective armistice agreements, see UN Document No. S/1794, which included part of a wider Israeli complaint against Egypt and Jordan that was submitted to the Security Council in October 1950.

7. See letter dated 3 April 1949, from Director General Walter Eytan to Foreign Minister Moshe Sharett (Document No. 267, Israel Foreign Policy Documents, ISA).

8. Report by Foreign Minister Moshe Sharett, 9 May 1949, regarding a meeting with King Abdallah in Shuneh on 5 May (Document No. 15, Foreign Policy Documents, ISA).

9. Report dated 1 July 1949, from Lausanne, by Walter Eytan to Foreign Minister Moshe Sharett, regarding a conversation with Jordanian representative Fawzi al-Mulki (Document No. 113, Foreign Policy Documents, ISA).

10. Report dated 9 January 1951, from Israel's representative on the Special Committee (established under Article VIII of the Armistice Agreement). (Document No. 11, Foreign Policy Documents, ISA).

11. See the relevant note in D. Ben Gurion's *Diary*, 13 February 1951 (Israel Defence Forces Archives). The murder of King Abdallah in July the same year could only have strengthened the Prime Minister's skepticism.

12. It is extremely important to emphasize the preliminary nature of the initial tracing of the armistice lines on the ground. The exact location could not be determined without meticulous plotting and offered many opportunities for dissent. This issue will be discussed in detail below.

13. Security Council Official Records, Meeting No. 517 (30 October 1950). Some comments on the above views of General Riley will emerge, more or less indirectly, as concrete armistice problems are discussed below.

14. UN Document No. S/2048, Part II.

15. See Security Council Official Records, Meeting No. 517.

16. UN Document No. S/1907. The discussions in the Security Council, which resulted in the resolution appearing in that document which was adopted on 17 November 1950, also covered issues concerning armistice questions between Egypt and Israel.

17. At a meeting of the MAC on 25 April 1949 Jordan agreed to the necesssary (small) adjustment in the armistice line.

18. See the text of Article VIII in Chapter 3 and Appendix 1; also, the report dated 12 March 1951, from M. Sasson and R. Shiloah (Document No. 83, Foreign Policy Documents, ISA).

19. UN Document No. S/2833.

20. UN Document Nos S/3139 and S/3180 (1954).

21. See Note 10 above.

5. Armistice Without Article VIII

With Article VIII remaining dormant at best, defunct in practice, issues unresolved by the Armistice Agreement took center stage as sources of constant friction, with occasional deadly flareups. These issues resulted from the imperfect interim armistice settlement and resurfaced from time to time, reflecting the ups and downs in relations between Israel and Jordan along the armistice line.

THE AREA BETWEEN THE LINES: GOVERNMENT HOUSE

Neither party was fully satisfied with the status of the Government House area between the armistice lines, which was of interest primarily because of its commanding location overlooking the Old City. Furthermore, it constituted a large and well-located urban area coveted for civilian and economic development. Finally, some roads linking Jordanian territory ran through the area, and it offered convenient access into the Israeli-held part of Jerusalem. As the area was demilitarized under UNTSO supervision, each party was anxious lest the other gain some advantage there by stealth or ruse. UNTSO, for its part, was alert against any attempted encroachment on its own positions there. Thus, early in the life of the armistice, Israelis and Jordanians were united in disliking the vacuum created in the Government House area. The parties, therefore, without consulting UNTSO, decided to divide the area between themselves, except for the Government House compound itself where UNTSO was based.

UNTSO objected to this scheme and persuaded the Jordanians to back out, but meanwhile Jordanian soldiers had already taken control of the portion alloted to them in the bilateral arrangement.

In response, on 6 June 1949, Israel installed troops and positions in its allotted section and set about fencing it off and ploughing vacant land there which had been the site of agricultural experiments conducted by the Hebrew University. A diplomatic crisis ensued, and the issue was discussed by both the Armistice Commission and the Special Committee, in one of its first attempts to deal with areas of potential and actual conflict. For strategic reasons Jordan was anxious to have Government House on the Jordanian side, should the armistice lines ever be made permanent, while letting UNTSO use it as long as necessary; UNTSO seemed agreeable to this approach. It is unclear why UNTSO supported Jordan in this matter. However, no firm agreement was reached and the situation reverted to the previous status quo. The entire Government House area returned to its previous demilitarized status, with civilian activity and the presence of civilian police permitted in the Israeli and Jordanian sectors.

On 7 February 1953, Israel made a fresh attempt to improve its position in this area by taking military control, under police disguise, of the abandoned Arab College within its sector. The considerations behind this move were defensive and tactical. As a pretext, Israel alleged Jordanian infringement of the agreed accommodation in the Mount Scopus enclave in northern Jerusalem, where Israel had detected the unauthorized presence of Jordanian soldiers and an influx of Jordanian civilians. Under political pressure from Washington, Israel backed down.[1] Diplomatic friction continued throughout the years over rights and prerogatives of the UN in the Government House compound, as the UN insisted that none of the parties, not even their accredited representatives to the MAC, could gain access there without UNTSO's approval. Nevertheless, Israelis and Jordanians both held that the entire site was theirs, its status to be determined by an eventual agreement.[2]

The UN insisted on its authority as guarantor of the 'special status of the area around Government House,' relying on a decision by the preceding truce monitoring organization back in 1948.[3] UNTSO reinforced its claim to authority when around Christmas and New Year the COS hosted two consecutive balls, to which the delegates of the parties to the MAC were invited to attend separately. They would not be admitted without invitation, and neither were they invited together; the intention was to send a clear message that the parties had no say over the site and would not be permitted to convene there together to again plot to evict the UN. These balls were attended or boycotted according to the fortunes of the relations between the UN and the parties at any particular point.

The annual balls were not the only occasions to test the limits of UN authority in that problematic area. In the 1960s, two events required cooperation of the Jordanian and Israeli delegates at the MAC, much to UN displeasure, testing those limits to the full. In a meeting of the sub-committee of the MAC in 1962, the Israeli delegate, Captain Israeli, proposed joint action to fight the processionary moth, a pest which infested pine trees in the Jerusalem area causing great damage to the preciously few hand-planted wooded hills there.[4] As the Jordanians were oblivious to the blight and ways to combat it, Israel suggested a meeting at which Israeli experts could show their Jordanian colleagues infested trees and present the materials needed to eradicate the moth. The Jordanian delegates were sceptical at first, doubting in particular that a neutral place could be found for the meeting. But when the parties' agricultural experts met under the auspices of the MAC, some of them discovered that they had been coworkers at the British Mandate Department of Agriculture 20 years earlier. Emotions overtook the gathering and the Jordanians grew eager to have their Israeli friends teach them about the plant disease, which they knew could cross the border into their territory at any time. The Israeli delegates, somewhat disingenuously, suggested that the ideal location would be Government House, where a lush pine wood surrounded the premises. After some hesitation, aware of the UN's reluctance to accept this intrusion into their fiefdom, the Jordanians agreed. The UN followed suit, not wanting to be seen as hampering a health measure agreed upon by the parties.

On another occasion that same year, a horse belonging to an Arab farmer in the adjoining village of Silwan was apprehended in Israeli territory. Normally, trespassing animals would be kept in quarantine for 40 days to ensure they carried no contagious diseases before they were handed over to their owners in the presence of UN Observers. But the village in question happened to be the home of the Jordanian Senior Delegate to the MAC, General Muhammed Dawud.[5] Dawud personally intervened on behalf of his fellow villager and regarded the expeditious return of the animal as a matter of personal prestige and honor. The Israeli delegate, the same Captain Israeli, saw this as an opportunity both to please his colleague and at the same time to again test the UN's position concerning Government House. The Jordanian delegate agreed to expedite the handover, suggesting that it be done the next day, skipping all formalities, in the UNTSO compound. The UN officers reacted quite unpleasantly, arguing, on the authority of their COS himself, Swedish General von Horn, that the handover should be held outside the UN area as the 'horse could ruin the gardens of the compound.' The diplomatic crisis gathered momentum and was referred to higher authorities on all sides. The Jordanian delegate elected to keep quiet while Israel did the fighting for him. The UNTSO COS finally caved in – under protest – when faced with the threat that international journalists would be summoned to see how the UN was hampering the implementation of an agreement reached by the parties.

Friction and complaints persisted on both sides in situations not covered by clear agreements. Israel set up a roadblock on its side of the demarcation line to ensure that UN and other traffic to and from the UNTSO compound was not used for unlawful purposes. Among other things it was important to check the identity of Israeli civilians who were allowed into the demilitarized area, where an experimental farm and student dormitories were located. Occasionally a Jordanian military vehicle was spotted traveling on the new road from Jerusalem to Bethlehem, paved by the Jordanians through rocky ground as a substitute for the old road which was in Israeli hands. Sections of this road crossed the demilitarized zone, but the Jordanian military had no other recourse, and most of the time Israel did not insist. Similarly, Arabs from the tiny village of Jabal al-Mukabbar, just outside the perimeter fence of Government House, on occasion crossed into the Israeli side with their herds, or attempted to plough patches of rocky land in the Israeli part of the zone. Equally unacceptable was an Israeli enterpreneur's unauthorized start of construction, in 1963, of a hotel on the Israeli slope of the zone, which might serve civilians who did not live permanently in the area. Bitter deliberations were held in the MAC on this matter, and the construction work was not completed at the time.[6] Still, as a rule, probably due to the immediate proximity of the UN headquarters, a peaceful routine prevailed in daily life in that highly sensitive area.

Through historical irony, or perhaps just as a quirk in the rapidly evolving events in the agitated Middle East, on 6 June 1967 – 18 years to the day after Israeli forces entered the western part of Government House to implement an agreement with Jordan on its partition – Jordanian forces burst into that area, drawn into battle by the Egyptian belligerence against Israel which sparked the Six Day War. No Jordanian pretext was advanced to justify this move. The Jordanians were simply going after what they had always regarded as the most strategic asset in southern Jerusalem. Inelegantly, their first objective was the UN compound itself, whose occupants had backed Jordan's demand for control over the site in an eventual partition of the area. The surprised UN personnel quickly ran for cover.

Israel reacted swiftly and dislodged the Jordanians from their short-lived gains – proving to them once again that it was not for nothing that the location appears on the maps as the 'Hill of Evil Council' – and handed the area back to UNTSO, which had sided with the Jordanian claim. But by then, as elsewhere in Jerusalem, the armistice lines had been wiped out. It was Israel that now tolerated the UN headquarters in what had become Israeli territory. Jordan's claims to that area, as to all its conquests on the West Bank and Jerusalem since 1948, were finally renounced in August 1988, when King Hussein, terrified lest the Intifadah of the Palestinians against Israel might expand into his fief in Transjordan, announced the end of his tutelage of Western Palestine.

THE MOUNT SCOPUS ENCLAVE

The status of the Mount Scopus enclave, as an Israeli island within Jordanian territory, was even more uncertain than that of the Government House area. Whereas the latter was seen by both sides as belonging to them jointly pending an agreed partition, Jordan argued that the entire Mount Scopus demilitarized zone was part of its territory; Israel regarded its sector as 'sovereign Israeli territory.' Article VIII provided for the 'resumption of the normal functioning of the cultural and humanitarian institutions on Mount Scopus and free access thereto' under 'agreed plans and arrangements,' which implied a *de facto* functional integration of the Israeli sector within western Jerusalem, or at least so the Israelis expected. How else, indeed, was one to understand 'normal functioning,' or a major university and a major hospital enjoying 'free access?' However, since Jordan blocked the reopening of these institutions, Israeli expectations in that regard were replaced with frustration and inevitable resentment.[7]

To further complicate matters, a dispute developed as to which of two maps of the 'island' was the binding one. Israel held that it was the one attached to the Mount Scopus demilitarization agreement of 7 July 1948 initialled by Franklyn M. Begley, a UN official who assisted in the preparation of the agreement. The Jordanians preferred a map drawn on 21 July 1948 in connection with a subsidiary agreement between the local Israeli and Jordanian commanders, relating to the no man's land strip between the Israeli and Jordanian sectors of the demilitarized zone. That map reduced the original area of the zone, to the benefit of Jordan. It was initialed by the above-mentioned Mr Begley and the Jordanian military commander, but not by the Israeli commander. Why the UN official apparently certified two conflicting maps was not clear.

He may have been guilty of nothing more than human error or an oversight. As to the Israeli and Jordanian commanders who had met to discuss arrangements for the area separating their sectors, it does not seem logical that they should have digressed into amending the original Mount Scopus agreement. At any rate, since the Israeli commander did not sign the 21 July map, it was not binding, and there the matter rested. Norwegian General Odd Bull, the UNTSO COS since 1963, who saw his headquarters in Government House taken over by Jordanian troops in 1967, commented that the disagreement over the two Mount Scopus maps gave rise to 'most of the problems in the Mount Scopus region.' He felt, also, that it was 'incomprehensible ... that the Head of UNTSO had not at the outset insisted on one valid map.'[8]

The Mount Scopus area was significantly different from the Government House area in another respect: it included within the Israeli sector an Arab community which was unfriendly, to say the least. The Mount Scopus Agreement allowed the 'present population of the [Arab] village of Isawiyya' to remain in place, but 'no additions will be made to the village population except by agreement of both parties.' Here was another potential source of trouble, namely illicit infiltration of Arabs, with or without Jordanian encouragement, to increase the population of the village. The agreement did not define agreed modalities for monitoring the level of the permanent population and its natural growth, as opposed to ingress of outsiders seeking substitutes for homes lost in the war, or infiltrators. It had become customary in the Armistice Regime that the situation on the ground counted much more than the legalities of the Agreement; if the Agreement offered the option of increasing the population of the village 'by mutual agreement,' one could be sure that the population would be increased, with or without agreement. Arabs were likely to assume that no one would take the unpopular initiative, legal as it may be, to evacuate poor refugee families, including young children and destitute old people, from their places of refuge.

In addition, and again for lack of specific and detailed arrangements, the sides would disagree about the authorization and limits of agricultural cultivation and grazing by those Arab inhabitants in the Israeli-held area. Israel also worried that the Jordanians might introduce into the village, under civilian cloak, all sorts of undesirable elements. Next, among the humanitarian institutions within the Israeli sector of Mount Scopus one could count, in a sense, a cemetery of Allied war dead from the First World War, where many British, Australian and New Zealand troops of General Allenby's command are buried. The cemetery was neatly maintained by the Commonwealth War Graves Commission based in Britain. Access to it was needed for gardening and occasional repairs to structures and graves, and for annual memorial services. Visits and memorial services posed no problems, but regular maintenance presented questions regarding the nationality of the workers, their residence, procedures for access to the area and related matters. While the Commonwealth War Graves Commission saw itself as the exclusive arbiter in most of these matters, Israel felt that it was solely responsible for all activities and security on the Mount Scopus 'island'. The Jordanians, for their part, were anxious to encourage any erosion of Israel's authority on Mount Scopus, in this case under Commonwealth pressure. But in the end, failing an agreed solution on the one hand, and due to a tremendous sympathy the Jews in Palestine had for General Allenby and his troops on the other, Israel undertook to carry out essential maintenance work in the cemetery unilaterally with the scant and overburdened manpower at its disposal in that isolated enclave.[9]

The UN was not in a position to contribute much to the settlement of these issues, since its powers and role on Mount Scopus were far from clear. The area in question was not mentioned in the Armistice Agreement aside from the vital but problematic

Article VIII, where it was reserved for treatment by the Special Committee. Consequently, the day-to-day terms of reference for UNTSO concerning Mount Scopus were anchored in the 7 July 1948 Mount Scopus Agreement. Violations of the Security Council-ordered truce (paragraph 1 of Article I of the Armistice Agreement) and eventual 'agreed plans and arrangements designed to enlarge the scope of this agreement and to effect improvements in its application' (paragraph 1 of Article VIII) were a separate complex. Paragraph 3 of the Mount Scopus Agreement laid down that armed Jewish and Arab police in the demilitarized zone 'will be placed on duty under the United Nations Commander,' and 'the UN flag will fly on the main buildings.' For the rest, the UN Commander had the responsibility of arranging for supplies, replacement of personnel and visits by 'properly accredited individuals.'

This vague regime was a recipe for misunderstandings, friction and violence, as events were to show. Its very general stipulations were neither elaborated nor superseded by anything better, as envisaged by Article VIII. At the height of tension in the course of those 19 unhappy years, Lieutenant-Colonel G.A. Flint, the Canadian Chairman of the MAC, lost his life 'while attempting to end ... firing and rescue some Israeli policemen' from Jordanian fire. Four Israeli policemen lost their lives in the course of that incident.[10]

The Mount Scopus regime was vague because nothing in it determined the authority of the UN Commander; none of the parties would submit to his directions in matters related to their security; no one could define who were the 'properly accredited' individuals permitted to visit the Mount Scopus enclave, which opened wide possibilities of fraud; no one could say whether the 'policemen' stationed there by both parties were members of the civilian police force or otherwise, nor what weapons they were allowed to carry; and there was no authority to enforce any agreed understanding of the parties if one of them failed to honor it. The UN Commander was a commander only in theory, since none of the police forces of the parties accepted orders from him, and he was not free to circulate on Mount Scopus without prior agreement and coordination with the parties to the armistice, allowing them ample time to deploy or hide as they wished.

From the point of view of both Jordan and Israel, the two square kilometers of the Mount Scopus enclave were considerably more important strategically than the much larger demilitarized area surrounding Government House. 'If Israel managed to get control of Mount Scopus it would mean that Jerusalem was more or less encircled,' wrote General Bull in his memoirs as the UNTSO COS.[11] But Israel's position on the Mount, as a demilitarized island within Jordanian territory, was much more precarious in comparison with its situation in the Government House enclave which was continguous to Israeli territory and directly accessible in case of emergency. Also, it was believed initially that the presence of UNTSO headquarters provided a measure of deterrence. Conversely, the Jordanians as well as the UN personnel understood that should the Israeli garrison on the Mount be put in jeopardy, Israel would act swiftly to ensure linkage between its territory and the enclave, possibly triggering large-scale battles that no one wanted. For these reasons, in spite of the violent exchanges such as the one cited above, and in spite of the vulnerability of the fortnightly Israeli convoy to Scopus under UN auspices, not once did Jordan attempt to launch an all-out assault on the Israeli enclave or the convoys, nor did Israel mount an attack to create such a link, until the momentous events of the 1967 war.

Thus, once it became clear that Jordan was not going to allow implementation of the armistice provisions relating to Mount Scopus, Israel spared no efforts to strengthen its juridical and military position there within the limits imposed by the Mount Scopus Agreement. Hence, Israel strived to maintain a favorable balance of precedents, creating new ones when possible. Jordan's concern was the opposite, namely to prevent an expansion of Israel's effective presence on and around Mount Scopus. Against this background, three major foci of friction soon developed: relief and supply convoys to the Israeli sector, activities related to the village of Issawiyya, and the patrolling of the Israeli sector by the 85-man police contingent which guarded the premises.

The bi-weekly convoys routine was launched in late 1948, under UN inspection designed to ensure compliance with paragraph 1 of Article II of the Armistice Agreement, under which no military or political gains were permitted during the truce ordered by the Security Council. The convoys were barred from carrying weapons, ammunition and military equipment of every description, as well as mail, maps or plans which might convey military information. From the outset it was clear that this would be difficult if not impossible to enforce. There were endless possibilities for hiding military equipment of every description in the armored buses which brought each fortnight a convoy of personnel to relieve half the Israeli contingent on duty in the enclave. Civilians going up ostensibly to maintain laboratory equipment or to look over important book collections in the university libraries could be anything but what they were said to be. Neither UN personnel nor Jordanian experts were able to verify what they were told. Even the canned and otherwise preserved foodstuffs sent up could contain unacceptable items. The UN personnel supervising the convoys, sometimes even sampling the cans of food, could also be distracted to a degree which would compromise their vigilance.

At first Jordan was not involved whatsoever in the inspection of convoys – quite rightly, it would seem, as supplies were the exclusive responsibility of the UN commander, in accordance with paragraph 4 of the Mount Scopus Agreement.[12] Then followed the sorts of developments typical to the flawed implementation of imperfect agreements. The Arab signatories, dissatisfied with the outcome of a war which they had expected to win, began to see the UN involvement as a plot designed to deprive them of victory over Israel.[13] On 14 October 1950, the UNTSO COS William E. Riley, the American general mentioned above, responded to Jordanian dissatisfaction regarding the Mount Scopus convoys by formulating new convoy arrangements. Henceforth two Jordanian observers, as well as two Israeli observers, were to be present when UN personnel inspected the convoys before they departed from the Mandelbaum Gate area near MAC headquarters in no man's land. Then, on 11 November 1950, Jordan demanded that armed Jordanian soldiers be allowed into the Israeli enclave to watch the unloading of the convoys. This created a crisis and the convoys were suspended. Finally, under pressure from General Riley, the Jordanians relented on condition that no visitors be permitted to join the convoys, as had been the practice until then. The general appeased them by issuing a formal definition of who might be regarded as legitimate visitors and by setting a ceiling on the number of visitors to be allowed on each convoy.

The sensitivity of the convoy issue was highlighted on 4 June 1952, when a barrel of fuel, one of seven to be inspected for clearance, aroused the suspicion of a UN Observer who felt it was heavier than the others. UNTSO personnel wanted to check this barrel more closely, but the Israelis promptly withdrew it from the convoy. The barrel was moved to the MAC building, and UN personnel proposed to force it open to see what exactly it contained. Israel objected and Israeli military police intervened; the barrel kept its secret, if it had one. The Israeli position stemmed from principle: UN personnel could only inspect what was going up to Mount Scopus, not materials and containers which were not going up, even if initially intended to be brought to the Israeli sector there.

This disagreement reflected a divergence of perception which surfaced at times between UN and Israeli officials. The former instinctively felt on such occasions that they were called upon to translate their judgement into orders. Israel's firm view was that the proper as well as the effective and desirable role of UNTSO personnel was to act not as policemen but as intermediaries seeking to build bridges between the signatories to the Armistice Agreement, without hesitating to take a firm public stand against one of them when events made it necessary and armistice procedures made it possible.

Interestingly enough, on 3 March 1967, three months before the outbreak of the Six Day War, UN Secretary General U. Thant wrote to the Acting Head of Jordan's Mission to the UN that: 'our task is to try to bridge differences and not to aggravate them or to score points for or against either side.' His approach was different from that of his predecessor, Dag Hammarskjöld, but what he meant by scoring points remains unclear.[14] Hammarskjöld not only embraced an interventionist approach to his perceived role of peacemaker in the world, but also instilled in the UN missions operating under his guidance, including UNTSO, an aggressive sense of justice to be applied when two parties were in conflict. It was not enough to build a bridge between contending countries; it was necessary also to expose the culprits, to redress the wrong, and to side with the innocent or the victim. Naturally, in the course of his years as Secretary General, when he repeatedly shuttled between the leaders of Israel and the Arab countries, each side enjoyed the role of the innocent victim and denied any guilt of aggression ascribed to it by the UN. The struggles between UNTSO and the parties to the Mount Scopus Accords and other issues were affected by those sensitivities.

The village of Issawiyya on Mount Scopus was a thorn in the side of the Israelis in the area. It was a large, hostile presence within an isolated Israeli enclave surrounded by Jordanians and guarded by only 85 Israeli policemen. A UN inspection of the enclave at the end of April 1953 revealed that the population of Issawiyya was 1,000-strong, whereas in 1948 no more than 600 individuals had been identified as legitimate residents. The UN did not propose to take any action in this matter. According to an Israeli report, UN officials noted that to remove the unauthorized residents would increase the burden of Palestinian refugees in the care of the UN Relief and Works Agency (UNRWA).

It may well be that the Issawiyya villagers were only concerned about their daily livelihood, and were unaware of the political hair-splitting struggles between the UN, Israeli and Jordanian officials regarding maps, agreements, words and formulae. However, seen within the context of a besieged, embattled and overworked Israeli garrison on the Mount Scopus enclave, every little event was likely to be blown out of proportion, and any innocent step taken by the villagers could be misconstrued as part of an evil plot to undermine Israel's precarious hold on the Mount. But, according to the old adage, one may be actually persecuted even if one is paranoid. Be that as it may, there was no dearth of equivocal incidents of all sorts, which easily escalated into crises and poisoned further the already embittered and tense atmosphere in and around the Mount.

For example, controlling movement to and from Issawiyya was another source of friction, as was the creeping extension of land use by villagers for cultivation or grazing. Some villagers attempted to evade a long-established system of annual renewal of permits to farm lands within the Israel-held perimeters, designed to check unilateral creation of new facts on the ground which, if not removed immediately, would constitute a new status quo. Questions such as who would approve or carry out necessary repairs to the road leading to Issawiyya acquired political significance as instances of tangible exercise of authority. Routine patrolling was another aspect of the same issue when Israeli patrols encountered villagers during their rounds. Whether by direction from outside or at their own initiative, the villagers exhibited defiance of the Israeli patrols all too frequently, raising complaints at every opportunity in order to gain ever-greater independence from Israeli meddling in their affairs, something which was often seen by Israelis as intentional attempts to erode their authority and responsibility or to provoke dissent between Israeli and UN officials. One potent tactic which had that effect was the villagers' prolonged and firm objection to the operation of an Israeli road barrier during night hours on the way from eastern Jerusalem to the village. The repercussions of these confrontations were so inflammatory that at times they reached the desk of the UN

Secretary General, as in the case of 4 April 1965, when an Israeli patrol near Issawiyya came under Jordanian fire.

Patrols throughout the Israeli sector on Mount Scopus were carried out by Israel as a means of asserting its control over the area. The Israelis felt that their control and rights were eroded in those areas where they could not patrol because of Jordanian fire or UN objections. They considered that such erosion, if unchecked, would eventually invite further Jordanian encroachment, gradually establishing a new situation detrimental to Israeli interests and probably harmful to the security situation in that part of the enclave. This was particularly relevant with respect to the aforementioned area between the line drawn on the 7 July 1948 map and the one shown on the 21 July 1948 map. The Israelis called that area, which was adjacent to the university buildings on their southern flank, 'Gan Shlomit.' On 24 July 1956 two UN Observers and a Jordanian liaison officer were wounded by a Jordanian land mine as they were proceeding to evacuate Jordanian soldiers who had trespassed into the area. Tension continued to mount and, early in December 1957, UN Secretary General Dag Hammarskjöld made a quick trip to Amman and Jerusalem in an effort to defuse the situation. With the agreement of both parties he arranged for Ambassador Francesco Urrutia, Columbia's Permanent Delegate to the UN, to proceed to the area as his personal representative in order to negotiate a restoration of full implementation of the Mount Scopus Agreement of 7 July 1948. On 18 January 1958, Mr Urrutia reported successful results, but unrest on Mount Scopus continued.

In June that year another serious incident occurred there – already alluded to above – which took the lives of Colonel Flint and four Israeli policemen. Mr Hammarskjöld was in the Middle East at the time and he took the opportunity to hold fresh discussions with the governments of Israel and Jordan on the Mount Scopus situation; this took place on 21 June 1958. A period of greater calm followed, but the basic problems remained a constant irritant. A second high-ranking special mission representing the Secretary General was dispatched to Israel and Jordan early in 1965 (the Spinelli–Rikhye Mission) to seek greater cooperation between them in armistice affairs. Not much could be achieved before the momentous events of June 1967, which turned the situation upside down and eliminated all those thorny issues in one stroke while giving rise to others of quite another kind.

On 21 April 1965, an Israeli officer attached to the Israel–Jordan

MAC reported that UNTSO's representative for Mount Scopus had discussed with him UNTSO's views regarding Israeli patrols in the area. According to an UNTSO, official patrolling was not mentioned in the Mount Scopus agreement, and as it provoked the Jordanians it should not take place.[15] Five months earlier, on 30 November 1964, UNTSO had demanded in a letter that a traditional display of lights on Mount Scopus for the Hanukkah festival be switched off to avoid the danger of an adverse Jordanian reaction.[16] On 15 May 1967, General Odd Bull felt it necessary to complain in writing to Israel's Director of Armistice Affairs about an illuminated Star of David and other symbols displayed on Mount Scopus to mark Israel's Independence Day.[17] The insinuation, or subtle threat, of violence if Israel did not refrain from activities which it disliked had become a common Jordanian tactic designed to erode Israel's rights and authority along the armistice lines, based on the calculation that the UN would always react by calling on Israel to 'show restraint' to avert the outbreak of violence.

The UN indeed did not conceal its sensitivity to Jordanian threats, and its overriding preference for calm – regardless of Israel's concerns – if necessary. An exchange of letters in September 1966 between General Bull and the Israeli Director of Armistice Affairs puts the issue into sharp focus. The former wrote on the 16th, that in his opinion there should be no interference with land cultivation by the Issawiyya villagers to which there was no mention in the 7 July Mount Scopus Agreement, except in the context of security. Again, who was to determine Israel's security needs? Should Israel do this by herself or put herself at the mercy of UN judgement? On 19 September he was answered that whatever is not mentioned in that document precisely required the assent of the party concerned – Israel – or an understanding between the parties. Bull was also reminded that there were Jordanian commitments in Article VIII of the Armistice Agreement which still remained unfulfilled.[18]

The Jordanian sector of the demilitarized zone on Mount Scopus, encompassing principally the Augusta Victoria Hospice which had been turned into a hospital, saw vastly fewer difficulties for the simple reason that it was contiguous to Jordanian-held territory. It was regarded as Jordanian territory for all practical purposes and did not require special defensive measures or any contact or cooperation with UN officials. The one Jordanian concern was to erode the Israeli position on Mount Scopus, which they regarded as a thorn in their side. Their strategy was: (1) to get the villagers of Issawiyya to trespass into Israeli-held territory as 'innocent civilians going about their legitimate business under constant Israeli threats'; and (2) to elicit UN support for endless maneuvres calculated to restrict Israel's activities and make life in the Israeli enclave untenable. Having scuttled Article VIII of the Armistice Agreement, they turned to reducing the impact of the July 7 Agreement, which was less favorable to them than the one of July 27. Ultimately they aspired to occupy the territory by force when Israel tired of holding on to it under constant harassment. All this took place under cover of impressive military fortifications on the fringes of their sector, which would play a vital role in the battles of June 1967.

To sum up the Mount Scopus issue: Israel acted in a way calculated to maintain every shred of its limited strength in that strategic area, at heavy cost if necessary, as a bastion planted behind enemy lines. To attain that goal, the fortress had to be equipped, trained, rehearsed and kept in a permanent state of alert, disregarding the Mount Scopus Agreement if and when necessary. Jordan, on the other hand, equally regardless of obligations under the agreement, felt that it could weaken Israel's hold on Scopus by the threat and use of violence, and by exploiting the primary concern of the UN for peace and quiet. It was this situation – built on fears, suspicions, calculations, interests and concerns not necessarily connected to the Armistice Agreement or the Mount Scopus Agreement – which ultimately determined the everyday working of the armistice on Mount Scopus, as in the Government House area.

NOTES

1. The relevant documents on this issue are in the ISA, although they had not yet been declassified when this study was being completed.
2. It may be recalled that when Jordan eventually decided, in June 1967, to enter the Six Day War on the side of Egypt, its first military move was to capture the Government House compound and its surroundings. See, Uzi Narkiss, *Soldier of Jerusalem* (Jerusalem: Israeli Ministry of Defence, 1991), p. 329 [in Hebrew].
3. Letter dated 11 September 1956, from UNTSO COS, General E.L.M. Burns to the Director of Armistice Affairs at Israel's Foreign Office (ISA).
4. The processionary moth is a worm which decimates pine trees by devouring their needle leaves and building poisonous nests around them. To curb the dissemination of that blight, the contaminated clusters of leaves have to be nibbed and burned.

5. Dawud was later Prime Minister of Jordan during the 'Black' September of 1970.
6. The hotel was inaugurated after the 1967 war, appropriately under the name of *The Diplomat Hotel*.
7. Memorandum dated 22 March 1965, from the Israeli Director of Armistice Affairs to the Israeli Prime Minister (ISA).
8. General Odd Bull, *War and Peace in the Middle East* (London: Leo Cooper, 1973), pp. 63–4.
9. In many of Israel's major cities there are streets and avenues named after General Allenby, honouring him for liberating Palestine from what many Palestinian Jews regarded as 'the Turkish yoke.'
10. Bull, *War and Peace*, p. 64.
11. Ibid. p. 63.
12. For the full text, see the Mount Scopus Agreement (Appendix 2).
13. See report dated 9 January 1951, from Israel's representative on the Special Committee (established under Article VIII) to Walter Eytan, Director General of the Israeli Foreign Ministry. (Document No. 11, Foreign Policy Documents, ISA.)
14. See, UN Document No. S/7831.
15. See, Foreign Policy Documents, ISA.
16. Ibid.
17. Ibid.
18. Ibid.

6. Armistice Realities in the Metropolitan Area

In the densely populated urban area of Jerusalem, where the populace and military positions were just meters apart, opportunities for both inadvertent human mistakes and vicious mischief were rife. Indeed, much of the work of the MAC was focused on ten kilometers of the 920 km under its jurisdiction. This work involved resolving technical issues regarding the armistice, implementing preventive measures to avert conflict, and, when incidents did break out, taking firm and immediate measures to contain them. There were three technical problems in the Jerusalem metropolitan area, in order of importance:

1. the exact location of the eastern (Jordanian) and western (Israeli) armistice demarcation lines on either side of the long no man's land which separated them;
2. what, if anything, was to be done with no man's land areas between these lines; and
3. enforcing agreed restrictions on the size and composition of armed forces within the ten kilometers of the demarcation line specified in Article VII and Annex II of the Armistice Agreement.

Incidents along the demarcation lines which touched upon one aspect of these problems naturally had ramifications on the others. For example, an accidental trespassing into no man's land could raise questions of interpretation of the location of the respective borders of the parties, and also incidentally challenge the legality of the military deployment of the parties on the border or within no man's land. Incidents arising out of presumed encroachments on no man's land areas could be explained, though not necessarily justified, as immediate reactions to what were seen as dangerous cases of trespassing. But heavy fire across the lines, unless in obvious self-defense, and acts of violence perpetrated by persons who had crossed the lines for that purpose, had to be judged as gross or flagrant violations of the armistice, depending on their severity. Violations of restrictions on the size and armaments of forces near the demarcation line did occur and were registered from time to time, but did not generate serious difficulties as the threat to the peace or to human lives was potential, not immediate. On the Israeli side violations were generally occasioned by ceremonial needs, such as military parades requiring concentrations of troops and weapons, but devoid of hostile intentions. For the Jordanians the motive was typically internal security, when the government deployed troop reinforcements to control restive Palestinians on the West Bank and in Jerusalem. Thus, even though the work of the MAC was overburdened by the need to note, investigate and discuss these complaints, playing the required formal games of due procedures and undue filibusters, there were no real issues to be discussed. In both cases, these apparent violations were of a temporary and transitory nature, and as soon as the circumstances that occasioned them ended, the violations also ceased.

However, other armistice violations were not only serious but permanent or recurring, requiring constant attention. At some points along the demarcation line, common sense led the parties to agree to permit residents of one side to live in buildings, and in some cases even to occupy military positions, which were partly or wholly in no man's land. The exact course of the line was not in dispute, and in any case did not pose a problem, since the parties had allowed the requirements of daily life to overtake judicial stringencies. For example, on 7 July 1951, the two parties jointly prepared a map showing which side could allow its citizens to reside in which buildings within no man's land. The agreement, which consisted of a signed protocol of the relevant discussion in the MAC, probably eliminated, or at least attenuated, a potential source of friction which could have cost human lives if not dealt with preventively.

Elsewhere, friction was not unusual, springing from jealous but understandable determination not to let the other party get away with illicit gains, or from over-readiness to use any pretext to inflict injury on the other party. A lone unarmed person stepping a meter or two into no man's land could be pretext enough. Since the entire length of the urban boundary was constantly watched by armed soldiers posted in or atop the houses along this urban stretch of the armistice line, trespassing drew an immediate response, often before the MAC could intervene to calm the tempers and defuse the situation.

As it turned out, Israel which was the party interested in marking and fencing the line, was the party interested in avoiding incidents. It was discussed earlier how Israel's neighbors were reluctant to cooperate in systematically surveying and marking the armistice line, lest it be implicitly recognized as a permanent boundary which *ipso facto* lent legitimacy to the State of Israel. In the Jerusalem area, the only agreed line was one drawn with a thick pencil on a 1:20,000 scale map. This made the location of the line on the ground unclear. For example, on 21 January 1955, six years after the armistice went into effect, the Israeli–Jordanian MAC adopted Resolution No. 214, stipulating that a structure partly covered by the line would be considered as falling entirely inside it. Under more rational circumstances, one could imagine that the parties to such an agreement would have lost no time in jointly clarifying the exact location of the armistice line to avoid dangerous misunderstandings. However, in the Jerusalem area and elsewhere, wrangling over the course of the line on the ground was endless, mostly in the context of incidents. Therefore, as plotting the armistice line on the ground or ascertaining encroachments were undertaken formally under the auspices of the MAC, UN Observers had always to be directly involved or else no agreement between the parties could be expected.

But the involvement of UN Observers could also be fraught with crises between them and the parties. Indeed, armistice violations consisting of armed action across the demarcation lines, of the type described above as 'gross' or 'flagrant,' also brought into the fray UNTSO personnel in a process consisting of:

- verification of facts alleged in formal complaints; and
- casting the deciding vote, or abstaining from voting, in the MAC when the Commission was ready to make its judgement on the case.

A positive outcome for the complaining party could usually include a condemnation of the other party or of the deeds imputed to it. Both parties were sensitive to formal condemnations by the MAC, but UN personnel were not entirely comfortable with its role as judge between the parties in conflict, bearing in mind possible adverse political repercussions and reactions on the part of resentful or offended governments ready to confront UNTSO. David Brooks, in his book *Preface to Peace*, relying on press reports and official statements as well as UN documents, found that Arab pressure played a role in the retirement of General Riley as UNTSO COS in April 1953; whereas Israel was instrumental in the early retirement of his successor, Danish General Van Bennike, replaced by Canadian General E. Burns, who soon became the target of Egyptian criticism. A more junior officer who served as acting UNTSO COS for about a year in 1956–57, American Colonel Byron Leary, had to give up his position under Jordanian pressure.[1]

It was also noted earlier that a series of gross armistice violations in 1951 did not generate MAC action until a fierce Israeli retaliation forced the issue. Another series of such violations occurred in the Jerusalem area during the spring and summer of 1953. On 23 April, two Israelis were murdered by infiltrators from Jordan. On 7 June, Jordanian infiltrators murdered another Israeli and wounded three more. In July two Israeli soldiers were killed and a third wounded. Later that month a civilian Israeli watchman was killed on the outskirts of the city. Worse armistice violations occurred the following year. On 30 June 1954, Jordanians fired two-inch mortars from the Old City wall into the streets of western Jerusalem. One Israeli woman was killed and 20 people were injured. Israeli Prime Minister David Ben-Gurion, in a public statement on 1 July, described this assault as an 'outrage against civilization.' Jordan responded on 2 July with more heavy fire into western Jerusalem, killing one Israeli soldier and wounding four civilians, including two children. This time Israeli troops returned fire and some random hits were reported on church buildings in the Old City.

Then came international reactions. UN Secretary General Dag Hammarskjöld called upon the parties on 2 July to put an end to the exchange of fire. The Jerusalem Consular Corps considered a joint protest to the Israeli government over hits scored on religious structures in the Old City, but Israel averted this action by warning the US, Britain and France of the risks inherent in such a move. The public suggestion that Israel was attacking holy places might encourage Jordan to consider itself free to fire with impunity from the Old City on positions in western Jerusalem, while their firing positions were sheltered by the presence of religious sites.[2]

France's one-sided behavior in this instance was not without precedent. The Consular Truce Commission established by the Security Council on 23 April 1948, and consisting of the representatives of Belgium, France and the US, had floated ambitious proposals which included the demilitarization of Jerusalem as a whole, a complete ban on the presence of army and police within a radius of 50 m from all holy places, the establishment of an international police force to protect the holy places, and evacuation of certain military positions on both sides of the line. All these ideas proved to be politically impossible. It was believed that France played the role of prime mover in this diplomatic episode, while the Vatican was behind it all, in the hope of breathing new life into the old plans for the internationalization of Jerusalem.

The MAC discussed complaints submitted by both parties over the bloody events of 30 June and 2 July, and when resolutions came to a vote on 17 July 1954, UNTSO COS, General Bennike, did not know who opened fire, and consequently the MAC was unable to make even a mere moral contribution to the strengthening of the Armistice Regime in Jerusalem.[3] Later that year, General Bennike initiated a determined effort to bring about a special Area Commanders' Arrangement for Jerusalem and its vicinity 'to prevent, if possible, or in any case to suppress immediately, all outbreaks of firing and other hostile acts in the Jerusalem area.' A text was ready in February 1955, and on 18 April he was able, finally, to report success. The agreement had entered into force by oral affirmation at a meeting of Israeli and Jordanian representatives, without being signed by anyone. Jordan would not sign because the UN was not a signatory, and Israel insisted that the Agreement, being a 'local commanders' one, must be strictly bilateral, to emphasize the unambiguous responsibility of the parties toward each other to cooperate directly in its implementation.[4]

The next serious eruption of violence in the Jerusalem area occurred in September 1956, as a culmination of a series of incidents along the Israel–Jordan armistice line which had necessitated swift, forceful, daring (and costly) Israeli reprisals against Jordanian military installations. This was a peak period of widespread Arab–Israeli tension, orchestrated by the Soviet-supported nationalist and pan-Arab regime of Gamal abd-al-Nasser in Egypt. Soon, he was to nationalize the Suez canal, unleashing a grave international crisis which led to the coordinated invasion of Egyptian territory by Britain, France and Israel, spearheaded by Israel on 30 October 1956. Since Israel had openly adopted a policy of retaliatory raids, having concluded that no other recourse was available to it in the face of mounting violence along the armistice lines, the spiral of hostilities kept shooting higher. In that period which preceded the 1956 Sinai–Suez War, the main events along the Israel–Jordan border were:

- On 10 September 1956, a total of 13 Israeli soldiers were killed and three wounded in two separate Jordanian attacks.
- On 11 September, 21 Jordanian soldiers were killed and one wounded in an Israeli raid on a major Jordanian police fortress.
- On 12 September, three Israeli Druze watchmen were killed at a well-drilling site.
- On 13 September, 12 Jordanian soldiers were killed and four wounded in an Israeli raid on another major Jordanian police post.
- On 23 September, four people were killed and 16 wounded by Jordanian fire on the participants of an international archaeological seminar held at Ramat Rachel in Southern Jerusalem, while they were examining excavations in the open, and were largely exposed and defenceless.
- On 24 September, an Israeli tractor driver and an Israeli woman were killed by raiders from Jordan.
- On 25 September, Israeli troops again raided a Jordanian police fortress and army positions south west of Jerusalem, killing 39 soldiers and policemen, and wounding 12.

All Israeli raids were acknowledged for what they were. Not so Jordanian attacks. The one on the archaeologists in Ramat Rachel is of particular interest within the framework of this study. The Jordanian authorities asserted that the killing was the work of a single soldier using a light machine-gun, in a fit of madness, and they presented to the Chairman of the MAC medical documents to back their claim. On that basis the Chairman made a public statement about the incident in which the Jordanian version was included. The statement was issued on the day of the incident, before a full investigation could be carried out, and without any prior discussion of the incident in the MAC. Evidently, UNTSO was concerned urgently to dampen angry spirits and to counteract

Israeli counsels of retaliation, and hoped that such a statement would achieve that purpose. It did not. Moreover, it prompted Prime Minister Ben-Gurion to send a letter of protest on 25 September to the UNTSO COS, General Burns, in which he strongly criticized the haste to accept the Jordanian explanation and confer credibility on it, without the facts and Israeli observations and reservations on the case being thoroughly examined.[5]

Eye-witnesses on the Israeli side, including foreign Christian clergymen who were participating in the archaeological conference, reported that they had clearly seen two light machine-guns firing, not just one as alleged by Jordan, and also a rifle discharging single shots. The Israeli authorities were certain that the carnage could not have been caused by a single long burst of fire out of a single weapon. Other witnesses had noted Jordanian soldiers firing their rifles from fortified positions.[6] The MAC discussed the Israeli complaint on 10 October 1956, at emergency meeting 272, and on the strength of the Chairman's deciding vote adopted a Jordanian amendment asserting that the guilty soldier had acted in consequence of 'mental breakdown.'[7] When a UNMO who was supposed to verify facts, cross-examine witnesses and act on the findings, also became an amateur psychiatrist and unwisely took sides in an affair which he had no credentials to comprehend independently of the findings, he and the entire machinery he represented lost credibility and broke down.

As expected, Israel did not think that this affair was handled by UNTSO with responsibility, wisdom, impartiality and fairness. As already noted, the day after the painful Ramat Rachel incident, another Israeli was killed and his friend wounded by marauders from Jordan. The result was that the following day an angry punishment was inflicted on Jordanian police and troops, significantly not in the internationally sensitive Jerusalem area, but not far from there. The armistice system was now in a state of crisis with which it could not cope successfully. By all accounts, there remained hardly any basis for a claim that the armistice agreements were a prelude to peace. Rather, it was the Sinai War of 1956 which brought about a period of relative calm along the armistice lines, through the impact of the crushing Israeli victory over the Egyptian army and the resulting deployment of UN troops in the area. Subsequently, fresh distraction from routine harassment of Israel sprung from the Iraqi revolution in July 1958, following which

British troops were flown to Jordan's rescue, and American marines were landed in Lebanon as a precautionary measure.

Those post-1956 years were also marked by the total paralysis of the Fedayeen bases in the Gaza and West Bank areas from which Palestinian marauders had launched the murderous attacks inside Israel which had triggered the spiral of violence in 1955–56, and which were cited by Israel as one of the reasons for invading Egyptian territory in October 1956. When these Fedayeen bases were destroyed during that war and Egypt was obliged to refrain from direct or indirect armed activity against Israel for the foreseeable future, weaker Jordan also had to clamp down on its own restive Palestinian Fedayeen and calm down her borders with Israel. One should also point out that the Sinai War brought about a decline of British and French prestige in the Middle East, to the advantage of the Soviet Union. The spectacular success of the Soviet space program, and the problems of the China Sea and of Eastern Europe, were also to push the Middle East to the back burner of world concerns and to cool down temperatures there.

By 1963, however, Jordan as well as Egypt was ready to resume violent anti-Israeli activism; this was most significantly manifested the following year by the formation of the Palestinian Liberation Organization (PLO) on Jordanian soil. Soon, sustained pressure from a number of incidents made itself felt in the Jerusalem area. Here was now a group whose organizational and technical capacity could be improved systematically, and whose status as an irregular body made it less exposed than Jordan's Arab Legion to such political measures as the UN and the Armistice Commission might take, or to retaliatory raids that Israel might launch in reaction to armistice violations. Admittedly, this new development had a more serious effect on Jordan than Israel, putting in jeopardy King Hussein's hold on his kingdom in general, and on the West Bank and Jerusalem in particular. This was due to mounting Palestinian nationalism among the preponderant Palestinian component of the Jordanian population. Whether the King was unwilling to control the new mood, or was simply unable to do so, the Armistice Regime began to shake once again to its very foundation.

On 1 April 1964, Israel's permanent representative to the UN, Ambassador Michael Comay, drew the attention of Dr Ralph Bunche, now UN Under Secretary for Special Political Affairs, to a reawakening of Arab violence across the armistice lines. He listed 17 incidents recorded between October 1963 through March 1964, five of which took place in the area of Jerusalem, including one at Ramat Rachel which cost the life of a Swiss tourist. On 11 July 1964, a Jordanian soldier crossed the line into West Jerusalem and kidnapped two foreign tourists, a man and a woman, later raping the woman. More violence was to follow.[8]

On 15 January 1965, a routine Israel army patrol near Mount Zion in the heart of Jerusalem came under fire from the Jordanian side of the line. Two days later, an Israeli patrol on Mount Scopus was attacked and its commander severely wounded. Following the first of these two incidents, General Bull traveled to Amman to urge restraint, and returned with a proposal for abandoning the usual patrol route pending clarification of the issue involved. Israel held that it was unacceptable to reward in that way a violent breach of the armistice for the sake of momentary quiet, and that the issue was already clear: the Jordanians had withheld cooperation intended to complete a survey and fencing of the demarcation line in the area.[9]

On 11 July 1965, intense firing from the Old City wall into the Israeli border quarter of Musrara killed two and wounded four. The fire was not returned. This time, the MAC issued a condemnation of Jordan, announced in an official statement. And so, the pattern repeated itself: Israel could be vindicated only if she buried her casualties quietly and complained; if she returned fire, even in clear self-defence, then it became 'unclear' who fired first, and the blame was shared by the parties, at best. However, if Israel reacted forcefully and out of proportion, it was likely to take the brunt of the condemnation. The public declarations of Egypt, the PLO, and other Arab bodies that they were hostile to Israel, were rarely taken as sufficient explanation for violence on Israel's borders. Each case was denied by the perpetrators, and covered up by the host country which permitted it, and the onus fell on Israel to prove intent.[10]

The border incidents continued, and only a few days after the fatal Musrara shootings, on 15 July 1965, the Jerusalem–Tel Aviv railway line was cut by an explosive charge. An electric cable led from the site up to the armistice line nearby. A year later, on 7 August 1966, explosive devices were detonated in apartment houses inside West Jerusalem. Again the footprints of the perpetrators led to Jordan. That autumn, on 28 October 1966, the railway line to Tel Aviv was sabotaged once more by an explosive charge, just outside Jerusalem.[11]

Throughout this period and right up to the great Middle East crisis in the spring of 1967 which culminated in the June 1967 Six Day War, complaints about less-violent and non-violent breaches of the Armistice Regime in Jerusalem and elsewhere, were submitted in considerable numbers almost incessantly, by both sides. They covered such matters as: unauthorized crossings of the demarcation line; creeping encroachments into no man's land; Jordanian military as well as civilian traffic through the Jordanian sector of the demilitarized zone in the Government House area; penetrations of Jordanian airspace by Israeli aircraft; the digging of presumed military trenches in no man's land; unilateral changes and improvements to structures; alleged trespass into no man's land; an Israeli attempt to take control of an additional building in the Government House area; and 'soft' Israeli acts of retaliation such as setting fire to structures across the line. In short, there was a continuous state of active mistrust. At least one knowledgeable Israeli official involved in armistice affairs, Colonel Y. Caleff, considered, in an internal report, that UNTSO's incompetence should be blamed for the malaise. He felt that the Israel–Jordan MAC machinery was not being used professionally in the investigation of complaints, and the incompetence of its officials allowed the Jordanians to manipulate the MAC at will.[12]

However, the dominating feature of the uneasy armistice during its closing years, in the Jerusalem area as elsewhere, was the seemingly unstoppable Arab violence, pursued systematically as part of a larger design whose existence was never hidden. That design, again led by Nasser's Egypt with the reluctant participation of King Hussein, brought about the undoing of the armistice system altogether, though in a way different from that envisaged by the Arabs. The rapid succession of events in May and June 1967, in which Syria and the Soviet Union also played a major role, pushed Jordan into launching its fateful attack on Government House on 6 June 1967, followed by heavy shelling of West Jerusalem. Israel's swift and all-out reaction drove the Arab Legion from Jerusalem and the entire West Bank in three days of harsh fighting, and wiped out the armistice lines, whose precarious existence was no longer possible in any case. In one stroke all petty conflicts – over a few yards of no man's land, or a military position here or there, the pelting of rocks across the border, the problematic approach to Government House, the dangerous access to Mount Scopus, the exposure of civilians to adverse fire and the fear of coming too close to the border lest disaster struck – foundered within three days of fighting, and passed into history.

NOTES

1. David Brooks, *Preface to Peace* (Washington, DC: Public Affairs Press, 1964), pp. 61–5.
2. Representatives of the three countries met the Director General of the Foreign Ministry, Walter Eytan, on 2 July 1954. See his report in the ISA.
3. UN Document No. S/3278.
4. The Appendix 3.
5. ISA.
6. Ibid.
7. UN Document No. S/3670, Annex I, para. 4.
8. ISA.
9. Letter dated 18 January 1965, from the UNTSO COS General Odd Bull to Mr Kidron, the Israeli Director of Armistice Affairs; and the latter's reply (ISA).
10. ISA.
11. Ibid.
12. Colonel Caleff, member of Israel's mission to the UN – formerly General Staff Officer in charge of armistice questions – writing on 15 March 1967, from New York to Armistice Affairs at the Foreign Ministry in Jerusalem (ISA).

7. Managing the Armistice in Jerusalem

Most of the details concerning the daily work of the armistice bureaucracy can be gathered from personal recollections of those people whose lives were affected by the armistice in some way, or of the officials who dealt with its violations. UN records as well as the Israeli state and military archives, are replete with internal reports, for the most part confidential, which described the inside story of each event from every possible point of view. The author has himself lived through many of those events during his service as Israel's delegate to the MAC during the years 1960–65. Let us now consider how the MAC and its officials dealt with those incidents as they unfolded. We shall first sample the archives which tell a number of meaningful stories, and record how events were affected by incidents along the armistice lines. Amidst a generally grim record, some of these stories seem ridiculous, some comical, and some simply human, but one can be sure that at the time – under prevailing circumstances – they were taken very seriously indeed.

On 25 July 1956, Jordanian fire was directed at a group of Israeli workers near Mevasseret Yerushalayim, northwest of Jerusalem. When UN Observers arrived on the scene to investigate the incident, they were fired upon from Jordanian-held territory, twice, and one of them was wounded. On 1 August the MAC discussed the whole affair and voted to censure Jordan for the two attacks – and also Israel for having returned the first bursts of fire across the demarcation line. Israel took no part in the voting on this point, arguing that self-defence was an absolute right under the UN Charter which could not be challenged by the MAC. This incident, one of several where UN Observers were hurt, and sometimes lost their lives, went a long way to teach all concerned that the white flag held aloft by UN personnel in border areas or hoisted on their white-painted vehicles, did not guarantee their immunity or protection. In the MAC it was often said – partly in jest, partly in bitter truth – that in order for the white flag to be a real shield, it must be armored.

In February 1964, General Odd Bull informed Israel officially that he had obtained Jordan's agreement to let the Israelis clear an overgrown area (four meters by four) inside no man's land, which touched the Israeli demarcation line and had become an abode of disease-carrying rodents and stray cats. This was in the period when the parties met regularly in their sub-committee to deal with the processionary moth epidemic[1] which had infected pine woods in the border areas, and when goodwill – even warm relations – developed between the public health experts of both sides.

In June 1965, UNTSO protested to Israel that the Israeli flag flown over the Israeli sector of Mount Scopus on Israel's Independence Day was larger than the UN flag flown over that sector. In July of that year Jordan asked UNTSO officially to send a UN Observer into the metropolitan no man's land to retrieve balls accidentally thrown over the line by Arab pupils from a nearby school. Israel agreed to cooperate, but insisted that entry into no man's land could not be allowed without the participation of the Israeli and Jordanian representatives. The Jordanians considered that such a degree of fraternization would be too much, but since they did want the balls retrieved they agreed to let the job be done by UN and Israeli officials only.

In November 1965, UNTSO was upset by holes discovered in the fence near the abandoned Arab College in the Government House area. It transpired that the holes had been made by workers in the Israeli experimental farm nearby, who were tempted to avail themselves of the fine mushrooms they could see on the other side of the fence.

What these episodes have in common is a reflection of some of the intricacies of the human factor which developed over the years between all players at the institutional level of the business of armistice. The companions in that game, who obviously represented different, often contradictory, interests, also often yielded to human weaknesses or sensitivities, and formed a coterie of players who were privy to each other's concerns and personal worries, and often needed each other's help to overcome difficulties. Precisely because all of them knew the rules of the game, they also knew how to circumvent them when necessary in an elaborate system of give-and-take and looking the other way when 'improper' procedures were followed, or when human considerations outweighed procedural niceties. More often than not, the game consisted of respecting the rules on the surface, to satisfy the record, and then acting off-the-record in a much more humane and sensible fashion. In all cases, appearances had to be kept. And so, a web of informal and very personal links between all players concerned – the UNMOs, the Jordanian and the Israeli delegates, and their families – were often invoked to resolve matters that defied routine, regular and orderly solutions.

We have already shown in the context of Government House problems how the self-respect of a Jordanian delegate could be salvaged by a simple circumvention of Israeli quarantine regulations in Israel. The life of the MAC was marked almost daily by events of that sort. A young, inexperienced Israeli lieutenant (the author of this study) was assigned as the Junior Israeli Delegate to the MAC in1960 (without any previous preparation because a tragic car accident had felled his predecessor, the legendary Captain Levenson).[1] In the temporary absence of a senior Israeli delegate, it fell to the senior Jordanian delegate – Major (and later General) Dawud, twice the age of the newcomer and very much higher in rank – to coach the novice and to guide him with fatherly advice until he matured in the job. In meetings of the sub-committee, and in interminable informal talks between the two in Arabic, much teaching was done, much personal information was gathered by both parties, and many expressions of personal needs and their satisfaction were raised in those meetings. The UN personnel who chaired sub-committee meetings were often left in the dark when the Arabic-speaking duo plunged into a subject on their own. The Jordanian did not bother to explain his affability with the Israeli delegate which contrasted so strikingly with his severe and formal manner in regular meetings of the MAC.

One day the Israeli delegate was convened to an urgent meeting of the sub-committee without being told what it was going to discuss. Colonel Dawud was ahead of his Israeli counterpart, Captain Israeli, at the headquarters of the MAC near Mandelbaum Gate – a two-storey building in no man's land, conveniently located in the central section of the metropolitan demarcation line and easily accessible from either side. The UN personnel assigned to the MAC manned the building at all times, and were available for MAC business. Often UN officers would come in with their families, breathing life into the austere building that was flying a UN flag in the middle of the destruction and desolation characterizing the area between the lines. The delegates of the parties – Israelis more than their Jordanian colleagues – were in the habit of coming in without notice for a chat, to meet newly arrived UN officers or just to socialize.

Thus, on that early summer day there was no sign of anything extraordinary at Mandelbaum, though it seemed a little unusual that the senior Jordanian delegate was pacing about impatiently by the gate, expecting his junior Israeli counterpart. He welcomed him with a smile, and whispered in Arabic to him not to proceed to the meeting room on the first floor of the building, where the Operations Officer, New Zealander Captain Harry Dean, was nervously poised to preside over yet another exchange of recriminations between the Israeli and Jordanian delegates concerning some as-yet undisclosed mysterious issue. Steaming coffee in tiny cups had been served, and the fragrance of the cardamom in the Arabic-style coffee already filled the room as well as the adjacent passages. The Jordanian delegate told the expecting Observer that he had a few words to exchange with the Israeli delegate before the formal meeting began. Accustomed to this procedure whereby the delegates of the parties agreed informally beforehand upon the agenda and the outcome of a meeting when a practical issue was involved, the Observer discreetly kept his distance after making a courteous but vain gesture inviting the delegates into the room.

The Jordanian delegates always suspected that all meeting rooms in the MAC premises were bugged by the UN, and never considered them safe for a candid talk, in spite of the service provided by an Arab from East Jerusalem, who shared his job with an elderly Israeli woman from West Jerusalem. Muhammed was a simple-minded and affable man who smilingly and self-effacingly catered to the needs of the UN staff and the occasional guests from the two parties; Stella, a grumpy and bitter survivor of Auschwitz, always gave the impression that she did a favor with any minor service she was asked to render. Both seemed to be conscious of the uniqueness of their job in the service of peace, and were proud of it. There was a feeling of self-importance about them, born out of the secretiveness and discreteness of their comings and goings, and also of the sense of complicity which they shared. He, the easy-going Arab from the Orient, was forgiving and understanding to her bouts of anger; she, the Austrian-born refugee, ever suspicious, was condescending to him. But they somehow managed together to keep the place happy and functioning.

Right there at the gate, Dawud explained to the Israeli delegate that he had asked for an urgent meeting in order to arrange for a joint team of public health officers to spray anti-malaria chemicals in the Latrun no man's land along the old, now blocked, Tel Aviv–Jerusalem highway. While the team did its work, he continued, a very senior official from Jordan posing as chief of the anti-malaria team would like to meet his Israeli counterpart, likewise posing as an anti-malaria expert, wishes to discuss a matter of supreme security interest to the parties. The Israeli delegate consented to pass the message on, and it was agreed that the Latrun meeting would take place two days hence.

The formal MAC sub-committee meeting was swift and smooth. The UN officers had to admit that direct contact between the parties could facilitate and expedite armistice business. At the end of the meeting the Jordanian asked for yet another opportunity to exchange a few words unofficially, this time in the same room. His problem was pathetically simple: he had purchased a primitive hand-operated shaver in western Jerusalem before the city was divided in 1948, which he had used every morning since. However, the good machine broke down a few days previously and there were no spare parts to be found in eastern Jerusalem. The Israeli promised his help after the Jordanian discreetly handed the faulty shaver over to him, wrapped in a bag, trying to guess what the UN Observer present might have though was being trafficked under his nose. West Jerusalem was not the place where one could find a spare part for an obsolete shaver remembered only by very old folks. It took some searching in the Tel Aviv area before someone recalled that he had a relative who used a similar machine. The relative was contacted, but he would not give up his old shaver which he no longer used but to which he had suddenly become very deeply attached as a collector of outdated implements of all sorts. Only after much supplication strengthened by *raison d'état* and 'matters of national security', and a speech on Zionism accompanied by a hefty payment, would the old collector let go.

Very seldom was the Senior Jordanian Delegate so talkative and upbeat as on that sunny day at the Latrun meeting two days later. The Israeli delegation accompanying the official who was urgently summoned to the talk, was accompanied in a separate civilian vehicle by the puzzled team of public health officers who could not understand the urgency of this anti-malaria battle in the wrong season, made its way through the bushy vegetation which covered the entire no man's land, including the path of the abandoned road. The wild landscape of hills was buried under a thick red carpet of anemones. Only the approaching red roof of the monastery, perched on the flank of the hill dominating the valley, was a reminder that the Israeli party had indeed arrived at the meeting place. The Jordanians were there, busy chatting with the 'foreign minister' of the Order of the Trappist monks who lived in the majestic structure of the monastery and dedicated their lives to praying to the Creator, maintaining silence to uplift their souls, while working in the more mundane hillside vineyards to sustain their bodies. It had become customary that when the parties met in the vicinity of the monastery, overlooking the valley of Ayalon where the biblical Joshua had arrested the setting of the sun and the rising of the moon, the 'foreign minister' of the monks, the only Trappist permitted to speak, came to meet the visitors.

The top officials of the parties recognized one another, apparently thanks to previous meetings. While they were busy exchanging their professional information and, possibly, negotiating the way their cooperation could come to fruition in the matter under discussion, the technical teams – who by now grasped the true purpose of the meeting – were happily engaged in collecting flowers and renewing old contacts with their Jordanian colleagues. With uncharacteristic care the delegates inundated the innocent UN Observers from both sides of the line with long dissertations on preventive medicine to keep them busy while the senior experts devised their strategy undisturbed, sufficiently far enough from any danger of interruption or indiscretion. In the course of those diversionary conversations Captain Israeli found ample opportunity to let his counterpart know that the private mission was successful and to hand over the precious shaver to the grateful Jordanian. After signing forms attesting to the success of the official mission, the parties went their separate ways, but not before acquiring a bottle each of Latrun monks' wine.

Some weeks later, at a time of relative quiet along the armistice lines, Captain Israeli celebrated the birth of his son, Abraham Avishai. All the staff of Observers attended the party under the spectacular Chagall windows at the Hadassah Hospital in

Jerusalem, adding color and ceremonial flavor to the event with their sumptuous uniforms and medals from all corners of the globe. One of them passed word about the happy occasion to the Jordanian delegate, who could not attend for political reasons, much as he would have liked to. But he did not accept defeat. Again, he resorted to the device of an urgent meeting at the MAC headquarters. As soon as the last guests left the party, the happy father was asked by the UN Operations Officer to come immediately to a meeting at the office. The Jordanian representative was already present when the Israeli arrived, and he simply handed to his thrilled and grateful counterpart, with a smile, a huge giftwrapped package, mumbled a word of congratulation and left quickly after begging for strict secrecy for fear that he might lose his job, if not more. Such was the danger threatening a Jordanian Arab who gave a present to an Israeli Jew celebrating the birth of a son. The assurance was given, together with heartfelt thanks for his extremely friendly gesture. Unfortunately, a UN officer, hungry for publicity or simply careless or thoughtless, told the story to a journalist in Israel. It was published, and the expected Arab outrage followed. It took the emphatic denial of both the generous giver and the grateful recipient of the gift to lay the incident to rest.

Meetings of the sub-committee at the MAC, which became a weekly routine when the border was quiet, did not only deal with the personal issues of the delegates, or function principally as a cover for high-level political meetings. They were meant to deal with long lists of minor grievances on both sides, which were usually curable: straying animals across the borders; or, less frequently, straying people such as shepherds running after their herds, children unwittingly crossing the demarcation line, or others intentionally running away from their homes following a family row. All these cases were amicably settled. Straying animals or herds of cattle were usually handed over in the border area where they trespassed, to save transportation costs and quarantine procrastinations, in the presence of a UN officer who certified that the procedure had taken place as proposed by the sub-committee. On one occasion a UN Observer who had little experience with herding animals, undertook to count heads in order to certify their number (over 400), but was dismayed at his inability to keep the counted sheep together before they crowded with the others and muddled the counting. He was pathetically if understandably unable to accomplish his task, earning only the ironic smiles of the amused shepherds who had come to that spot to receive their animals. In jest, one of them suggested that the officer count the legs of the animals and divide the result by four. At the very edge of his patience and embarrassment, the officer accepted the advice and went to work; it was only the loud laughter of all present that convinced him to desist.

At other times it was incidents such as the one concerning schoolchildren's balls cited earlier in these pages which occupied the time of the sub-committee. Once, as the committee was in session at the MAC, the operations officer on duty rushed into the meeting to ask for counsel: on the telephone line was the mother superior of a monastery whose outside wall was adjacent to the Old City wall, the Jordanian demarcation line. One of the nuns had opened her window which offered the familiar scene of no man's land at the foot of the wall. In an irresistible early-morning yawn while looking out of her window, the nun saw with horror her false teeth falling into thick wild bushes down below. After an initial laugh at this grotesque situation, the parties rose to the occasion and went about their duty, accompanied by a dazed UN officer who kept repeating that he had never dreamt that his mission in the Holy Land would include retrieving false teeth from a bush. There was another minor problem involved: the nagging worry that there might be old land mines still scattered in that area, but that was overcome too.[2]

THE MANDELBAUM GATE

Straying persons were handed over, after much longer waits and following many discussions and interrogations intended to ascertain that they were neither spies, nor trained in the arts of spying while being held in enemy prison cells. As a rule, the handover took place at the Mandelbaum Gate, a nondescript square within no man's land, conveniently close to the offices of the MAC. The square took its name from Mandelbaum House, one of several two- or three-storey houses separating the Arab quarter of Sheikh Jarrah, in the northern part of East Jerusalem, from the Jewish neighborhood of Shmuel Hanavi. It had been an area of bitter fighting in 1948. When the armistice was agreed, it was left undivided between the forward fighting lines. Entry into the square was barred on both sides by roadblocks, and the square itself was made the only officially recognized passage between Israel and Jordan, much like Checkpoint Charlie in divided Berlin. It was now the point of handover of persons and animals from one party to the other, a daily crossing point for clergymen, diplomats and UN personnel, the point of assembly and departure of the fortnightly Israeli convoy to Mount Scopus and the annual Christmas crossing of the Christians of Israel to Bethlehem (Catholics just before Christmas Day, and the Orthodox later in January).

In a way, Mandelbaum Gate told the story of the armistice in Jerusalem. It was the point of encounter and occasional human contact between Israel and Jordan, and when the border flared up elsewhere it was here that tension was the most tangible. Here military positions faced each other across the square and the nervous and weary soldiers manning them could shout greetings or curses at each other, as the general atmosphere and personal moods prescribed, or – less frequently – shoot at each other point blank. It was here that the many international and local facets of the divided city were revealed as day after day, except on Yom Kippur (the Jewish Day of Atonement, when all Israeli ports, airports and points of entry are shut down), busy notables of all nationalities sporting their national dress, their clerical gowns or the blue-and-white (ironically the colors of Israel's flag) of the UN, crossed the square in one direction or another, in an endless stream of cars bearing diplomatic or UN number plates. Others had to change Jordanian into Israeli plates, and vice versa, upon their crossing from one side to the other. They first crossed one check-post, usually nodding or smiling, or loudly greeting the police guard at the gate who knew them all as the years wore on, then crossed the 50-yard square in deadly silence, suspiciously glancing in all directions, before relaxing as they crossed the second check-post to the other side.

Only the parties to the armistice were spared the routine shock of sudden transition from one culture to another via military positions and under loaded guns, necessary to accomplish the most mundane of tasks: errands, shopping, returning home, picking up a child from school or from a friend's home, taking children to a show, going out to a concert, visiting friends in their homes, or moving between the MAC and one's headquarters or the headquarters of UNTSO. Nationals of either party were not allowed into the other's territory. Only the delegates of the parties to the armistice were allowed into the square, together with their assistants as circumstances required (the assistants were not allowed any further). Those occasions were not very frequent; some were for *ad-hoc* needs, like returning a straying person or animal, or the body of a killed infiltrator, or undertaking joint preventive action against disease or pollution inside no man's land north or south of the Mandelbaum Square. Other crossings, such as the Mount Scopus convoy, or the massive crossing of Israeli Christians at Christmas, were planned ahead of time. Only once, during the visit of Pope Paul VI to Jerusalem in 1964, were special arrangements made in the square to welcome him into Israel from the Jordanian side of Jerusalem.

THE MOUNT SCOPUS CONVOY

Usually on the first and third Tuesday of each month, the Mandelbaum Square turned into a fair-like site, except that stern-faced Jordanian officers stood by to scrutinize the three dozen Israeli policemen who were going up to relieve half the personnel who had been up on Mount Scopus cut off from the world during the previous four weeks. UN Observers were also present, usually headed by the Chairman of the MAC who was *ex-officio* representative of UNTSO for Mount Scopus affairs, acting under the authority of UNTSO's COS. The Chairman presided over the preparation of the convoy. The Israeli party comprised the contingent of policemen going up to relieve the garrison on duty, and designated experts and technicians going up to do maintenance work and return with the next convoy a fortnight later.

The Israeli personnel had their personal belongings spread on their kitbags ready for meticulous inspection by the UN officers, under the vigilant eye of the accompanying Jordanian officers who could not touch the personal effects of the Israelis, but could direct the UN officers – as they saw fit – to double-check items or be more thorough in their inspection. The severity of this procedure could depend on the mood, whim or genuine concern of the officer heading the Jordanian overseers. With the completion of the inspection, the policemen rearranged their stuff and silently mounted the armored vehicles awaiting them in the square, as their names were called by a UN officer from a roll previously submitted by Israel.

The trucks loaded with the supplies for Mount Scopus were also searched by UN Observers accompanied by Jordanian officers. They were first unloaded in the square, and their contents scrutinized systematically and checked against lists provided by Israel against the rules and regulations prescribing what might or might not be allowed to go up, and then reloaded. The trucks themselves were inspected separately. Barrels of fuel, always carried to meet the domestic needs of the enclave, were given special attention after the barrel incident described above. Other barrels carried cooking oil. Next came sacks of wheat, other cereals, dried vegetables, flour (bread was baked in the enclave), fresh fruits and vegetables, cartons of preserved food and all manner of basic and luxury supplies to keep a garrison of 85 policemen and half a dozen visitors more or less happy in their enclave until the next convoy. Sometimes special food supplies, like the Matzot (unleavened bread) for Passover, wine, or sweets prepared for the holidays of Purim and Hannuka, would raise eyebrows and warrant questions; but over the years both the Jordanians and the UN personnel learned what to expect on certain holidays and had no problem with these special items.

The question of food inspection was always a thorny one, and it remained insoluble. The dilemma was clear: if the UN, under Jordanian prodding, were to open every can of preserved food, there would be no more preserved food, and there was no way to feed the garrison with fresh supplies within a biweekly convoy regime. If every sack of flour or sugar were bored through for inspection, much of it would be spilled irretrievably. But, left unchecked, all these containers could carry large amounts of prohibited supplies, including ammunition, spare parts and disassembled weapons; and the Israelis had earned quite a reputation, during the Mandate years, as innovators in the arts of hiding and disguising weapon parts and ammunition. Indeed, but for those skills they would have been defenceless before the invading Arab armies in 1948, their artillery, tanks and combat aircraft. A related question which was in the air, though never officially asked, reinforced the suspicions that the convoys could not all have been completely 'clean': that is, since no replacement of arms or ammunition was ever allowed on Mount Scopus, how would the Israelis there defend themselves in an emergency?

The dilemma was addressed on an *ad-hoc* basis, and it took forbearance, goodwill and humor to side-track it and allow the convoys to proceed. At first, it was agreed that the UN Observers would inspect the whole by sampling a few items at random. But then, all the opened cans in the Mandelbaum Square, especially under the scorching sun of the Israeli summers, would be spoiled before they reached their destination. Everyone understood that in a regime of serious rationing, carefully calculated to last the two prescribed weeks, and perhaps longer in case of a border flare up, the Israelis could not afford to lose part of their precious supplies to the vagaries of a whimsical inspection. But, on the other hand, since it was fair to expect the Jordanians to insist on some sort of effective supervision of what was being hoarded on Mount Scopus under their nose, a compromise was struck: UN Observers alone would open the sampled containers in the kitchen of Mount Scopus, so that they could be put to immediate use. The Jordanians had wished their representative to be present, but since he was banned from entering the Israeli sector of Mount Scopus, Jordan had to accept this constraint. Comic incidents ensued, for example, when conscientious UN Observers who wanted to taste all the contents of the cans they opened to verify validity of their posted ingredients, fell ill from the gastronomically inadvisable mixture of orange jam and mackerel preserves.

The description of the Mount Scopus convoy operation cannot be complete without mentioning the military preparations made around it. On the Jordanian side of the square could be seen Arab Legionaires perched on their light trucks carrying machine-guns, who were to lead the convoy through their territory, followed by UN cars flying UN flags. Next came the two Israeli armored cars carrying the Israeli personnel and driven by Israelis, followed by UN vehicles flying UN flags, and an Arab Legion escort. At the end came the Israeli supply trucks driven by UN personnel.

From the moment of departure, Israeli infantry and armored units, backed by artillery and ground-support combat aircraft on alert, were tensely ready to intervene should the convoy be attacked on its way through the densely inhabited Sheikh Jarrah quarter of East Jerusalem. The convoy, whose speed was dictated by the very slow armored buses, took close to half an hour to cross the four-kilometer route. The same tension enveloped the convoy, the Mandelbaum Square, and all the command posts of all the parties, from the moment the convoy started its way back with the personnel who had been relieved and the empty trucks.

This tension was not without justification. In addition to the uncertainties of crossing hostile territory and the related precautions, there was the traumatic memory of an ambush of such a convoy back in 1948, just before the end of the British Mandate, when dozens of medical personnel trapped in the halted armored vehicles were incinerated alive. Arab crowds carried out that atrocity in retaliation for a murderous onslaught by the dissident Jewish Irgun against the Arab village of Deir Yassin on the western outskirts of Jerusalem. That attack resulted in a terrible massacre; it occurred before the establishment of the State of Israel, when uncontrolled militias on both sides had their way. Although there were now recognized authorities on both sides committed to a formal armistice agreement policed by the UN, and a regular regime of biweekly convoys planned and protected within a regime negotiated and accepted by both parties, such traumas take time to die.

On the Israeli side massive intervention was planned and prepared for every convoy, to make sure that tragedy would not repeat itself; the Israeli forces were poised to move into Sheikh Jarrah and secure the link to Mount Scopus, while artillery and air support were to keep that area inaccessible to potential Arab Legion reinforcements. Also, Israel made sure that the Mount Scopus garrison could hold its own until they could join with the incoming Israeli troops. At the same time, Israel insisted that Israeli drivers rather than UN personnel should sit at the wheel of the 'armored cars'[4] carrying the Israeli relief personnel. The Jordanians understood the Israeli position and took all precautions, leaving nothing to chance. However, they ensured that the Israeli drivers would not be able to detect any Jordanian military installations on the way, by leaving them just a slender slit open in the armored plate in front of the steering wheel during the journey through Jordanian territory. These 'armored cars' were ordinary trucks or buses protected from bullets and rocks by steel plates crudely fastened on them, with narrow slits left open for the drivers. Their original purpose was to keep Jewish traffic moving on vital roads threatened by Arab bullets and rocks before the termination of the British Mandate. Those that remained serviceable were quite useful before the nascent Israel was in a position to import real armored vehicles.

THE CHRISTMAS CROSSING

The only time during the year when the officials at Mandelbaum

Gate seemed to follow a normal routine, totally oblivious of the armistice and its vagaries, was the Christmas and New Year season. Indeed, thousands of Israeli Christians dressed in all styles, from traditional Arab to the most modern and fashionable, crowded the square for the formalities that would allow them to be in Bethlehem on Christmas Eve, and to return immediately after the New Year. It was not a MAC affair, because the arrangements were made by the civilian authorities on both sides of the border, but MAC officers were present watching for any possible mishap. Since the Jordanian authorities would not recognize Israeli passports, Israeli citizens had to be provided by the government with documents which were acceptable to the Jordanians; these were called *laissez passer*. Allowing people resident in Israel to participate in Christmas celebrations in Bethlehem was probably the only case of Jordanian compliance with the ill-fated Article VIII of the Armistice Agreement providing, among other things, for free access to religious sites. This is why the Christmas crossings by Israeli citizens were extremely important to the authorities of both sides. For the Jordanians it was a matter of showing goodwill without compromising their vow not to allow any Jews in the kingdom. For Israel it was proof that with sufficient goodwill all the provisions of the paralyzed Article VIII could be respected, which would defuse tensions along the armistice lines not only during the Christmas season but during the rest of the year.

The crossings to and from Jordan brought about a change of mood in Mandelbaum Square. No longer were there brief formal encounters between officials to effect a quick handover under the suspicious scrutiny of the military posts on both sides. Now, on the occasion of Christmas, there seemed to be new rules, or no rules, to the conduct of the masses of pilgrims. If on normal days an abnormal vigilance prevailed on both sides, lest someone trespassed into no man's land, on the abnormal day of the Christmas crossing, the place suddenly became normal: people wandered about the square in large numbers, completely unmindful of their proximity to the armistice lines. They clustered round family members and friends, talked and laughed for as long as they wished and as loudly as if they were in their home village square, not in the awesome and notorious border passage. They went through the formalities with a nonchalance that covered up both nervousness about what lay across the border, and the thrill at the prospect of meeting long-unseen family members. The procedures were of a civilian nature – the checking of documents, customs inspection, and a briefing regarding conduct when in Jordan and when crossing back into Israel. In short, the square had become a regular civilian border crossing point, and no hint of the usual nervousness about security overshadowed the place.

On the day of return, the square was even more joyful and lively. People talked about their encounters in Jordan, compared prices and modes of life in their villages with what they had witnessed and learned during their brief pilgrimage. All seemed engulfed in euphoria over the extraordinary privilege extended to them as the only Israeli citizens who were allowed to leave their country by an overland route into a neighboring Arab country. Visibly happy with the experience and heavily loaded with presents and purchased goods, they made their way to the temporary Israeli customs office set up for the occasion, where their new acquisitions would be inspected and customs duties paid for some of the goods imported. Most of those returning seemed to have put on new clothes, not only in celebration of their happy return home but also to escape paying duty on the new items they wore. Some women who appeared excessively obese to the experienced eye of the customs officer were asked to shed their clothes in a closed cabin put up for the purpose and were caught, as every year, with entire rolls of new fabric wrapped around their waists to avoid paying customs duties. As soon as the re-entry procedures were over and the last returning pilgrims had boarded their vehicles, the square fell back, at a stroke as it seemed, into the desolation and vigilance and tension which characterized it most of the time.

Working with the MAC also meant maintaining close relationships between the delegates of the parties and UN Observers. We worked together under the most adverse conditions during border incidents and official investigations launched by the Armistice Commission, and often clashed with one another when people were biased in the interest of their respective countries, or when UN representatives took positions unacceptable to either, or both, parties. But it was precisely this pressure-cooker environment which brought them close together and forced them to expose their human weaknesses. This degree of intimacy also predisposed them to share thoughts and, at times, to enter into a state of complicity. One case in point will illustrate this pattern of unstated complicity in the midst of the most difficult disagreements and adverse debates. In the early 1960s Israel decided to make a military parade in Jerusalem the focus of her Independence Day celebrations. The Armistice Agreement had stipulated a restriction on the size of forces on either side of the border in Jerusalem, which meant in practice that the planned concentration of troops and armaments that were to participate in the parade would contravene the Armistice Agreement.

On previous occasions Israel had argued that the spirit of the Agreement would not be violated if Israel gave assurances that the armaments to be paraded would not be in functional condition as weapons and would be withdrawn immediately once the parade had run its course. But on this occasion the Jordanians would not agree. They insisted on following the letter of the Agreement – despite their flat refusal to implement Article VIII of the Armistice Agreement and the fact that their forces in East Jerusalem were armed with weapons exceeding the permitted technical characteristics, and were paraded occasionally in the streets of the city. Israel had never seriously protested against this, recognizing that without those weapons the Hashemite Kingdom might not be able to keep the lid on local Palestinian nationalists who opposed the King.

After serious consideration of the matter, Israel decided to go ahead with the parade and launch a pre-emptive discussion in the MAC so that any Jordanian complaint regarding the parade could not be taken up before the parade had completed its course. To begin with, the Jordanians would have to see the offending military hardware rolling into West Jerusalem before they could launch a formal complaint. Next, UN Observers would have to verify the factual basis of the complaint in order to confirm that a breach of the Armistice Agreement had been committed. Then, discussion in the MAC could get under way, culminating in a resolution calling on Israel to withdraw the forbidden armaments without delay or face an annoying discussion in the UN Security Council and possibly some unpleasant results.

As luck would have it, vigilant Israeli observation posts spotted and photographed an armored car sporting Arab Legion markings and equipped with a cannon, which was of a make not allowed in Jerusalem, patrolling near the Damascus Gate. With this evidence in hand, Israel lodged a formal complaint to the MAC and called for an emergency meeting of the commission to discuss the matter. The Jordanians now launched their own complaint. All concerned realized that the issue now depended on how soon the Israeli complaint could be disposed of so the MAC could take up the question of the Israeli parade and abort it by appealing to the UN Security Council. Both UNTSO and the Jordanians duly understood the position but had to conform with the agreed rules and procedures, which they did without blinking an eye. In private one of them said, 'Why did we need all this?'

The Israeli delegation prepared itself thoroughly for gaining the time needed to run the parade before the MAC was free and ready to take up the Jordanian complaint. To this end it brought to the first meeting of the commission a very able diplomat, Arthur Levran, who had years of experience in futile debating at the UN General Assembly and the various UN agencies. The Chairman of the MAC, Colonel Burns from New Zealand, sensed the magnitude of the task ahead and wisely seated next to himself the Legal Adviser of UNTSO, Mr Vigier, a very polished French jurist with a reputation of not being very favorable to Israel.

The Jordanian delegation was business-like and confident that its case was so clear-cut that UN support for it was obviously fully assured. The Jordanians just had to wait out Israel before playing their trump card, perhaps even compel Israel to call off the parade she had announced with much fanfare, and then march home victorious. They were confident that the Israeli complaint would be dismissed quickly since the UN Observers had 'found no evidence on the ground' to support the Israeli complaint, as the prohibited Jordanian armored vehicle had been removed from the scene. As the reinforced quorum of the MAC opened its deliberations under its obviously displeased Chairman, the floor was duly given to the first complaining party, Israel, in accordance with the rules set by General Riley back in the 1950s.

The Israeli delegation immediately asked its diplomat-adviser to take the floor on its behalf, and he began with a series of procedural matters, expressed in superb, somewhat playful English, using wit and understatement and humorous sarcasm which electrified the room and elicited not a few smiles; much to the distress of the Jordanians who began to understand that the debate was not going to be conducted and concluded as rapidly as they expected. Then the Junior Israeli Delegate, Captain Levenson, began reading out a very long litany of Israeli complaints about past Jordanian violations of the armistice in Jerusalem. Interest in the debate gradually waned, and the Jordanian delegates, as well as the

Chairman of the MAC and his adviser began exchanging notes nervously, begging with their eyes for an end to this unexpected Israeli tactic. Neither of them had any legal recourse, as the rules of procedure for the MAC – agreed by both parties – did not allow any time restrictions on the parties in presenting and explaining their case. However, a series of pauses were requested by all participants; the Israelis became tired after taking many turns in addressing the commission in a marathon of argumentative statements; the Jordanians were tired of listening, and frustrated with what they were made to listen to, seemingly with no end in sight. The UN personnel, to whom the Jordanians were looking for succour, thought perhaps of invoking the intervention or guidance of their superiors with a view to putting an end to this widely publicized debate, whose outcome was eagerly awaited by diplomats, foreign chanceries, journalists and the public at large.

When the debate resumed in the afternoon, Israel went on reading its complaints and commenting on the general dysfunctioning of the armistice and the MAC, while the attention of the other participants was directed elsewhere. The Israeli delegates could have cited the entire Bible, and no one could have told the difference, as long as they kept talking and asking for a pause at reasonable intervals. The first day ended in the fatigue and disappointment of the Jordanians and the UN personnel. The Israeli party felt its tactic was working, and convened during the night to plan the next day's citations and arguments. Informally, both the UN personnel and the Jordanian delegates pleaded with the Israelis to speed up the submission of their case, in order to free the MAC to discuss other important business on its agenda. But no one disputed Israel's right to defend its interests according to the rules. Nevertheless, the chairman of the MAC hinted that he might use his prerogative to intervene in the proceedings and bring the discussion to a close by deciding that it was time to vote. The Israelis rejected this idea out of hand.

The next day, while Israeli newspapers were announcing the rehearsal of the parade and asking the public to attend, the MAC convened again. The festive mood of the previous day had disappeared, for the general expectation was for more of the same. However, the Chairman seemed determined to close the case that same day in order to allow for a well-deserved debate on the Jordanian complaint at last; still in time to adopt a resolution that would block next morning's parade. The Jordanian delegation apparently was less optimistic, sensing from their personal acquaintance with their Israeli colleagues that nothing was going to stop that parade. Either for this reason, or because they had been impressed by the impact that the Israeli diplomat had made the day before at the MAC – and, perhaps, mainly under the influence of the Arab fascination with rhetoric which at times could be valued more highly than action – they resolved to show the MAC that an Arab diplomat could match the Israeli, and so the debate had to continue. On the second day they produced their own diplomat, a polished gentleman and an accomplished diplomat, Dr Hazem Nusseibeh,[3] who had served his country as ambassador in several capitals. The Israelis were happy to let him have the floor for as long as he pleased, and he soon plunged into a lengthy dissertation on the merits of the UN, the importance of the armistice, and the vital function of the MAC. All this in perfectly accented impeccable English.

When he was through, the monotonous Israeli filibuster resumed its grind based on endless quotations from the records of the MAC and the minutes of UN Security Council discussions, long into the night. The Chairman and the Jordanians repeated that they would remain at the MAC table for as long as it took until the Jordanian complaint about the Israeli parade was tabled for debate. By two o'clock in the morning, and despite successive cups of coffee served and sipped, the exhausted participants were all resting their weary heads on the table or reclining back in their chairs for a moment of relaxation. It was a surreal, if not grotesque, scene: respectable people, impeccably dressed, slouching around like homeless vagabonds under the bridges of Paris at night, their dishevelled hair touching that of those who were their opponents in the bitter debate; and senior officers in their impressive uniforms, their medals dangling, at times emitting metallic sounds, as the tired men slumped exhausted over the conference table. From time to time one or another of the weary participants would straighten up and regain a momentary coherence, before sinking down once more into his restless slumber, careful not to disturb any of the others. The MAC servants, ever ready to serve some food and coffee to anyone who could enjoy them, watched in dismay the evaporating aura of authority and prestige which had habitually marked their illustrious bosses and their important guests.

By the next morning interest in the whole affair seemed to be fading; however, due to inertia, the discussions resumed. At some point, the Chairman announced that he had had enough of Israel's procrastinations and that it was time to conclude the debate. Israel's complaint did not get the support of the Chair, therefore no resolution condemning Jordan was adopted. As the parade began, the Jordanian complaint came to the fore. The proceedings were extremely brief, as in a court of summary trial. No evidence needed to be heard, it was all clear and, the text of the condemnation of Israel having been agreed beforehand between the UN and Jordan, it was adopted forthwith by majority vote. The resolution also called upon Israel to withdraw its forces without delay in order to restore the situation to what it had been three days earlier. The Israeli delegates, who did not dispute the facts, naturally opposed the condemnation, arguing that they had not violated the spirit of the armistice; but they also announced that the Israeli troops had completed their ceremonial duty and were already on their way out. This episode remained for many months to come the reference point for the absurdities and the ineffectiveness that could hamper the less than perfect Armistice Regime in Jerusalem; but in no way did it affect the personal relationships within the MAC or the routine work in the sub-committees.

Life in the MAC and within the UN community in Jerusalem had a considerable impact on the agenda of the Israeli delegates. True, most UNMOs lived in eastern Jerusalem, where the availability of spacious housing at low cost and the amenities of colonial life – with drivers, maids, cooks and gardeners – were affordable to nearly all of them, and made the Jordanian side much more attractive. However, for their services, shopping and cultural needs they looked to western Jerusalem. Parents of children drove them back and forth to school every day, wives would rather buy foodstuffs that they were familiar with in the supermarkets of western Jerusalem than shop in eastern Jerusalem's colorful and fragrant oriental markets. The latter were reserved for strolls, for souvenirs and for household needs other than food. The UNMOs and their families often went to western Jerusalem for concerts, and the unmarried men among them found it much easier to befriend Israeli women than the conservative and closely watched women in traditional Arab society. But, like all Jerusalemites at that time, when the city virtually closed down in early evening, the UNMOs learned to socialize indoors. Some of them could be found in the few bars of western Jerusalem, or those of the famous *American Colony Hotel* and the *Intercontinental Hotel* on the Mount of Olives in the eastern party of the city, but for most, socializing meant visits to friends and dinner parties with their colleagues.

Very often, UNMOs, especially those with operational appointments, would drop by the Israeli Delegation offices for a drink or a chat, sometimes unannounced. Some of them were invited by the Israeli delegates for meals at home or in a restaurant, often in the company of their spouses and sometimes with their children as well. This created opportunities for the UNMOs to escape their isolation or to find entertainment for their families. Many cases are known of lasting friendships forming between the guest and host families, much to the delight of both. In a very few cases UNMOs elected to live in western Jerusalem, for personal, cultural or political reasons. They were much more open to reciprocate invitations they received to the homes of Israelis, while their colleagues in eastern Jerusalem could not extend the same courtesy. In either case, the Israeli delegates were called upon every so often to assist in the solution of some personal problem or to intercede before this or that official to facilitate technical and logistical arrangements. On the Jordanian side, while the UNMOs developed the same kinds of relationships with their Arab colleagues, these were often restricted to the official level and less open to inter-family relations and mutual visits at home, due to the Arab predilection for not mixing business with family life.

NOTES

1. See Chapter 5 above.
2. Shimon Levenson served in the Israeli delegation to the MAC for some 25 years and was renowned for his phenomenal memory of people and events. Anyone who dealt with armistice affairs on the Israeli side had to rely on his knowledge and experience. On the strength of his record, he was hired in the 1970s by the UN Office in Bangkok to battle against the drug traffic in the Golden Triangle. Later on it turned out that he had been recruited by Soviet Intelligence during his service there to spy against his own country. He was convicted by an Israeli court in the 1980s, and sentenced to serve a term of 12 years in prison. He was released a broken and sick man in 1999.
3. The same story is recounted in Narkiss, *Soldier of Jerusalem*, p. 38.
4. Dr Nusseibeh – from a clan of notables which has been famous in East Jerusalem for centuries – served the Jordanian government in various capacities until he was eventually appointed Ambassador at the UN and then Foreign Minister, in spite of his Palestinian origins

8. Living under Armistice in Jerusalem

Beyond the formalities of the Security Council, UNTSO, MAC, foreign chanceries, diplomatic work and military activity, the Armistice Regime directly touched the lives of the Jerusalem citizenry. The city continued to grow and prosper, while people continued to work, raise their families and travel, hoping for the best under the difficult circumstances while preparing for the worst. Indeed, for many years after the trauma of the 1948–49 siege of western Jerusalem,[1] inhabitants continued to hoard food and water and avoided walking too close to the Arab Legion's positions. Those who lived in close proximity to the border areas – Musrara, Sanhedria and Shmuel Hanavi in the north; Abu Tor, Talpiot, and Mekor Haim in the south – for many years kept protective walls of sandbags at the entrances to their buildings, reinforced the glass of their exposed windows with materials such as tin and plywood, or even blocked their windows to leave only narrow slits in the direction of the potential danger. Residents of the border areas were not generally among the well-to-do, but in addition to earning a hard living and doing their household chores they often had to stand as night guards in their neighborhoods, where danger was always palpable. Still, in daytime they might exchange greetings with their Arab neighbors across the fence or with some well-disposed Arab Legionnaire posted just a few meters away.

Most of these accounts can be gathered from the contemporary press, which was replete with the feats of the common people in the face of frequent armistice breakdown, as detailed in the Introduction above; or with personal recollections of the residents who experienced, day in, day out, the anxieties and the frustrations of living in the divided city. Some stories were told by, or could be distilled from, the official reports of the UN as we have attempted to do in the previous chapter. But the most poignant ones were inscribed on the city walls themselves, which witnessed the full effects of the ineffective Armistice Regime, from the terrible to the trivial, from the bleeding of the victims to the pervasive disruptions in city services. The infrastructure had been disrupted during the war and could not be restored thereafter. Streets had been bisected, with concrete walls separating their eastern and western halves. The electric company, the telephone exchange, the main post office, the courts, the prison, the police headquarters, the best hospitals, the shopping areas, and the few entertainment centers, remained in Israeli Jerusalem; while Jordanian Jerusalem was deprived of them. Conversely, the prestigious Rockefeller Museum remained in eastern Jerusalem, along with the Jewish holy places, from which the inhabitants of western Jerusalem were now banned. The Hebrew University and Hadassah Hospital remained in a problematic Jewish enclave on Mount Scopus, out of service and surrounded by hostile forces which would have hampered their operation in any case. The historic cemetery on the Mount of Olives, the most coveted place before the war for Jewish burials, was also in Jordanian-held territory.

The fresh memories of the war, sprinkled with sporadic clashes along the demarcation line, could not but remind every one, at every moment, of the abnormal era they were living in. The artificial and desperate attempt to find substitutes for the lost joint institutions and services, such as the municipality, government offices, the water supply, certain schools and medical services, public transportation and sewer systems, in itself was living proof that this all was temporary, and that normalcy would prevail only when the organic and natural growth of the city was restored. Hence, the provisional character of the armistice arrangement – itself truncated by the failure of Article VIII from the outset – guided the thinking of the city planners as well as of the common citizenry. But, as the years wore on, the necessities of life, reinforced by the fact that western Jerusalem had also become the capital of the new State of Israel, forced the populations on both sides of the line to produce more or less adequate substitutes. Eastern Jerusalem built its own municipality and electric power grid, hospitals, and telephone, transportation and judicial system, which were integrated into the Jordanian superstructure; while western Jerusalem had to construct new campuses for the University and the Hadassah Hospital, new burial grounds, and so forth. At the same time Israel had been deluged with large numbers of new immigrants and many of them were settled in the evacuated border areas of the city, or in the old Arab neighborhoods of South and West Jerusalem.

WESTERN JERUSALEM

Jerusalem under armistice was also undergoing drastic change as the nascent Israeli government moved into the city. This necessitated temporary housing for the thousands of government officials and, indeed, many ministries, while permanent premises were under construction for the Knesset, government offices and public institutions. The very installation of the hub of the Israeli authority – except for the Ministry of Defence – a few hundred yards from the demarcation line, was something of a political statement. It calmed the fears of the Jerusalemites, especially those on the border, and instilled in them self-confidence and hope. Self-confidence, because if the élite of government had settled there, the siege and the calamities of 1948 would never be allowed to be repeated; hope, since a capital city could not be left for ever exposed to the imminent danger inherent in the fragile and disappointing Armistice Regime. So, it was reasoned, either a more solid permanent arrangement had been agreed upon which would allow a return to normal, or the opportunity might present itself in the future to reverse the unfortunate results of the war. In the noisy street politics of those days, the government in place (led by David Ben-Gurion) embraced the first assumption, while the Herut right-wing radicals (headed by Menachem Begin) vociferously advocated the latter.

One of the major lessons learned from the war in and around Jerusalem, and its aftermath, which had an immediate effect on life under armistice, was the need to widen and strengthen the Jerusalem 'corridor' west of the city, which was surrounded on the other three sides by hostile enemy territory. To do this, it was necessary not only to ensure a dense continuum of Jewish settlement all along the metropolitan demarcation line described above, but also to build a string of new settlements to the northwest and the southwest of the city. These would guard the approaches to the city during the armistice and constitute a living dam against any new attempt, in case of war in the future, by the Arabs to resume their siege of the city. These steps, which were pursued assiduously and without fanfare, also helped reassure the armistice-stricken inhabitants of West Jerusalem that the horrors of the Arab ambushes on Jewish convoys to the embattled city – since the declaration of the Partition Plan and up until June 1948 – would not be repeated.[2] To that end, the new highway to Jerusalem was widened, and several new alternative roads were built to provide access to the city from the west and southwest, in case of emergency, when the main highway, which was in full view of the Arab Legion along its last few kilometers before its entrance into the urban area, might be exposed to enemy fire.

Western Jerusalem had changed immensely both along the demarcation line and in the hinterland, both due to the massive building by Israeli of huge tent-towns and barracks to accommodate the inflow of Jewish refugees from Europe and the Islamic lands, and the conversion of some previously Arab neighborhoods into refugee centers for the newcomers as explained in the Introduction. Some of those encampments, like Talpiot on the southern confines of the city, were located very close to the demarcation lines and, along with many other privations, their impoverished inhabitants had to face the risk of being shot at by the Jordanians every time an incident flared up in the vicinity. In time, at the end of the 1950s, these temporary camps were converted into vast housing projects, and the same population moved in, still in close proximity to the armistice line, but better protected from the elements and from the hazards of the Armistice Regime. All the southern neighborhoods of West Jerusalem, which had previously had Arab or mixed population – such as Talbiya, Abu Tor, the German Colony, the Greek Colony, Bak'a and Katamon – were now completely Jewish, and new construction started to spring up to accommodate the waves of incoming immigrants.

In the westernmost limits of the city, the Arab villages of Deir Yassin and Lifta, which had been attacked and destroyed by the Jewish forces in the early phases of the battle for Jerusalem, now lay in ruins. The Givat Shaul neighborhood had completely replaced the former and expanded to the limits of the latter. The Arab village of Malha to the southwest, had also been evacuated by its inhabitants during the war and populated by new Jewish immigrants from 1949. This village, which was also included in the expanded city limits, became a focus of endless cases of infiltration during the 1950s from across the nearby border with Jordan. The infiltrators were mainly former inhabitants who came to 'visit' their former lands, or steal property from the new settlers, or to avenge their own expulsion/flight/evacuation from their lands and houses a few years earlier. From the 1950s the former neighborhood of Beit Mazmil became a thriving suburb of Jerusalem, renamed Kiryat Yovel, where thousands of new immigrants built their new houses.

At the entrance to Jerusalem, the neighborhoods of Romema and Sheikh Badr were also completely Judaized and expanded; the latter became the site where the Israeli Knesset, government offices and, lately, the Supreme Court, as well as the new campus of the Hebrew University, were constructed. This area was renamed Givat Ram. On the southwest border of Jerusalem, the village of Beit Safafa – together with Abu Ghosh further to the northwest – were all that remained of the string of Arab villages which had blocked the western approaches to the city, whose population had not fled during the war. The armistice line in that area crossed the middle of the village, dividing families and disrupting social and commercial life. While the remaining Arab population on the Israeli side was integrated, municipally if not socially, into western Jerusalem, the Jordanian part of the village remained independent of eastern Jerusalem.

In retrospect, one wonders today how the entire Jewish city of West Jerusalem doubled and trebled its Jewish population in a matter of a few decades – from 100,000 in 1948 to nearly three times that many in 1967 – on the ruins of the Arab villages that were destroyed during and after the 1948 war, or in the same neighborhoods that had belonged to, or had been occupied by evacuated Arab populations, without leaving on record any signs of public expressions of remorse, regret or soul-searching. Indeed, judging this demographic metamorphosis as an end-result, one is puzzled at what today seems to be, at best, a manifestation of insensitivity, on the part of the new settlers; or, at worst, an almost inhuman act of displacement of others. It is only during these past few years that Israeli historians have begun digging up the documentation of those formative and fateful events, and with a cool-headedness borne out of maturity and self-confidence, have been re-evaluating the data relevant to that history and reinterpreting them. In the process a number of taboos have been violated, and a few icons have been shattered, causing not a few explosions of anger among the Israeli public.

In this new ambiance of debate, no one writing on these sensitive issues can escape from the need to account for some of the inevitable puzzles and to throw into the arena some sort of plausible explanation, even if it raises eyebrows or generates fits of rage in certain circles. There is no doubt today that the old myth of the Arab refugees all fleeing of their own accord, has crumbled; for there is evidence that the massive evacuation of Arab neighborhoods in Jerusalem – and elsewhere – came in the wake of terrible fighting which, naturally, frightened the civilian population of the warring parties into moving out of the war zone. However, while the Jewish population had nowhere else to go, and therefore held its own with its back to the wall, the Arabs innocently believed that they did have a choice – that is, to seek temporary refuge in neighboring Arab countries until the end of hostilities. Due to the optimistic fighting spirit instilled in them by their leaders, the Arabs also believed in their chance to return home after the fighting had ended. Therefore, without getting into the question of the morality or lack thereof of certain specific military tactics followed by both parties, it is evident that the massive exodus of the Arab population of West Jerusalem was generated by genuine fear that was fuelled by horror stories which were often exaggerated.

It is equally evident that, regardless of how we judge today the overall picture of that war, we can only torment ourselves with the disastrous human price it exacted, but we cannot conclusively indict the players on the scene at the time that war was unfolding. For, while the Arabs were being evicted or running for their lives, Jewish immigrants who had escaped or survived the Nazi hell were streaming to Israel and avid to settle down and find some degree of stability, safety and certainty. It was hard to expect those drowning people to relinquish the life-saving raft that was offered to them in consideration of others who occupied it first. Similarly, the Jewish leadership which was poised, against all odds, to establish a fragile state and protect it against invading Arab armies, could not be expected to be so magnanimous as to allow themselves to be moved by human considerations that might put in jeopardy their own plans for survival. On the other hand, at the end of the war, and during all the interminable debates, conflicts and wars in the ensuing 50 years, allowance should have been made by the Israeli leadership for the misery and suffering of the Palestinians, even if it found them impossible to redress under conditions of war. To express sorrow for the misery of the enemy, or condolences for his losses, would not have diminished the justification of the war of defense led by the nascent Jewish state by one iota. Nor would it diminish the pride and morale of its present-day armies.

One has also to acknowledge the almost total elimination of the Arab and Muslim nature of the neighborhoods that were taken over by the Jewish troops in West Jerusalem. For, not only were entire villages razed on the outskirts of the city as mentioned above, to signify that they would never be allowed to be rehabilitated and repopulated by Arabs, but many Muslim mosques, cemeteries, tombs of local popular saints, and other sites of historical or cultural value, were either destroyed, or Judaized, or converted to other uses. The most notorious example is the vast Muslim cemetery in Mamillah – today Agron – Street, which was partly destroyed and partly turned into a park, with the rest abandoned to weeds and decay. Names of streets and neighborhoods were also Judaized: Katamon became Gonen; Sheikh Bader, Givat Ram; Beit Mazmil, Kiryat Yovel; etc. Once again, one could understand that the Jewish newcomers who survived the Holocaust and the 1948 war would be eager to make a new start, in a cultural environment transformed to fit their new national ambitions; but one should also feel empathy for the Arabs who looked from afar upon the new occupiers of what were their lands, houses and shrines, and for the frustration they must have felt at their inability to alter the new situation. In a further bout of sympathy, one could even understand the repeated attempts of those destitute Arabs – in armistice language they were called 'infiltrators' or 'marauders' – over the years to regain their properties or, at the very least, take revenge on those who had disinherited them. The fact that they had lost the war, even the fact that they had started the war, are immaterial to the destitute and the uprooted.

In an attempt to skirt the gloom of the armistice, and to heal the wounds left by the severing of eastern Jerusalem from the city center, the Israelis extensively developed their Jerusalem. Many, both in the municipality and in the government, wanted Jerusalem to match the liveliness of its epicurean Tel Aviv rival with its well-earned epithet of 'a city without a break'. It was in those days that the stinging remark was made in the bohemian milieux of Jerusalem that: 'the only advantage of Tel Aviv is its good road to Jerusalem,' a reversal of the same saying that could be heard among the renowned hedonists of the coastal metropolis of Israel. In spite of the tensions and the occasional shooting incidents, a large auditorium, Binyanei Ha'uma, was erected at the entrance to the city. Here, large-scale festivities were launched for the tenth anniversary of the Jewish state in 1958, and many daring cultural and international activities were held, as if there were no armistice and the city were not half-surrounded by enemy guns at close range. Tourism into the city picked up, many hotels were built to welcome tourists and pilgrims, local and international, and a semblance of normality set it, although broken at times by bloody incidents along the nearby demarcation line as mentioned in the Introduction. A few foreign embassies, notably from Latin American countries, added to the international flavour of Jerusalem, already teeming with UN Observers, the foreign consuls of many Western countries, tourists from all parts of the globe, pilgrims, clergymen and nuns.

EASTERN JERUSALEM

Eastern Jerusalem was also licking its wounds after the war. But, unlike its western counterpart, it remained quite stagnant during the armistice. While, during the armistice, western Jerusalem had more than doubled in both territory and population, due to the priority status granted to it by Israeli authorities and the determination of its inhabitants to draw a curtain over the past and look forward, the eastern side of the city was neglected. It had been a backwater under the Turkish Ottoman Empire and under Jordan it had become a backwater once again, despite the previous 30-year interregnum of the British Mandate during which it was the center of the mandatory government and the seat of the High Commissioner. King Abdallah, and then his successor Hussein, while paying lip-service to the city and its holy places, were wary of promoting its political importance, lest it be embraced as the center of Palestinian nationalism on which they were trying to clamp down. For the Jordanian King, who added the Holy City to his title when he annexed the entire West Bank to his kingdom, Jerusalem was, first of all, a focus of prestige: it was the place where his valiant Arab Legion had not only held its own against Israel, but had also forced the embattled Jews to withdraw from their positions in the Jewish Quarter in the Old City, and evacuate the

Jewish communities north (Atarot and Neve Ya'akov) and south (the Etzion Bloc) of it.[3]

In later years King Hussein sought legitimacy as ruler of Jordan as the descendant of the Hashemites in the Hejaz and by claiming the title of the Curator of the Aqsa Mosque, the third holiest shrine of Islam. Even after he lost the mosque in 1967, he kept claiming his right to redeem it in any eventual settlement with Israel.[4] But right after the 1948 war, and all throughout the armistice years, eastern Jerusalem was little more than an Arab Legion outpost which was watching the restive Palestinian population as much as the Israeli-controlled western part of the city. The Jordanian task was facilitated by the fact that much of the Palestinian leadership of the Jerusalem which was, as a whole, hostile to the aspirations of the King in Western Palestine, had left the city during the fighting and lost its control over Arab Jerusalemites. Certainly, some members of prominent Jerusalem families such as the Nuseibehs, Husseinis and Khalidis had stayed, or returned after the war. However, after the exile of the mufti Sheikh Amin al-Husseini and the killing of his nephew, Abd-al-Qader, in the battle for Jerusalem, no leadership to speak of stayed behind to act as communal leaders, launch development programs, or galvanize political forces for the future of Arab Jerusalem. Some Jerusalemites were co-opted by the Hashemite regime. These included Anwar Nuseibeh, who was for many years the Governor of Jerusalem, and Muhammed Dawud, the Senior Delegate of Jordan in the Armistice Commission, a POW in Israel in 1967, and later Prime Minister of Jordan in 1970. Others either moved to the center of power in Amman, or, like the Khalidis, made brilliant careers in academia, trade or diplomacy abroad. The very fact that they agreed to be co-opted and serve under the Jordanian government meant that they had lost their nationalist drive and their ambition to take risks by independent struggle.

Unlike the western side of the demarcation line, which saw expansion, growth and development, the eastern part of Jerusalem, most of all the border areas, experienced few, if any, changes. The Jordanian positions along the demarcation lines, which had been in place since the June 1948 truce, were still in their same encampments, except that they had been expanded and fortified over the years. The only noticeable changes in eastern Jerusalem during the early years of the armistice were demographic and cultural, not physical. All traces of the centuries-old Jewish life in the Old City were extirpated and Jewish holy sites destroyed or

severely damaged. All Jewish synagogues were razed and access to
the holy Wailing Wall for Jews was forbidden. The site's identity as
a Jewish holy place was denied by the Jordanians and it became
exclusively Islamic, known only as the venerated place where the
mystical horse of the Prophet, which had transported him on its
wings from his native Mecca to Jerusalem, had waited for its rider
to descend from his heavenly encounter with the angels. Attesting
to that event, a sign carrying the name of the horse, Al-Buraq, hung
on the Wall until removed by the Israelis in 1967.

The dejudaization of the eastern part of Jerusalem included the
systematic desecration of the Mount of Olives cemetery: *The
Intercontinental Hotel* was built by the Jordanians on the site, and
other tomb stones were pillaged to be used for construction and
paving roads, both by the Arab Legion and the local populace. So,
instead of allowing access to the Mount, as it undertook under
Article VIII, Jordan strove to destroy the site so that access would
become irrelevant even if permitted. The Jewish neighborhoods of
Atarot and Neve Ya'akov in north Jerusalem, were also dejudaized,
and their remaining structures made into military facilities for the
Jordanian army. All the previously Jewish places, religious sites or
otherwise, were allowed to be submerged demographically under
the flow of thousands of Palestinian refugees or villagers, mainly
from the Hebron area, who rushed to settle in the purely Arab city
of East Jerusalem. Thus, dejudaization was followed by
Arabization: thousands of Arabs were settled with their families in
all the above mentioned previously Jewish sites, notably in the
Jewish Quarter and the vicinity of the Western Wall. This was a
complete mirror image of what the Jews did in West Jerusalem to
Arab sites, except that there was no provision in the Armistice
Agreement to allow the departed Palestinians free access to their
former shrines or institutions.

THE COMMON METROPOLITAN BOUNDARY

In the north of Jerusalem, the strategically located Nebi Samuel (the
tomb of the biblical prophet Samuel), which Israel had
unsuccessfully attempted to conquer during the 1948 war, was the
equivalent of the Castel fortress on the Israeli side of the border,
and both dominated the armistice line as it approached the city. A
string of Arab villages on the Jordanian side, notably Beit Iqsa and

Beit Suriq, continued to control by fire, from across the border, the last stretches of the highway from Tel Aviv; while the Arab villages on the Israeli side were all destroyed during the battle for Jerusalem. Names like Beit Mahsir, Deir Ayyub, Castel and Colonia, had all passed into history, together with all the others that were now included within the Jerusalem city limits, as described above. The only two exceptions – Beit Safafa and Aby Ghosh – have been mentioned previously; the latter even had an extraordinary history of siding with the Jewish State during the war. This meant that anyone coming or leaving Jerusalem under armistice, on the Israeli side of the border experienced the hazard of gun-fire, since this was the main, shortest, and most frequented access to the Israeli capital. It is difficult to visualize today how the Jerusalemites, including their old and children, their political and military top leaders, their intellectual and economic élites, their artists and tourists, would have had to become resigned to this state of affairs under an Armistice Regime that was far from perfect and was often violated (as shown above).

On the Jordanian side, there were three major entrances to the city, two of which – from the north and the east – were out of range for light arms and mostly also outside Israeli observation range. From the north, the main thoroughfare coming down from Jenin, Nablus and Ramallah, was protected on either side by the formidable fortifications of French Hill and a second fortress across the road. It was also overlooked by Tel-al-ful, the magnificent heights on which the King had chosen to build his never-completed West Bank Palace. From the east, the road from Amman via the Allenby Bridge, Jericho and the large military encampment in Khan al-Ahmar to Jerusalem was in fact the main, and safest highway linking the Jordanian capital to its new acquisitions west of the Jordan, by way of Jerusalem. That meant that for the Jordanians, civilian and military alike, as for the occasional tourist on that side of the border, there was no danger, real or perceived, in traveling to eastern Jerusalem from these two directions. They were shielded physically by the distance from the border and the heights commanded by the Ramallah–Jerusalem highway; and, psychologically, by the sense of being in the hinterland when no enemy position was in sight. The third access from the south, which was exposed to Israeli fire, will be discussed below.

The urban area of Jerusalem has always been characterized by a cluster of hill-top neighborhoods, bearing their own names and usually providing their own community services, like independent villages or townships linked together by through roads and bound together under one municipal umbrella. Much like the ancient seven hills of Rome or the string of towns and suburbs which make up modern Berlin, Jerusalem has kept its geographic diversity within its urban boundaries; but, unlike its European counterparts, it has preserved, even cultivated, an extraordinary web of cultural, religious, ethnic, national, economic, status-oriented and linguistic groups. Therefore, the armistice lines, though cruel and arbitrary in appearance, did not much alter these divisions, although the displacement of some populations and their replacement by others definitely changed the nature, the environment, the demography and the cultural make-up of many of the neighborhoods. For example, the Jewish Quarter in the Old City still continued to be called Harat-al Yahud, within its historical borders, but it was now totally Arabized and Islamized. Conversely, the Arab-German Colony kept its name under Israel, but Sheikh Badr was rebaptized Givat Ram and was completely Judaized and Hebraized, although its geographic contours did not change.

The Northern Sector of the Line

These ethno-cultural changes, interestingly enough, occurred mainly in the neighborhoods which found themselves totally immersed in the new milieu of the armistice period. A new reality emerged from the truce and the armistice demarcation lines, which determined their new national identity deep into their side of the border, as the examples in the previous paragraph amply demonstrate. However, in the border areas which were affected only at their margins and not to their core, the pre-war situation continued to prevail to a large extent. At the northernmost tip of Jerusalem, bordering the armistice line, were the two religious Jewish communities of Sanhedria and Pagi (the acronym of Poalei Agudat Israel, an ultra-religious workers' organization). North of them and overlooking them at point-blank range, were the menacing Tililya and Shu'afat hills which had become fortified positions for the Arab Legion. To the east was the 50–200-m-wide no man's land, where a soccer playground had teemed with sports activities in better days, but was now an unfenced empty field infested with wild dogs and cats straying among the bushes and flowers in the rainy and spring seasons. In the summer and the fall it was dry and desolate, like the hills towering over it from the north.

For the Jewish inhabitants of these two remote neighborhoods, life under the guns was focused on Torah studies, in which people sought and found solace and hope. With large families and low incomes they were crowded into small apartments bordering on no man's land which faced east onto the imposing white rectangular building surrounded by numerous smaller structures which had served as the Palestine Police Training Base and Depot when Britain ruled the country. Now the UN flag flew above the main building as the UNRWA, which dispensed aid to the Palestinian refugees from the 1948–49 war, had taken it over. The area surrounding the building was occupied by Jordanian troops whose daily activities could be observed in detail by the black-hatted inhabitants of the two Jewish neighborhoods.

For them, armistice meant protecting windows facing Jordanian posts and directing their numerous offspring not to play directly under the watchful eyes of the Legionnaires a 100 m off. Armistice also meant that from time to time a stray animal would explode an old land mine, a relic from the war, or that a joint Jordan–Israel public health team would beat its way through the bush to spray anti-malarial substances after a particularly rainy winter. Still less frequently, someone from either side would find himself strolling across the fences, intentionally or absent-mindedly, into a mine-field and be in need of rescue. Usually these minor incidents were dealt with swiftly by the MAC, and settled before they flared into a violent eruption. Preposterous as it may sound, a feeling of safety under these conditions was provided by an Israeli Army observation post manned round the clock by a small body of armed soldiers, usually civilians on reserve duty, who would have been no match for their counterparts across the line if trouble arose. Yet, for the resigned, God-fearing residents of the area that seemed sufficient.

Across no man's land and south of the UNRWA compound, lay the houses of the Sheikh Jarrah Quarter, one of the bloodiest sectors of the war. It had been captured and lost by both sides, during the battles for Jerusalem even before the end of the British Mandate.[5] The armistice lines left all of the quarter in Jordanian hands, commanding the vitally strategic road to Ramallah on the one side, and the only access to the Mount Scopus complex on the other. For the Israelis it was not so much the coveted site of the tomb of

Shimon the Righteous as the link to the embattled Israeli enclave on Mount Scopus, and the object of meticulous military planning in case they had to move to rescue the besieged garrison or the fortnightly convoys under UN auspices which ensured its survival. The Jordanians were well aware of that, hence their resolve to defend it come what may. But, for the civilian populace living there – barely a few thousand – there was a feeling of being squeezed from the west and the east by an imminent Israeli threat. They knew that the Israelis had failed ultimately to keep the neighborhood in their hands when they attacked from the west in 1948, but they were petrified by the imposing and humiliating presence of the Jewish fortress of Mount Scopus at their back, which dominated not only their houses, but the entire northern section of the city. And they were also aware that when the chips were down, the Israelis would not hesitate to seize their neighborhood in order to secure the link to Mount Scopus. In the day-to-day conduct of their lives, however, they were not much concerned about the armistice line which ran just in front of their houses. They may have looked with envy and nostalgia on the sprouting new development west of them, contrasting the almost total immobility on their side, but none of that disturbed their routine.

Somewhat different was the situation in the twin Arab neighborhoods of the American Colony and Wadi Joz, immediately south of Sheikh Jarrah and facing the famous Mandelbaum Gate and the Shmuel Hanavi Quarter in West Jerusalem. Ironically, this was named after the same Prophet Samuel whose name was used for the Jordanian position of Nebi Samuel which threatened Shmuel Hanavi from the north. Although they did not front the demarcation line side-by-side – Wadi Joz being located east of the much larger and more prosperous American Colony – both felt the same squeeze as Sheikh Jarrah by virtue of their location between the Israeli lines to the west and the Mount Scopus fortress to the east. The American Colony, a lush green spot in the generally arid East Jerusalem, which sports spacious villas and mansions, was the place chosen by foreign consulates – notably the British and the American – and the wealthy landed, intellectual and commercial élites of the local Palestinians, for their activities and lodging. Here were held the famous literary salons, the sumptuous dinners and receptions; and here were plotted some of the most fateful policies adopted by the Palestinians. One of those houses which belonged to the Husseini family, was to become the famous Orient House.

The public institutions of the colony – such as the *American Colony Hotel*, the St George Cathedral, the St Stephen's Monastery, and the Rockefeller Museum at its southern limit – also made it an important spiritual, economic and cultural center which was most attractive to foreigners in East Jerusalem and the object of awe and envy for the local populace. It was in the Rawdah School here that the irregular Arab militias which fought for Jerusalem in the 1948 war established their headquarters. Because of its close proximity to the Mandelbaum Gate, it also became the access for UN personnel to the MAC offices and the passage for their peregrinations between the two parts of the city. Moreover, the inhabitants of this respectable quarter were not the types to stray into no man's land or to take unnecessary risks, or to challenge Israeli soldiers across the line, or to run after lost animals into the wild. All these factors combined to lend this part of Jerusalem a peaceful and quiet atmosphere, hardly matched anywhere else in East Jerusalem but comparable to the wealthy neighborhoods of West Jerusalem, such as Rehavia, Talbiyya, Qiryat Shmuel, and Beit Hakkerem further to the west. For these reasons, among others, the no man's land bordering the American Colony to the west was among the most calm and tranquil areas along the metropolitan demarcation line.

The Israeli side of the border told a different story. Behind the first line of Israeli posts guarding the western side of the Mandelbaum Gate, matching those occupied by the Arab Legion on the opposite side bordering with the American Colony, were the slum neighborhoods of Shmuel Hanavi, Mea Shearim and Musrara which extended westward all the way to the center of the city. These were large and crowded clusters of old ultra-Orthodox Jewish neighborhoods, or old Arab houses, occupied by the Jews during the war; also, ugly, cheap and very large housing projects hurriedly built after the war to populate the border areas and to accommodate the waves of new immigrants reaching Jerusalem. Also noted for their imposing presence, were a series of old communal houses for the ultra-Orthodox, like the Hungarian Compound, and foreign institutions such as the Italian Hospice which dominated the entire border area from its impressive heights. Those parts of these Israeli neighborhoods which bordered the American Colony also enjoyed its advantages and could usually borrow, as it were, some of its serenity. But the southern part of Musrara, at the mercy of the Old City Wall, knew many troubled and bloody days.

This part of West Jerusalem was particularly sensitive, due to its close proximity to some of the central nervous systems of the city: the City Hall, the central Post Office and Telephone Exchange, the Police Headquarters and the Courts of Law (municipal and district; and the Supreme Court which was, and is, the crown and pride of the Israeli judicial system). Immediately behind them were the two major hospitals of Jerusalem, the new temporary Hadassah and Bikur Holim, whose vital importance stemmed from the isolation within enemy territory of the largest and most competent medical establishment in the city – the crippled Hadassah Hospital on Mount Scopus. This area also included the liveliest shopping and entertainment center of town, with its famous triangle formed by the three major avenues of West Jerusalem: Jaffa, Ben-Yehuda and King George V. All three streets were busy, lined with Jerusalem's finest stores, cafés, banks and movie theaters; but they also bore scars of the war. Ben-Yehuda and King George V Streets had witnessed the horrors of car-bombs which had hit major buildings even before the birth of Israel; and Jaffa Street had been the scene of a similar tragedy when the near-by *Palestine Post* building was blown up by Arabs in 1948. Scores had been killed and hundreds wounded in that atrocity.

The fresh memory of these traumas had led the Israeli government to construct a high concrete wall at the beginning of Jaffa Road, just behind City Hall and in front of the Legionnaires in their protected positions on the city ramparts at the northwestern corner of the Old City wall, who could otherwise wreak havoc in West Jerusalem at will. In this way, life in central Jerusalem was shielded from enemy positions in its heart. Not so in the southern part of Musrara, which remained helplessly exposed. Fortunately for that otherwise doomed part of the border area, Israeli positions had been placed on top of a badly damaged wing of Notre Dame de France – the largest, tallest and most massively constructed building on one of the highest spots in the city. This Notre Dame Convent with its hundreds of cells had known very bitter hand-to-hand fighting during the war, much to the displeasure of its occupants who had come to worship God not to see their fellow humans engaged in an orgy of killing.[6] At the end of the war, on the eve of armistice, Israel had taken possession of the wing of Notre Dame which rose above the teeming Damascus Gate, a stone's throw from Musrara.

It was the threatening presence of the Notre Dame positions

which mitigated the topographical inferiority of Musrara. It dominated not only the entire neighborhood, but also the frightening northwestern corner of the city wall which was fenced off by the concrete screen built in West Jerusalem. Only Suleyman Street separated the convent from the wall and, since that street was covered on the armistice map by a line carelessly drawn with a thick china marker, that line widened every time it was touched. The inevitable result of this was an abundance of disagreements as to the exact location of the armistice line at given points. More than once these disagreements produced exchanges of fire which threatened the life of innocent civilians. Musrara residents experienced some very serious and painful border clashes, some of which have been detailed in a previous chapter.

The Mount Scopus Sector

We cannot conclude this discussion of life in the northern sector of Jerusalem without devoting a few words to those who were isolated in the Mount Scopus enclave immediately east of Sheikh Jarrah and the American Colony. As we have seen in previous chapters, while life in the southern Jordanian compound of Augusta Victoria in the demilitarized zone was more or less normal by virtue of its contiguity to Jordanian-held territory, life in the northern Israeli sector was quite hazardous, threatened by uncertainties, and pregnant with dangers, real and perceived. We have already discussed in some detail both the procedures surrounding the biweekly convoys to Mount Scopus and the security problems which produced violations of the armistice, and UN involvement in dealing with them. But the 85 Israeli personnel who guarded the enclave also had a personal life, a daily routine to pursue, a tremendous responsibility to discharge – aware of the depressing fragility of their existence and impatiently waiting for the relief convoy.

Basically, the compound – about one square kilometer in area – was divided into three units:

- The large Hadassah Hospital at the northernmost end of the Mount, with a smaller building on each side, occupied the highest point in the area. This ensured full control of the entire landscape west, north and east, all of which was enemy territory. Adjoining it to the north was the only road leading to the top, which passed through Sheikh Jarrah and then alongside the Commonwealth War Cemetery, also located within the perimeter of the Israeli sector. This road cut the Hadassah compound in two: the main building east of it and a few smaller buildings to the west which overlooked Sheikh Jarrah and offered a spectacular view of West Jerusalem. Like Moses on Mount Nevo, the men of the Mount Scopus garrison could view it but not go into it unless relieved by convoy in due course. To the east, the roof of the immense Hadassah Hospital suggested to the imaginative among its guards a platform, or a launching pad, from which they could fly off over the awesome and desolate Judean Desert and splash right into the mirror-like water of the Dead Sea. Immediately east of Hadassah, on the descending slope towards the desert, lay the second unit of the Hadassah compound.

- The village of Issawiyya was a sprawling Jordanian rural settlement inhabited by native Palestinians and many war refugees. Outwardly, it affected a disarming innocence, but in reality it was a hot-bed of fervent hostility towards the Israelis who were supposed to overlook it, like a virtual Trojan horse. It is hard to imagine now why the Israelis agreed to include that hornets' nest within their territory. They could either have insisted on taking it empty of people, or simply refused to include it in their enclave. True, that would have cut by one-third the area under their control, but then their line of defence would have been shortened considerably and the population of the enclave would have been homogeneous. Such an enclave would have been much easier to manage in every sense.

The Arab village within the Jewish sector of Mount Scopus did indeed prove to be a liability rather than an asset. In all clashes between the civilian population and the soldiers, the former always seemed to be in the right. Troops can have the upper hand in these clashes, but by winning in such circumstances they are bound to become the losers in the final analysis. One can surmise that only the naivety of the military commanders who signed the Mount Scopus Agreement, or the hope that its Article VIII would soon secure free access to the enclave and put an end to military confrontations, could have induced the Israelis to acquiesce in the existence of the anomaly called Issawiyya. The Jordanians were to draw only benefits from this situation; their civilians pitted themselves against the Israeli guards, and almost invariably they earned support from the UN in all instances. They could not have devised a nastier problem for the Israeli presence on Mount Scopus which they regarded as a dagger held against the Israeli back and a rich fountain of humiliation.

- South of Hadassah on the single road which ran along the crest of Scopus, at a distance of about 500 m, stood the cluster of buildings which had been the campus of the Hebrew University since its inauguration in 1925, until it was compelled to transfer to West Jerusalem. The western buildings overlooked the olive groves on the slopes leading to Wadi Joz; the eastern buildings overlooked the amphitheater where the inaugural ceremony of the university had taken place in the presence of the British High Commissioner, Lord Herbert Samuel, Dr Chaim Weizmann, the veteran Zionist leader, and Professor Albert Einstein. The eastern compound also offered various defence options southwards in the direction of the Jordanian sector of Augusta Victoria.

In normal times the impressive natural fortress of Mount Scopus needed at least an 800-man, four-company battalion for its defence – one company in three shifts for each of its sections and one company in reserve against an attack. In addition, it was necessary to have specialist crews to man heavier weapons such as mortars, heavy machine-guns, light anti-tank guns and perhaps some pieces of artillery. All this, and service and maintenance personnel, were required for such a force defending an isolated position under constant danger of attack. But the reality of the armistice allowed for only 85 'policemen' – fewer than the complement of a single infantry company – who had to carry out all the duties involved, in total isolation and under constant danger. Its routine tasks were many:

- To man at all times a network of observation posts covering the entire perimeter of about 2,000 m in circumference, which encompassed the Hadassah and University units and the road between them, leaving Issawiyya out of the permanent scope of vigilance. Even so, breaking the total number of guards into three more or less equal shifts, that left some 25–30 men – assuming they were in good health – to bear the burden of guard duties. This came to one man to every 80–100 m (or double or triple that distance), whereas proper practice would have required two or three men to do the job on a hilltop more or less devoid of vegetation – other than the trees around the clusters of buildings – which made observation and defence all the more hazardous, especially since the approaches to the hilltop were sporadically covered with trees and bushes, which made it easy for attackers to surprise the defenders.

- To prepare and be prepared at all times for a surprise attack by the Arab Legion, which had enough military hardware and manpower in the immediate vicinity to carry out such an attack at short notice. This meant that the defenders, including those off-duty, had to be alert round the clock with their weapons ready for use. With this in mind, very precise contingency plans were drawn up to meet all eventualities, which stressed the absolute need to hold out until a massive Israeli intervention could be mounted.

- To conceal the main weapons of defence – not all of them necessarily allowed under the Mount Scopus agreement, yet kept close enough and ready for use when needed. During some of the serious incidents of gun-fire on Mount Scopus, cited above, use was made of these 'forbidden' weapons, so everyone knew they existed, but no one would admit that they had slipped through the strict regulations devised for the Mount Scopus convoys.

- To meet all requirements of food and drink, hygiene, health and recreation, and to maintain a routine within which everyone knew his duties. It was like living in a submarine where space was limited and supplies scarce, with everyone counting the days and hours to resurfacing into the real world.

- To train the personnel in the use of their light weapons as well as the forbidden ones, and to rehearse again and again rapid deployment in case of emergency. Since this could not be done in daytime under the eyes of the Jordanians, it was necessary to lose some precious sleeping hours. The Jordanians often complained to the UN about the 'strange noises' that the night breezes of Jerusalem had transported to their ears from Scopus, and they demanded UN inspection. But nothing improper was ever found. However, this game of hide-and-seek consumed much of the stamina of the force and demonstrated to the men the need to keep alert and watchful at all times.

- To send out patrols beyond the immediate perimeter of Mount Scopus; to keep a watchful eye on the area around; and to deter or prevent encroachments by Arab farmers and herdsmen. These patrols also ventured into Isawiyya and its immediate surroundings. Violent clashes often ensued (some of which have been discussed above) when the Jordanians misinterpreted the intentions of Israeli patrols. The reverse could hardly occur, since the encircled Israelis in their inferior situation would not dare drum up any large-scale incident that might cost them dearly.

The Central and Southern Sectors

The western side of the Old City Wall, which constituted the Jordanian demarcation line from Notre Dame in the north down to Mount Zion in the south, created an asymmetry between the two parts of Jerusalem as far as living under the armistice was concerned. For the wall was heavily guarded by Arab Legionnaires, and while it gave a sense of security to the Arabs who lived in the intramural quarters, it posed a direct and imminent danger to the inhabitants of the western part of Jerusalem, who were exposed to small-arms fire practically along its entire course. Moreover, the people who lived inside the wall were physically shielded by it and, except for an occasional venture outside the ramparts, they would not even be conscious of the fact that they lived in a border area, nor that armistice rather than peace was the frame of reference for their relations with the neighbouring community. They could conduct their lives so comfortably inside their shaded alleys and noisy bazaars, that even when an exchange of fire took place outside, it sounded to them too remote to warrant their attention, much less to cause a sense of anxiety. When they lifted their eyes to the wall from the inside all they could see was the reassuring figures of soldiers posted behind well-fortified positions high up. The Israeli landscape offered a somewhat less reassuring picture.

Lying between the City Wall and the Israeli side of the city there was a 100-m-wide strip of no man's land in a ravine that looked like a natural moat protecting the towering David citadel and its contiguous Jaffa Gate. The lowest terrain was still covered by the ruins of the Jewish commercial centre of Jerusalem, burnt down by the Arab rioters during the 1936 Palestinian uprising against the British, and since then deserted as a dangerous border area. The large Tannous building at the edge of no man's land had become partly an Israeli military position and partly a pitiful slum, home to

West Jerusalem's poorest. The adjoining Mamillah Street, which used to lead to the now destroyed commercial centre, and the web of alleys branching out of it, had all become a vast array of decrepit workshops, garages and shanty houses. A little to the west, one could see the imposing structure of the famous King David Hotel, which had housed a part of the British administration during the Mandate; the splendid tower and domes of the YMCA compound; the American Consulate General in West Jerusalem (a second one was located in the American Colony in East Jerusalem); the superb mansion housing the French consul-general and his offices, built in the 1930s to match the glamour of Government House; and any number of other public institutions, like the Biblical Institute next door to the French Consulate.

In normal times, an Israeli driving southward to the main King David Street, which was partly exposed to the City Wall, could only delight in the splendid view open to him: the Citadel and the nearby Kishleh police station and prison dating from Ottoman times; and the Jaffa Gate, which had to be breached to allow Emperor Wilhelm II of Germany into the Old City with his coach, and where the last unsuccessful attempt was made by Israel to break into the besieged Jewish Quarter during the war. To the south, the picturesque Yemin Moshe quarter, envisioned and financed by Sir Moses Montefiore as alternative housing for those Jews who had been crowded into squalid conditions in the Old City. An elegant windmill constructed on higher ground nearby alongside the main thoroughfare to south Jerusalem became a famous landmark. Parts of this otherwise exciting landscape were much less agreeable to the eye: on top of the magnificent City Wall, especially on its south-western corner, (occasionally trigger-happy) Arab Legionnaires were watching at all times. So anyone venturing south into the neighbourhoods of Talbiyya, Abu Tor, Bak'a, the German Colony, Talpiot, Arnona, Ramat Rachel, Mekor Hayim, the Greek Colony, and the vast barracks for new immigrants (the infamous Ma'abarot), had to look anxiously over their shoulder while passing along that stretch of the road. Some of the most serious incidents in Jerusalem – involving loss of life – under the armistice, occurred right there, along the line or within no man's land to the east.

Immediately south of the wall lay the Mount Zion complex of holy places, dominated by the Dormition Church and Convent. Tradition has it that the tomb of King David is located there, and that the Last Supper was celebrated nearby; here too, the area was at the mercy of that notorious corner of the City Wall. Only when one climbed down to the Hinnon Valley did one begin to lose sight of it and enter into the Abu Tor complex on the slope leading up to Government House. The hinterland on both sides of the line did not offer any particular points of friction: on the Jordanian side there was the sprawling and arid village of Silwan, home of the Senior Jordanian Delegate, Muhammed Dawud; on the Israeli side, the railway station, the Government Printing House, the British Consulate for West Jerusalem (another British consular mission, a more active one, is located in the American Colony, in the eastern part of the city), and the Scottish hospice – all overlooking the breathtaking view of southern Jerusalem, from Mount Zion and the imposing City Wall, to the crowded neighbourhood of Abu Tor, an essentially Arab quarter divided by the war, with the armistice line running right through its middle.

Due to its strategic importance between the Old City and southern Jerusalem, and its large Arab population, Abu Tor became a problematic focal point of armistice violations where several military positions were located right in the midst of the civilian population of both parties, who lived in too close proximity to avoid friction. Furthermore, the Israeli section of Abu Tor houses was situated higher than its Arab counterpart, which gave the Israelis – military and civilian – a clear advantage. There are two ways of explaining the friction in those conditions (for lack of clear evidence showing who caused the trouble): the one favoured by the Israelis was that due to their topographic inferiority and the anxieties this generated, the Arab residents sought to redress the imbalance by aggressiveness. The Jordanians advanced the more straightforward thesis that Israeli military and civilian population simply took advantage of their dominating position to challenge their adversaries across the lines. Be it as it may, many emergency meetings of the sub-committee of the MAC were held in the middle of the night in an attempt to calm tempers and to reject assertions of civilians and military on both sides that the 'others had started it.'

For the most part, neither side was interested in exacerbating the situation in that section of the line. Even when it was the policy of the Jordanian government to act more aggressively along the borders, Abu Tor was not a convenient spot for a test of strength because of its topography. In such cases Jordanian citizens preferred caution, satisfying themselves, usually, with rock-throwing across no man's land where it was narrow. In other instances children 'mistakenly' crossed the border at play, or purportedly ran away after a row with their parents and crossed the line to make trouble for them as a 'punishment'.

To avoid these dangerous occurrences, in the early 1960s Israel began to build a fence down from Mount Zion into Abu Tor, but Jordan opposed the project, arguing that the demarcation line must not assume the character of a political frontier. In any case, unbridgeable differences between the parties regarding the location of the armistice lines on the ground blocked any practical progress – much to the chagrin of the Israeli area commander, Colonel Yoseph Nevo, who had valiantly fought for Jerusalem in the 1948 war. What was to be the Nevo Wall – inspired, it was said, by the contemporaneous Ulbricht Wall in Berlin – never got off the ground.

From Abu Tor the demarcation lines bifurcated to form a two-kilometre-wide area between the lines, known as Government House, whose legal status has been described in a previous chapter. Not only were the demarcation lines too far apart to create any friction by proximity, but on both sides the population was not as dense as in the other sectors to the north; and in fact there were vast tracts of land left empty. The presence of the UN Headquarters in the vicinity also helped maintain tranquillity in that sector. On the Israeli side, the outer limits of sovereign Israeli territory, before entry into the area between the lines, were marked by the large compound of the St Claire Convent, the Allenby Barracks (which had been taken over from the British at the end of the Mandate and were now inhabited by families of Israeli military officers, or earmarked for military purposes), and the tiny neighbourhood of Arnona. On the Jordanian side it was pure wilderness, except for the southernmost houses of Silwan and Abu Tor, which hardly touched the demarcation line.

Breaches of the armistice, which were few, occurred within the Government House area itself where the parties had secured their civilian rights; for example, in Mount Scopus to the north. But, here, no special arrangements were needed for access to the area, either from one side or another, due to the contiguity of each party's section to its own sovereign territory. On the Israeli side, the entrance was controlled by a road block manned by a policeman and access was restricted to UN personnel on their way to and from

UNTSO Headquarters, and to students who lived in the experimental farm. Curiously enough, the same policeman stood guard at the roadblock during most of the armistice years. He was a bizarre, eccentric, self-made (and self-taught) intellectual; an aberration in the police force, who spent his days reading history and philosophy books, content to lift his roadblock a few times a day and devote all the rest to his study. On the Jordanian side, the Bethlehem road and the tiny village of Jabel al-Mukabbar were the only objects of disagreement, which was rarely attended by violence. The fact that the Jordanians did not post a guard at their entrance to the area between the lines meant that they were practical about it all: since the traffic to Bethlehem had to go along that only available road built to replace the shorter one now in Israel's hands, there was no sense in stopping it. Israel accepted this as a fact of life, and when it complained to the MAC it was about the villagers of Jabal al-Mukabbar straying onto the Israeli side with their cattle, or encroaching with the intention of adding another patch to their meagre land. Usually, these incidents did not involve much violence beyond throwing a few rocks or hurling some juicy swearwords.

South of Government House, the two demarcation lines joined into a single line that ran due south, leaving in the west the southern part of the large Talpiot neighbourhood, and in the east the twin Arab villages of Sur Bahir and Umm Tuba. Between Talpiot and Ramat Rachel at the southernmost tip of Jerusalem, about one kilometre of the road was almost empty, since no foci of tension existed on either side, except for an occasional encroachment, innocent or deliberate, by local herdsman. Then the border swung round the hilltop where Ramat Rachel was perched, and abruptly turned to the north-west towards the southern quarters of West Jerusalem. Ramat Rachel, with its water tower offering a superb view of Bethlehem and Beit Jallah, had become a lively tourist spot, which at times whetted the war-like appetites of the Legionnaires across the border and resulted in serious border incidents like the ones described above. Ramat Rachel, a kibbutz uniquely situated in an urban area, had been destroyed during the war in heavy fighting with the invading Arab forces. Its destruction was commemorated on a wall of the renovated dining room by a patch of scars left by Jordanian bullets and shells.

On the Jordanian side of the border facing Ramat Rachel at close range stood the frightening Mar Elias fortifications manned by the Arab Legion. It was from there that a Legionnaire fired at the participants of an international conference of archaeologists held there in 1956, inflicting death and injury on dozens. That hill, behind which an ancient monastery stood hidden, was the axial position of the Jordanian Army in southern Jerusalem. Its location faced Ramat Rachel at the same elevation and also barred any hostile approach to Bethlehem and Beit Jallah. From there on, leaving the vast encampments of new immigrants west of Talpiot, the border meandered through a deep ravine that cut through the Arab villages of divided Beit Safafah and Bettir, skirted the southern part of the westernmost neighbourhoods of west Jerusalem, and continued westward beyond the city limits. This southern border had been set out in order to leave the railway to Jerusalem in Israeli hands, with a protective 200-m strip of land to the south of it.

This sensitive sector and the populations living in it were not totally free from incidents and anxieties. The new immigrants who inhabited the Talpiot Ma'abara were the immediate neighbours of the divided Beit Safafah and as a result suffered not a few times. To their daily chores and troubles in the difficult conditions of those days when food and other necessities were rationed, was added the fear that their children might stray across the adjoining border into hostile territory. The new Israeli hilltop settlements of Ora and Aminadav – which faced their Arab counterparts Sharafat, Wallaja, Battir and Beit Safafah – suffered during the 1950s from Arab infiltrators who harassed the western neighbourhoods of Jerusalem, triggering shooting incidents and causing loss of life.

Only when the much-frequented new Hadassah Hospital was built in Ein Karem (another abandoned Arab village in that area that had become a Jewish neighbourhood in west Jerusalem) did the area emerge from isolation and its population know some respite.

All passengers (be they Jerusalemites or visitors) on the slow, antiquated train from Jerusalem that took two hours to reach Tel Aviv or four hours to reach Haifa experienced a justified concern for their safety. The highway linking Tel Aviv and Jerusalem was also exposed to Jordanian military positions along its final stretch into the capital, as already noted earlier; but, somehow – perhaps because the busy road was preferred to the largely idle railway – people felt more secure on the buses. To allay fears, the railway company regularly ran a small trolley patrol along the line to ensure security ahead of every scheduled train. However, in the eyes of the inhabitants of Jerusalem the railway line remained problematic, and travel on it was to remain slow and somewhat adventurous during the entire life of the Armistice Regime.

NOTES

1. The siege is best described in Collins and Lapierre, *O Jerusalem*; especially Chs 18–30.
2. These events are described in poignant detail in Collins and Lapierre, *O Jerusalem*, especially in Parts Two and Three.
3. See Chapter 1 above, and the relevant chapters in Collins and Lapierre, *O Jerusalem*.
4. Eventually, King Hussein introduced a clause to that effect in the peace treaty he signed with Israel in 1994.
5. See Collins and Lapierre, *O Jerusalem*; especially pp. 303–4, 330 and 381–5.
6. Ibid., pp. 459–60 and 470–3.
7. Ibid., pp. 416–18, 421 and 424–30.

9. Evaluations of the Armistice Regime: The Israeli and Jordanian Perspectives

The Israel–Jordan Armistice Agreement was born with fundamental weaknesses, making its premature demise unsurprising. Its fatal flaws were apparent in everything from the initial intentions of the parties, to the conduct of the negotiations, to the provisions and implementation of the Agreement itself. It remains to be understood whether and to what extent the parties expected or even intended such an outcome, or whether they truly desired a workable settlement but simply failed to achieve it. Each of the key players – Jordan, Israel and the UN – had unique interests and expectations from the process, as will be set out below.

THE HASHEMITE AMBITION

King Abdallah's personal ambitions in Palestine are perhaps the key to understanding his resolve to annex Jerusalem as his principal war gain, his decision to grant it top priority in troop deployments on the Palestine front, and his disregard for the provisions of the crucial Article VIII of the Armistice Agreement. It is clear from all the documentation released so far, including the King's own memoirs which will be cited below,[1] that he regarded Jerusalem as the great prize of the war, and was intent on occupying and retaining as much of it as possible, so long as his hold on the Islamic sites there was assured. It is similarly clear that when he was compelled to sign the armistice, he had no intention of implementing Article VIII. Once Egypt had signed an armistice with Israel, Syria and Jordan were in no position to continue the war on their own. Abdallah needed an armistice desperately, but could not achieve one without accepting Article VIII. However, full implementation of Article VIII would have restored normalcy to Jerusalem and restricted the presence of the Arab Legion while allowing people of all faiths and nationalities to move about the metropolitan area – including its holy sites – freely, and the Jewish institutions on Mount Scopus and the Mount of Olives to function as before. Abdallah feared that such a scenario would promote Israeli dominance – demographic, economic, cultural and political – and might pull the city increasingly into the Israeli orbit. Maintaining tight Jordanian control over the eastern half of the city, keeping it an isolated backwater town, was more likely to ensure the King's grip on that area pending a permanent solution.

The Hashemites, the ruling family of the Hijaz, probably began to develop ambitions towards Jerusalem during the reign of King Abdallah's father, Emir Hussein, Sharif of Mecca, who headed the Arab Revolt against the Ottoman Empire in support of the British war effort during the First World War. Sharif Hussein may have had designs on Jerusalem as part of the pan-Arab kingdom the British promised him in return for his support. When French imperial ambition thwarted Britain's plans for a pan-Arab kingdom, Britain compensated the Hashemites by installing Hussein's sons, Faisal and Abdallah as the rulers, respectively, of Iraq and the Emirate of Transjordan (a new principality the British carved from their Palestine Mandate).

Emir Abdallah was never content ruling a sparsely populated desert principality, but rather sought to govern a more populous and fertile portion of the Arab world. His ambitions became more urgent following the expulsion of Sharif Hussein and the Hashemite dynasty from the Hijaz, the holy cradle of Islam, by the Al-Sa'ud dynasty in 1924. In the absence of participatory democracy or some other form of popular sovereignty, the legitimacy of Abdallah's reign rested on his family's religious claims as guardians of the holy city of Mecca. The loss of Mecca undermined his position, spurring him to seek a new religious focus which would strengthen loyalty to him across tribal and territorial boundaries and so restore his honor in the Arab world. To supplement his claim as Sharif, a descendant of the Prophet Muhammed, he set his sights on the al-Aqsa Mosque in Jerusalem, Islam's third holiest shrine.

However, Abdallah had a powerful rival in Western Palestine: the Mufti of Jerusalem, Haj Amin al-Husseini, the top religious authority for Palestinian Muslims and a powerful political leader, who also claimed descent from Muhammad. In his effort to gain control of Jerusalem, Abdallah had been looking for opportunities to involve himself in the affairs of Western Palestine since the 1930s. To that end he cultivated a friendship with the British High Commissioner in Jerusalem and attempted to discredit Haj Amin, his rival for the title of Curator of Aqsa. Acting like the ruler of a far more powerful nation, he engaged in active foreign policy initiatives to win support for his view that the two banks of the Jordan River should be unified to form one state. Simultaneously he began building up his legendary Arab Legion as a tool to fulfill his ambitions.

On 18 October 1933 Abdallah wrote to Sir Arthur Wauchope, British High Commissioner of Palestine (1931–38), about the impending 'danger' of German Jews flooding into Palestine and contributing to its Judaization. He was particularly concerned lest their 'customs and questionable moral standards might pollute the morality and sanctity of Palestine.' He reasoned that if such a cultured and well-organized people as the Germans had come to fear the Jews, despite their long acculturation into the German fatherland, the Arabs of Palestine had much more to fear, as they had hoped for prosperity after Versailles but found themselves instead confronted with increased Jewish immigration. Abdallah expressed his alarm at the scientific, industrial, artistic and martial expertise of those Jews, which he said posed a 'lethal' threat to the Arabs of Palestine. However, at that point he was still sensitive to the potential threat to his kingdom from an eventual Nazi penetration into the Middle East, including neighboring Palestine.[2] In 1934, Abdallah went a step further, claiming the responsibility for protecting Palestine from what he viewed as the threats posed by rising Jewish immigration. But already at this point one can note an ambivalence in the King's attitude towards the Jews: while favoring collaboration with them, he nevertheless feared their influence on Palestine, not only demographically, but especially morally and scientifically.[3]

On 25 July 1934, King Abdallah wrote once again to the British High Commissioner in Jerusalem, but this time as 'a Moslem Sharif in charge of the holy sites in Palestine and especially the Aqsa Mosque, as a leader who took a major part in the Arab Revolt, and as a person fully aware of the situation of his Arab compatriots in Palestine.'[4] Along with his litany against the Zionist lobby, the evident Jewish ambition to expand their National Home to include the entire area of Palestine, and the Jews' 'unbridled programme to purchase land from the Arabs,' he was particularly concerned that the influx of immigrants from different races and political convictions might stir up social inequities and political trouble. The Jews, complained the King, 'did not provide any proof as yet to the possibility of their merging with the native Arabs.' In other words, he was deeply troubled that in a land about which he entertained political ambitions, a Jewish minority was growing which might affect the docility of the local Arabs or promote such dangers to his rule as political pluralism, economic and cultural development, and scientific know-how that was free of his own patronage. But he also apprehensively recognized at the same time that Jews were busily purchasing land from the Arabs, not simply dispossessing them, as latter-day versions would have it.

A few years later King Abdallah expressed an even more direct and specific aspiration to rule Western Palestine as well as Transjordan, in a letter dated 5 June 1938 to Senator Abd-al-Hamid Bey Sa'id, President of the Moslem Youth Association in Egypt. This document, candid in recounting the fortunes and misfortunes of the Hashemites since their expulsion from the Hijaz, is worth quoting in parts:

> I received your letter concerning our proposal with regard to Palestine, which we formulated in view of our intimate knowledge of the situation there, something that makes us the most obvious instance to be referred to and listened to …
>
> I had arrived in Transjordan in 1921, after Syria fell to the French … Thanks to Allah, I succeeded to establish the Iraqi state under my late brother Faisal, and to set up a government in Transjordan whose expanse had been excised from the [area under the jurisdiction of the] Balfour Declaration and included … in the British sphere of influence.
>
> The first collision between the Jews and the population of Palestine occurred in Jaffa in the spring of 1921. But that one quieted down fairly soon. The implementation of the Balfour Declaration began without fanfare. While in 1921 the number of Jews did not exceed 100,000, it has now grown to 450,000 who have purchased fertile lands and settled on them, and also in the valleys and on the mountains extending from

Beersheba to the Hula Valley. So much so that as any Arab moves from one village to another, he encounters a Jewish settlement in the middle between the two ...

I have learned that the Jews demanded the continuation of the Mandate so that they could pursue their purchase of lands and bring in more immigrants. Palestine is facing the danger of being occupied by a foreign nation, and the solution hinges upon the removal of that danger ... and any delay will bring about the loss of Palestine in the literal sense of the word ... Therefore, I have considered it my national and religious duty to strive to resolve the problem through unification of Palestine and Transjordan. Thus, the population of Palestine will grow by half a million people, and they will have a say in the new state through a reinforced government, a parliament, an army, one budget, a sea-shore and borders protected from any illegal immigration. Then the new state will be able to breathe with relief and establish permanent relations with its neighbors ...

Do you side with my proposal, or would you rather support, like others, the continuation of the British Mandate and its corollaries: the threat of other occupiers, the continued inefficacy of the Palestinian leaders, and particularly their failure to prevent their brothers from selling more lands to the Jews, something that has already found expression in the new maps advanced by the Simpson and Peel Commissions of Inquiry? These reports prove definitely the scope of the land sales and the vanity of the Palestinian protests ... I was taken over by fear in the face of the emerging disaster ... and I have come to the conclusion that if we should allow the present situation to continue, Palestine will be full of Jews within two years.[5]

In November 1947 King Abdallah met secretly with a senior representative of the Jewish Agency (Israel's pre-independence government-in-waiting), Mrs Golda Meir, and assured her that he would take no aggressive action against the Jewish community in Palestine, emphasizing that the Mufti of Jerusalem was their common enemy. He expressed some support for the Partition Plan and made it fairly clear that should the plan be adopted, he would annex to his kingdom the areas allocated to the Arabs.[6] Contrary to conventional wisdom which maintained that Abdallah welcomed the return of the Jews to Palestine and was willing to collaborate with them, his aforementioned letters to the British High Commissioner show that he feared the Jews and regarded them as a thorn in his side, because they stood in the way of his ambition to annex all of Western Palestine, especially Jerusalem, to his realm.[7] But, since he assessed realistically the capacity of the Jews to hold their own, he was prepared to content himself with the Arab part of Palestine, and above all the Jerusalem area, as a first step towards turning his meagre kingdom into an important political and religious entity.

The British, whose support King Abdallah needed to carry out his plan, were caught in a bind: they had opposed the Partition Plan all along and therefore could not openly join the King in implementing it. On the other hand, as a responsible member of the UN, which had adopted the partition resolution, Britain could not oppose partition by force. Britain thus had no choice but to accept partition passively. They made it clear, however, that their passivity was tilted towards the Arabs, the pillars of Britain's Middle East policy. This preference was expressed in two principal ways: (1) Britain refused entry to Palestine of a UN commission charged with preparing the orderly implementation of the partition plan; and (2) British troops and police in Palestine did not prevent Arab guerrillas from infiltrating Palestine from the surrounding Arab countries, though they ensured that no military supplies would reach the Jewish areas of Palestine by sea.[8] Britain seemed to be confident that Arab regular forces aided by guerrillas would 'kill' partition without much difficulty, brushing aside the poorly-armed Jewish underground militias just emerging into the open. Partition would just go away leaving behind an Arab Palestine. However, Britain did support the proposed internationalization of Jerusalem as envisaged in the Partition Plan, as they expected to play a leading role in its implementation and subsequent administration.[9]

While the King and the British were crystallizing their respective plans regarding Jerusalem, a critical confrontation was emerging between the Jews in and around the city and the armed bands of the Mufti, Haj Amin. It was vital for the Jews to keep open the road to the city from the coastal plain, the only supply lifeline of the 100,000 Jews in the Jerusalem area who formed roughly one-sixth of the Jewish population of Mandatory Palestine. Sections of the road were dominated by Arab villages which served as bases for the

Mufti's forces, commanded by the charismatic Abdel-Qader al-Husseini, who sought to besiege the Jews of Jerusalem.

As the Arab siege of Jerusalem tightened in the winter of 1948, the Jews altered their position from rejection to support of the plan for internationalization.[10] The scarcity of supplies and armaments available in the beleaguered city forced the Jewish leadership to seek relief under the protection of an international regime for Jerusalem. This new Jewish position ran counter to King Abdallah's plan to keep the holy city in his hands.[11] As if this were not enough to threaten Abdallah's aspirations, the Arab League had begun to form a 'Liberation Army' in Damascus to invade Palestine, assigning responsibility for the Jerusalem area to the forces of the Mufti.

On the Jewish side, the new overall commander for western Jerusalem, David Shaltiel, was ordered by David Ben-Gurion (leader of the Palestinian Jews) to fight for the city street by street and house by house, to prevent the population from fleeing in panic, and to settle Jewish residents in every house evacuated by Arab residents, so as to create a continuum of Jewish positions along the entire urban front. In addition, the new commander was to secure links to the Mount Scopus enclave and to the isolated Jewish Quarter in the Old City, and to defend the approaches to Jerusalem.[12] These orders were the mirror image of orders received by Abdel-Qader Husseini, commander of the Arab forces led by the Mufti of Jerusalem. At the outset, the Mufti's forces were more successful than those commanded by Colonel Shaltiel. As long as Abdel-Qader could show that he was holding his own, and even eroding Jewish positions facing him, he could dismiss the dreaded prospect of an anti-Mufti intervention by King Abdallah's Arab Legion.

In February 1948 a meeting took place in London between British Foreign Minister Ernest Bevin and Tawfiq abu-al-Huda, Prime Minister of Transjordan, who was sent by the King to plead for British assent to an Arab Legion takeover of the portions of Palestine which the Partition Plan had reserved for an Arab state. The British government agreed, reasoning that Hashemite rule there would be preferable to a rule headed by the hated anti-British Mufti camp. However, Britain insisted that the Arab Legion must refrain from entering parts of Palestine earmarked for a Jewish state.[13] In the meantime, the commander of the anti-Mufti force that had been formed in Syria, Fawzi al-Kaukji, crossed to the west bank of the Jordan with parts of his army, under the indifferent eyes of the British. He was welcomed by King Abdallah in Amman and accorded the honors due to an enemy of the Mufti.[14] At the same time, the King was negotiating with the Jews regarding the manner of his annexation of the Arab parts of the West Bank. After a conference of the Arab League held in Cairo on 12 April, at which it was decided to dispatch regular Arab forces in support of the faltering Arab militias, the entrance of the Arab Legion into the West Bank and Jerusalem was imminent. In view of this situation, aggravated by ongoing Arab pressure in Jerusalem despite Jewish acceptance of an international regime for the city, Ben-Gurion reversed course and decided to fight for Jerusalem.

Now the Jews of Palestine were on a collision course with Jordan. King Abdallah, relying on the effectiveness of his Legion and on the evident Jewish respect for it, at one point offered autonomy for the Jewish community of Palestine if it accepted his sovereignty over Western Palestine, including Jerusalem. But, as soon as his offer was rejected, he knew that guns would decide whether or not he could realize his ambition in the Holy City. In her last meeting with the King before the end of the Mandate, Meir made clear that the Jews would not postpone their declaration of statehood; though they would respect the partition boundaries and would not object to Abdallah's annexation of the Arab parts of Palestine if war was avoided. However, they would fight even beyond those borders if an all-out war were triggered. The King was the only Arab leader to accept the Partition Plan, and in public he was reticent on the subject. As to practicalities, he needed a pretext for ordering the Legion into the territories he coveted which could serve as an umbrella of Arab consensus. He successfully blocked an Arab League declaration supporting the establishment of an independent Palestinian Arab state headed by the Mufti. This served his purpose pending the outcome of the war he planned; his Arab Legion would do the rest after the expiry of the Mandate. He was much encouraged by Britain's assessment that the Jews would not be able to stand up to the Legion.

Jordan's intervention began even before that fateful meeting between the King and Meir. On 4 May 1948, ten days before the declaration of the Jewish State which would offer the Arabs a pretext for sending in their armies, the Arab Legionnaires commanded by Abdallah Tal were poised to attack and destroy the Etzion Bloc of Jewish settlements south of Bethlehem and to remove this outpost defending western Jerusalem. The day the British departed, Jewish fighters took over some of the abandoned key posts and buildings in Jerusalem to improve their defence line in anticipation of the expected arrival of the Arab Legion. Colonel Abdallah Tal and his troops were on their way as soon as the Jewish State was declared, following the expiry of the Mandate and the departure of British officials and armed forces. However, it would take a good deal of Palestinian Arab supplication before King Abdallah overcame the hesitation born of his promise to the British not to order an assault on the city. The decision of the Arab Legion to take the Latrun positions straddling the highway linking Jerusalem to the coastal plain was a clear indication that Jerusalem was marked for isolation and conquest. Before the Jordanian takeover of Latrun, the area was evacuated by pro-Syrian irregulars of the Kaukji forces. There followed indiscriminate shelling of western Jerusalem for weeks on end, with the Jewish forces unable to respond in kind for lack of artillery. Obviously, the Arab bombardment was calculated to destroy Jewish morale in the city and thus obtain its capitulation.[15]

However, the Jordanian attacks, which included some daring raids, failed to change the basic deployment of forces along the metropolitan front lines. The exceptions were the Jordanian takeover of the Jewish Quarter in East Jerusalem, and the retaking of the Sheikh Jarrah quarter previously captured by Jewish forces. Attacks mounted by the Jews at that stage with a view to expanding their hold in Jerusalem, were failures. Arab neighborhoods taken by Jewish forces before the Arab Legion entered Jerusalem remained in their hands. The most painful failures were those moves intended to secure direct access to the besieged Mount Scopus area and to recapture the Jewish Quarter in East Jerusalem. Exhausted by constant fighting and near famine in West Jerusalem, faced by repeated failed attempts to reopen the road to Jerusalem from the west, and helpless before Jordanian shelling and bombing, with dwindling reserves of ammunition and other military requirements, the Jews accepted a UN call for a four-week truce mediated by Count Folke Bernadotte of Sweden and backed by the USA and Britain. For Ben-Gurion the truce offered the only opportunity to regroup forces, resupply Jerusalem and bring in some badly needed armaments – even in defiance of the terms of the truce. Sensing that victory was close at hand, the Arabs were reluctant to accept the terms of the truce. Nevertheless, King

Abdallah heeded his army chief's strong recommendation to consent; for Jordan's élite army was not trained for house-to-house fighting, and its commander feared that it might suffer fatally if it went on pitting itself against an enemy that was at least its equal in the art of close-quarter combat.

The much-awaited truce on 11 June 1948 – which literally saved Jerusalem from collapse under the Jordanian siege – came as a relief to the Jewish side after six months of unrelenting combat which had begun before the expiry of the Mandate and intensified thereafter. Abdallah Tal's protests failed to dissuade his King from personally ordering acceptance of the truce and obedience to its terms. The King arrived in Jerusalem immediately after the truce came into force. He praised Abdallah Tal for having saved East Jerusalem for the Arabs and promoted him to the rank of colonel. Then came the dramatic encounter of Abdallah Tal with his Israeli counterpart, David Shaltiel, to arrange a joint demarcation of the cease-fire lines in the city, on the basis of the military situation on the ground at the moment the truce came into force. This definition of the lines was duly reflected in the juridical terminology used by the UN for the cease-fire itself, namely 'cease-fire in place.' Those cease-fire lines would later be adopted by the Israel–Jordan Armistice Agreement as 'armistice lines.' Both the King and his army chief were of one mind – that fighting should not be resumed at the expiry of the truce; they started thinking about a durable settlement. But the Jews kept replenishing their supplies and brought up heavy weapons to strengthen their hand should fighting be resumed. Also, they completed a motor route circumventing the Latrun fortress which blocked the highway linking Jerusalem with Tel-Aviv, removing the threat of a fresh attempt to starve West Jerusalem of food and supplies.

Aware of these activities, and also of the nature of a peace plan under preparation by the UN mediator Folke Bernadotte, King Abdallah was doubly convinced that fighting should not be resumed on his front. The peace plan proposed the annexation of East Jerusalem to Jordan together with the largely arid southern tip of Palestine (called Negev by the Israelis) wedged between Egypt and Jordan. In addition, Jordan would enjoy free port privileges in Haifa harbor and convenient use of the international airport at Lod, near Tel-Aviv. This was fully satisfactory to the King and he saw no reason to assume the risks of fresh fighting. However, the Bernadotte Plan was rejected by the Arab League and Jordan was not in a position to leave the Arab fold and go it alone. The earnest advice – almost supplication – of the Arab Legion's British commander was not enough to tip the scales, and Jordan joined the Arab League countries in a resumption of the war on 9 July 1948. Ben-Gurion had resolved that should fighting be resumed at the termination of the cease-fire, Israeli forces would try to take the whole of Jerusalem and sufficient territory to constitute a wide, safe corridor between Jerusalem and the coastal plain, to rule out a fresh Arab siege of Jerusalem.

The Arabs' summary rejection of the Bernadotte Plan made it easier for the State of Israel to consider its options and to give priority to its own interests. It was an opportunity, for example, to consider authorizing Israel's armed forces, in case the Arabs resumed hostilities, to disregard the truce lines and establish more readily defensible ones. Ben-Gurion accepted Count Bernadotte's plea to extend the truce beyond 9 July, but expected that the Arabs would reject it, which they did.

With the resumption of fighting, Jordan's Colonel Abdallah Tal realized that it was now a whole new ball game. For every Arab shell on Jewish Jerusalem, ten shells fell on his side of the city. The new cease-fire imposed by the UN was hurriedly accepted by the Arabs, now in retreat on all fronts. Even so, it came too soon for the Israeli forces in Jerusalem, before they completed preparations for an all-out attack meant to bring the entire city under Jewish control. The new cease-fire came into force just as Colonel Shaltiel was ready to give the go-ahead. Still, before he was ordered to abort his maneuvers he managed to secure a wide, multiple-route access to the city. His last-minute attempt to launch an ill-prepared onslaught to salvage what he could of the Old City before the cease-fire entered into force, fell flat on its face. The boundaries of the cease-fire agreed by the Jerusalem commanders during the first truce remained largely unchanged thereafter. A few changes affecting the Jerusalem railway line in the southern part of the city and other matters of secondary importance were worked out in secret negotiations with the King in Shuneh, and eventually were incorporated into the Armistice Agreement. The special status of Mount Scopus was another issue addressed in those secret negotiations. An agreed solution to it found its way into Article VIII of the Armistice Agreement, discussed in detail above.

If King Abdallah's gains from the combined Arab war against Israel in 1948–49 fell short of his expectations, they were considerable enough for him to be eager to consolidate them in a formal armistice agreement negotiated under UN auspices. He was prepared to make some concessions if necessary to get the document signed and sealed as soon as possible. His Arab partners in the war returned home empty-handed, except for an attempt by Syria to put forward a dubious claim to water rights in the upper Jordan river. Article VIII of the Israel–Jordan Armistice Agreement formalized the main concessions made by King Abdallah on the road to armistice. Undoubtedly he felt it would not be too difficult for him and his advisers, in due course, to water down the meaning and application of those concessions, and he was not wrong. More serious by far was the fact that western Jerusalem was left in Israeli hands. King Abdallah could only hope that the wheel of history might yet be turned back in Jerusalem some day. This hope may explain the occasional eruption of shooting incidents that followed along the dividing line in the city, all of them started or permitted by the Jordanians – probably in the belief that a peaceful line was more likely than a stormy one to become a permanent border. The local topography offered an additional incentive to riflemen on the Jordanian side of the line.

In his memoirs King Abdallah repeated again and again that the 'Palestine question and its aftermath brought the harshest disaster to Arabs in recent memory.'[16] This does not sound like a judgement of someone who gained rather than lost from a war, or someone who was satisfied with his gains. Evidently he had aspired for more but accepted the truce and the armistice as the only way to avert a greater disaster. At the same time he left the door open for himself to violate agreements when they countered his designs; even to reverse them when opportunity beckoned. He stressed that one could pursue active war when one stood to benefit from it, or compromise and make peace when one could not.[17] This was his way of justifying the on-going talks with Israel even after the armistice, but those contacts never came to any positive end. A measure of his obvious reluctance to lay a stamp of permanence on the armistice lines can be detected in the almost comic behavior of his delegation to the Rhodes negotiations in 1949. On 3 March 1949, the head of the Israeli delegation to the talks reported to Foreign Minister Shertok that the Jordanian delegation refused to be officially presented to its Israeli counterpart by Mediator Ralph Bunche.[18] Shertok retorted that if 'the Jordanians pursue their uncivilized conduct, we shall stop the negotiations, and only resume them when we are convinced that they have learned something about civility.'[19]

The King continued, in the meantime, to resist the establishment of a Palestinian government after the truce, arguing that such a move was unwise before the land was liberated, for it would amount to accepting the Partition Plan.[20] One marching on the road to peace does not scheme for the elimination of his partner. In his Address from the Throne, asking his parliament to approve the annexation of the West Bank in 1950, the King made it abundantly clear that the union would take effect, 'without prejudice to the permanent settlement which will recognize the Arab rights in Palestine.'[21] This meant that the armistice was not necessarily the end of the road. The Jordanian behavior during the implementation of the armistice, especially in Jerusalem – notably the undermining of Article VIII which would have allowed the beginning of some form of informal normalization – was ample evidence of that trend of thought.

King Hussein, who held his grandfather in great admiration and vowed to pursue his course, did nothing to facilitate the implementation of the Armistice Agreement in the Jerusalem area, particularly Article VIII. The contrary was true, there were serious border incidents initiated by the Arab Legion in the course of his reign, and he constantly attempted to gnaw at Israel's sovereignty wherever possible, especially in the vulnerable Mount Scopus enclave and along the metropolitan demarcation line. It is enough to recall in this connection Jordan's plan in the 1967 war to take over western Jerusalem[22] and once again block the corridor linking it to the Israeli coastal plain. Jordan's ambition to annex Western Palestine obviously did not die with the signing of the Armistice Agreement.[23] Had the Egyptian and Syrian war plans been carried out successfully, as King Hussein was confident they would, Jordan's army surely would have marched westward to do what it failed to do in 1948.

ISRAEL'S PERSISTENT TRAUMA

Israel, too, had reason to be dissatisfied with the results of the 1948 war, especially in Jerusalem where it felt it could have taken the whole of the city had the second truce not been imposed by the UN so soon after the expiration of the first. Throughout the 1948 war,

Ben-Gurion gave priority to defending Jerusalem, including the road linking Jerusalem with Tel Aviv.[24] If King Abdallah wanted all of Jerusalem under the Hashemite crown to legitimize his rule, Ben-Gurion needed Jerusalem as the capital of Israel reborn in its ancient homeland and as the spiritual center of world Jewry. Ben-Gurion was prepared to support the internationalized option as the price for a peaceful revival of Jewish sovereignty in the land of Israel, as an effective international regime would have facilitated the maintenance of the Jewish majority in the city, tilting the balance there in favor of Israel. But, once the Arab countries challenged both partition and internationalization by war, Ben-Gurion no longer saw a reason to bow to the plan for internationalization. Instead, he became committed to rescuing the city in its entirety for inclusion in the Jewish State; and, after all the Israeli attempts to take the city failed, he termed the situation 'a lamentation for generations to come.' Nevertheless, when Israel signed the Armistice Agreement with Jordan, it was – together with the UN Mediator – much more hopeful than the Jordanians (and the rest of the Arabs) that the armistice indeed would be a temporary arrangement leading to permanent peace. Unidentified guidelines sent to the Israeli delegation for armistice negotiations directed the negotiators, among other things, to:

> Insist on complete freedom of movement, on foot and in vehicles, between the Israeli side of the border and Mount Scopus, in return for Israel allowing freedom of movement between the Arab part of the city and Bethlehem. The delegation is empowered to precede this demand by a suggestion that territorial continuity between Israel and Mount Scopus would be preferred, and Israel would be prepared to allow for a similar arrangement between Jordan and Bethlehem.[25]

The latter shows that, like King Abdallah, Ben-Gurion was pragmatic in settling for the possible. He felt bound to accept the second UN truce which the Arabs badly wanted, having found themselves confronted by better equipped and better organized Jewish forces. He knew that a few more days of combat might secure new boundaries for Israel which were tactically superior to those from the first truce and would greatly lessen the Arab appetite for more fighting. The Israeli public remained divided on the issue of the armistice lines, particularly in Jerusalem. Ben-Gurion and his coalition partners, much as they deplored the *de facto* partition of Jerusalem, did not entertain any concrete thoughts about reuniting it in the foreseeable future. The right-wing Herut party, led by Menachem Begin, whose standing in the country was much weaker than that of Ben-Gurion, nevertheless had considerable support for its vision of an Israel straddling the Jordan river and governed from a united Jerusalem located at its heart. Begin and his party had sufficient emotional appeal to mitigate their numerical disadvantage and lack of experience in public administration. But, Ben-Gurion and his ruling coalition were on record as being in favor of accepting the armistice lines as permanent political borders, if any of the Arab countries were prepared to recognize them as such.

However, until the 1960s, no Arab body was prepared to accept that Israel was an independent state even within the original partition borders, let alone within the *de facto* armistice lines. A clause in all the armistice agreements underlined their temporary character as a product of military considerations, and emphasized that they did not prejudice the rights and claims of the parties in future negotiations.[26] The Arab parties to the armistice agreements insisted on including this provision as a safeguard against any implication that the armistice involved political recognition, which would have constituted a powerful political and juridical barrier to fresh Arab attempts on Israel's life as a state. Israel regarded that same clause as the channel through which the Arabs would come, when ready, in a fresh attempt to destroy it, even if the armistice lines did not offer ideal starting points for military offensives. The armistice with Jordan, negotiated in the intimacy of the royal residence at Shuneh, gave the Israelis reason to believe that events would develop in this direction. However, they could not imagine at the time that the moderate and friendly King Abdallah who had signed a unique armistice agreement which left the door open to some arrangement that would deny room to the patent hostility reflected in the other armistice agreements, would so soon and so completely and bluntly renege on his pledge to seek a humane, friendly armistice leading to peace.

Faced with this reality, and following the usual Zionist tactic of building up strength gradually, Ben-Gurion turned to strengthening western Jerusalem, hoping that it would be able to hold its own in the face of any new Arab attacks. Its population had increased, makeshift transitory camps for new immigrants were converted into permanent housing, industrialization proceeded well, government offices were transferred from Tel Aviv, and large-scale public construction signaled that Jerusalem was given top priority in urban development as the country's capital city. At the same time, defences were reinforced, concrete screens were erected to protect some exposed locations, and Israeli positions along the metropolitan border line were strengthened and equipped with modern weapons. All this was calculated to create an atmosphere of confidence and a sense of security, in disregard of the hostile military positions.

NOTES

1. Abdallah's correspondence with Sir Wauchope is cited in the supplement to his *Memoires*, published in Amman (1 January 1951) [published in Hebrew under the title of *Soul Searching* just before his murder in Jerusalem].
2. Abdallah, *Soul Searching*, pp. 134–9.
3. Ibid., pp. 139–43.
4. Ibid., pp. 143–4.
5. Ibid., pp. 147–51. See also, Shlaim, *Collusion*, Ch. 5.
6. See Neil Caplan, *Futile Diplomacy*, Vol. 2 (London: Frank Cass, 1986), pp. 277–9.
7. For a discussion of this issue, see also Shlaim, *Collusion*, Ch. 5.
8. See Collins and Lapierre, *O Jerusalem*, Chs 16, 21 and 27, especially pp. 78, 298–9, 321 and 422–3.
9. Ibid.
10. Ibid., pp. 132 and 298.
11. Ibid., p. 149.
12. Ibid., especially Ch. 19.
13. For this episode, see Shlaim, *Collusion*, Ch. 5.
14. See Collins and Lapierre, *O Jerusalem*, Ch. 11.
15. For a detailed description of these events, see Collins and Lapierre, *O Jerusalem*, especially Chs 18–30.
16. Abdullah, *Memoires*, p. 29.
17. Ibid., p. 31.
18. Shiloah to Shertok, 4 March 1949 (ISA).
19. Shertok to Shiloah, 5 March 1949 (ISA).
20. Abdallah, *Memoires*, p. 35.
21. Ibid., p. 39.
22. This plan, which was part of the coordinated Arab war effort led by Egypt, will be discussed in further detail below.
23. See Samir Mutawi, *Jordan in the 1967 War* (Cambridge: Cambridge Middle East Library, 1987); especially Chs 7 and 8.
24. See Collins and Lapierre, *O Jerusalem*, especially Chs 16, 24 and 32.
25. Undated and identified document entitled, 'Directives to the Israeli Delegation for Armistice Negotiations with Transjordan (ISA) [Hebrew].
26. See Article II:2 of the Israel–Jordan Armistice Agreement.

10. Evaluations of the Armistice Regime: The UN Dilemmas

Since the beginning of its involvement in the Arab–Israeli conflict, the UN has had to contend with the following dilemmas:

- How could it represent the common will of the community of nations and, at the same time, serve the parties to the conflict?
- Should the UN seek to lead opposing parties to agreed solutions, or should it opt for imposed solutions under the moral pressure of votes in UN bodies, or for tougher pressure in the form of threats or sanctions authorized under the UN Charter?
- Are UN sponsored bodies which are involved in the Arab–Israeli conflict, such as UNTSO or the MAC, mere observers and reporters, or are they also authorized to indict and condemn?
- Could UN bodies and functionaries be parties to international agreements, thus acquiring a legal status of their own – for example, in the Mount Scopus enclave, at Government House, in the MACs – or must they always be seen as impartial helpers who cannot take independent positions beyond offering advice?
- Could military officers function in essentially diplomatic situations?
- Were the supervisory tasks of UN personnel open-ended in scope and duration, or are they subject to restrictions imposed by the parties concerned?
- Was the immunity enjoyed by UN personnel total and beyond question, or could they be called to account when they transgressed the boundaries of their mission?
- Could the credibility and impartiality of UN Observers be taken

for granted, or should they be subject to external scrutiny and sanction?

- Could the UN be trusted to decide matters solely on merit, or was it bound to be influenced by extraneous factors such as national interests in a particular situation, personal bias, the prestige of the organization, or pressure by interest groups?
- Was there a way of ensuring that UN personnel would not become personally involved – through emotion, political commitment, self-interest, vulnerability to pressure for one reason or another – in issues or situations handled by the organization?

At the time of the armistice the UN was a new institution on which high hopes had been pinned in the aftermath of the terrible tragedies of the Second World War. When the Middle East went to war in 1948 the UN was still inexperienced. Although most concepts like truce, armistice, cease-fire, no man's land, border demarcation and demilitarized zones were known from previous international crises, they were now to be applied in an area where young countries and governing administrations were just becoming acquainted with them in a practical sense. Hence all concerned were learning and teaching and applying them simultaneously. The UN no doubt was able to learn a good deal from the experience of the League of Nations, but that experience was neither very rich nor very successful; and the structure of the League of Nations did not include an institutionalized framework for international enforcement action, such as the UN's Security Council. Nor did the League of Nations have much experience in dealing with young sovereign states whose ways and traditions were not those of Europe.

Thus, the corps of the UNMOs in the Middle East had much to learn 'on the job' in the early years of UNTSO. Some of them even had to improve their knowledge of English which was the working language in Arab–Israeli conflict management. Soon after the Partition Resolution was adopted by the UN the organization sent its first representative to Palestine, Mr Pablo de Azcarate of Spain. Britain opposed this mission which was to help in the implementation of the plan. In any case there was little de Azcarate could do once the Arab states decided to send their armed forces into Palestine to smother partition at birth.[1]

In these new circumstances, the UN decided to send an official mediator to the area, to seek a peaceful solution to the Palestine question. The person chosen for the task was Count Folke Bernadotte of Sweden's royal family, head of his country's Red Cross organization. Unable to get the partition plan on track, he negotiated the first Arab–Israeli truce but was unable to enforce its terms, which forbade bringing fresh armaments into the area of conflict. In response to the many demands put forward by King Abdallah – among them full Transjordanian control of a united Jerusalem[2] – Count Bernadotte put forward a new plan. This last proposal was met by total rejection by the rest of the Arabs, as well as the Israelis, and cost him his life at the hands of Jewish terrorists in September 1948. Ironically, the Palestinians who were, and are still, considered the 'core of the conflict' and its trigger, were not found by Bernadotte to be particularly keen on their independence, which was overshadowed, as we have seen above, by the dominating figure of King Abdallah. Bernadotte wrote:

> The Palestinian Arabs had at present no will of their own. Neither have they ever developed any specifically Palestinian nationalism. The demand for a separate Arab state in Palestine is consequently relatively weak. It would seem as though in existing circumstances most of the Palestinian Arabs would be quite content to be incorporated in Transjordan.[3]

It was left to a new UN Mediator, the American Ralph Bunche, to lead the Egyptian–Israeli armistice negotiations in Rhodes to a successful conclusion; and this opened the way to successful armistice negotiations with Israel's other neighbors. His statement to the Security Council in August 1949, that 'the armistice regime will sweep away all vestiges of the war,'[4] expressed a fairly general expectation at the time. Reality was to disappoint all the optimists. It would seem that as long as the UN had Secretary Generals like the committed and active Dag Hammarskjöld – and all the more so as long as Dr Bunche served as UN Under-Secretary – that creativity and engagement characterized the role played by the UN in keeping the armistice alive. For, not only were they personally involved and ready to shuttle between the parties or send their special representatives to deal with fresh problems, they also had the wisdom to appoint COSs for UNTSO like General Riley in the 1950s, who did much to promote Middle East stability.[5]

Unfortunately, in the late 1950s and 1960s, laxity overtook armistice affairs precisely at a time when tensions mounted and UN firmness was needed. The COSs for UNTSO were appointed from neutral countries, who – like the Secretary-General himself – interpreted neutrality as indolence. When trouble arose, difficulties were referred to the Security Council and local initatives were taken not to resolve problems but to plaster over them or gain time in some other way until the next explosion. Gradually, the UNTSO COSs came to the conclusion that there was little they could do, and they were advised to keep the *status quo* and refrain from courting trouble by seeking remedies to difficult, fundamental issues. It may also be that whereas innovation was needed during the formative years of the armistice, in order to formulate ground rules and to set patterns of work, in later stages routine naturally took over and the UN could do no more than preserve what there was. In any case, the UN not infrequently aggravated situations rather than calmed them, or permitted inaction gradually to undermine healthy norms.

Every retired UNTSO COS wrote memoirs, passed judgements and drew lessons based on his experience and his observation of events. It would be instructive to refer in some detail to the COS who presided over the demise of the armistice – General Odd Bull – for a perspective on all the years of UNTSO activity before 1967. Special reference will be made to the armistice in Jerusalem, to which the retired general devoted Chapter 4 of his memoirs.[6] The general begins that chapter with the thorny issue of Mount Scopus. He recognized that the root problem was the dispute over maps. The Israelis held that the agreed map was the one attached to the Mount Scopus Agreement of 7 July 1948, and initialled F.M.B. (Franklin M. Begley was a member of the UN Secretariat who assisted in the preparation of the agreement). The Jordanians maintained that another map was the valid one, namely the map used on 21 July 1948, when the local military commanders of both sides reached an agreement regarding control of the strip of land lying between their respective zones on Mount Scopus. That map was initialled by the Jordanian Commander and by Mr Begley, but not by the Israeli Commander; consequently, Israel consistently refused to recognize it. The 7 July map covered a larger area than the later one, which meant that Israel claimed control over a strip of territory in the demilitarized zone, while Jordan insisted it was part of her territory.[7] In view of the countless incidents which developed in the dispute strip, many of which led to loss of lives, it is tempting to put the following questions to the UN, based on the views of General Bull himself:

- Why did Mr Begley sign two contradictory maps; and if he intended the later one to supersede the earlier, why did he not put his position in writing, officially?
- How could it be that two different maps were allowed to stand, under UN auspices, as evidence of an agreed demarcation of areas of control?
- Why did UNTSO fail to initiate discussions between the two parties in an effort to settle the dispute?

General Bull blamed his predecessors for allowing the dispute to fester, but he – like them – took no action to remedy the fault, and did not explain why. In his memoirs he just noted that very few problems arose on Mount Scopus during the term of duty of General Riley as UNTSO COS.[8] What the Israelis regarded as their right to patrol the area of Issawiyya on Mount Scopus, within Israeli-controlled territory according to all relevant maps, General Bull viewed as provocation – 'they were bent on provoking and intimidating the villagers,'[9] as he put it. As could be expected, he also critized the Israelis for closing the road between the village and Jerusalem at night, and for preventing the villagers from repairing their road, and judged that 'the actions taken by Israel in the name of security, only had the effect of stimulating insecurity.'[10] But he said nothing of the villagers' encroachments on lands that were not theirs, of riots organized by them against the Israeli authorities – instigated most probably by the Jordanian authorities. A dramatic increase in the village population – obviously by ingress from the outside in violation of the Mount Scopus Agreement – likewise was passed over in silence by General Bull. His sympathy for the poor population of the village certainly was understandable, but his duty was to see that agreements signed under the armistice were respected, since the size of the village population affected Israeli security in the beleaguered Mount Scopus enclave. Also, indifference to violations of agreements surely invites more violations. In the time of General Riley (1948–53), there were indeed fewer incidents because someone made sure that there were fewer violations on both sides.

Another major problem concerning Mount Scopus arose from Jordan's refusal, referred to above to allow 'resumption of the normal functioning of the cultural and humanitarian institutions on Mount Scopus and free access thereto' as stipulated in Article VIII of the Armistice Agreement. Jordan, when pressing her case concerning the agreement of 7 July 1948, refused to acknowledge any link between that issue and her obligations under Article VIII. Israel maintained that, quite apart from the need to decide which of the two different maps signed in July 1948 was the right one, it was not reasonable to demand respect for one Mount Scopus agreement while refusing to respect another. However, Jordan wanted to disown Article VIII, which had become politically untenable for her, but insisted on the terms of the separate agreement. The UN found it easier, and therefore more convenient, to disengage from the question of Article VIII which was explicit and central to the armistice itself; but Israel would have refused to accept an armistice that did not include Article VIII. The UN bureaucracy bowed to Jordan's refusal to honor its obligations under that vital article because, in the words of General Bull:

> It is certainly most regrettable that the activities of the cultural and humanitarian institutions on Mount Scopus were not resumed. The same could be said of other areas – the Wailing Wall in the Old City of Jerusalem, for example. But in the political conditions prevailing between 1948 and 1967 this would simply not have been possible. UNTSO had quite enough to do ensuring the safe passage of the fortnightly convoy to and from Mount Scopus to relieve 50% of the garrison and bring in supplies.[11]

This candid admission of helplessness by the COS of UNTSO had a far reaching significance on more than one level:

- An expression of regret is a mark of honesty, to be sure, but honest acquiescence in the violation of contractual commitments is poison to another aspect of honesty – which is the very soul of meaningful commitments – namely the failure of the UN to enforce its implementation.
- On a practical level, non-compliance by one party with the cardinal clause of an agreement is bound to weaken the agreement as a whole. It is against reason in such a situation to expect the aggrieved party to respect its own commitments regardless of the breach committed by the other.
- It seemed from time to time that UN officials regarded the armistice not as a serious and binding arrangement between states, but rather as a somewhat vague understanding whose

meaning might change from time to time in response to political circumstances or pressures. Leading powers on the world scene, naturally, were the main sources of such pressures, all the more so since most, if not all, of them were permanent members of the UN Security Council. It should also be remembered that the membership of the UN included a considerable number of Arab and Moslem states whose sympathies and support were automatically available to the Arab signatories of the armistice agreements supervised by UNTSO.

- If the UN was indeed unable to fulfill its tasks under the armistice because: 'its hands were full with the fortnightly convoy,' then UNTSO should have applied for more manpower and equipment to meet its obligations, rather than relegate the application of the vital Article VIII to some uncertain future when the UN felt more relaxed about its schedule.

Far more justifiable was Odd Bull's assessment of Israeli behavior and UN deficiencies in supervising the operation of the convoys. He had suspicions – which he said were confirmed – that the Israeli vehicles which made up the Mount Scopus convoys had secret compartments in which forbidden weapons and materials were carried into the supposedly demilitarized zone. He noted that while, in the earlier convoys, the UN observers could not check the vehicles but could watch their unloading once they arrived at Mount Scopus, at some point the Israeli police on the Mount made it a rule to ask the arriving observers in for coffee, which resulted in unobserved unloading once or twice. This was then used as a precedent to justify Israeli insistence that the observers arriving with Mount Scopus convoys must stay away when these convoys were being unloaded. The UNTSO COS Odd Bull took the position that his organization must carry the blame for this dereliction of duty.[12] After the unification of Jerusalem in the Six Day War, the Israeli army put on show some of the items that had been smuggled up to the Mount Scopus enclave in convoy trucks; among them were all the components for two Jeep vehicles mounted with 105-mm non-recoiling cannon. The worst aspect of this state of affairs was not so much the Israeli trickery in itself, as the fact that it meant UNTSO let down the Jordanians.

General Bull attested that the Mount Scopus agreements were further eroded, always in Israel's favor, and complained, among other things, that while the responsibility for the security of the

Mount Scopus enclave was his, he was not allowed freedom of access to it and freedom of movement in it. He justified his inaction by citing the advice of his French political adviser, Henry Vigier, who felt that the best General Bull could do was to help maintain the *status quo*.[13] But the general did not explain how or why he let the *status quo* erode. His insistence on respecting the terms of the Mount Scopus Agreement was not matched by an equal concern over Jordan's refusal to discuss the implementation of Article VIII under which Jordan was to allow free access to the enclave and a revival of the excellent institutions that lay idle there. By acquiescing in Jordan's refusal to honor its commitments under Article VIII, and thus condemning those institutions to neglect, UNTSO in fact contributed to the creation of an impossible situation on Mount Scopus.

Could it be that the UN preferred a state of affairs from which it derived authority, to a situation that would render UNTSO unnecessary? Perhaps the UN could not permit itself to handle the Jerusalem situation in a straightforward manner for fear of provoking the unforgiving displeasure of its Third World members and their supporters. Whatever the reason for allowing Article VIII of the Armistice Agreement to petrify, it did seem to many that the UN would sooner accept an abnormal situation in which it had a say, than risk a painful loss of prestige. It kept reporting Israeli violations of the Mount Scopus Agreement, such as the display of electric lighting in the shape of the Star of David over the Israeli enclave to mark Independence Day. General Bull saw in that display 'a clear infringement of the armistice agreement,'[14] but did not cite the specific provision violated by the offending Star of David. Apparently, he felt that any Israeli move or gesture that irritated the Arabs should be regarded as a violation of the armistice in the sense that it provoked tension, whether or not it contravened any of the armistice provisions. For example, he marked the day Israel started pumping water from its own sources in the north to irrigate arid areas, as 'the beginning of the escalation of the conflict which was to erupt in June 1967'[15] (that is, the Six Day War). On the other hand, he found no fault, apparently,with the creation of the PLO and the murderous attacks it carried out inside Israel from Jordanian territory. Instead, he focused at length and in considerable detail on a position Israel was reinforcing in the Jerusalem metropolitan area, which attracted the attention of the Secretary-General of the UN and of the Jordanian Prime Minister –

and consequently also the attention of the Israeli Foreign Minister[16] – as if, in those summer days of 1965, that particular position rather than the Arab campaign of terrorism and sabotage against Israel was the cardinal threat to peace.

Israel had strengthened its position inside its territory at a point on the route of the Mount Scopus convoys, when it was feared that an attack might take place. Considerations of higher diplomacy induced Israel to yield to UN pressure; but Israel remained puzzled by General Bull's priorities. In this instance his energies had been devoted to a marginal matter, rather than to the fundamental issues that would soon destroy the armistice. He regarded the five weeks during which he had dealt with that banal incident as the 'most difficult time he spent in the Middle East,'[17] after which he needed a vacation in his native Norway. Back in Jerusalem and faced by 'reports of explosives presumably placed by Palestinian saboteurs inside silos and houses in Israeli villages,' all he had to say was that Israel demanded that the Jordanian government take full responsibility for these acts committed from its territory in flagrant violation of its armistice commitments, but that Jordan disclaimed such responsibility.[18] The result was a draw. Each side said what it had to say, as if there were no clauses in the Armistice Agreement to be consulted nor steps to be taken against the offending parties. General Bull held talks with the Jordanian Prime Minister, to convey to him the Israeli assertion that Jordan was responsible. He would not go beyond this, as he would have done in other cases, and therefore all he could report was that the Prime Minister was unable to accept Israel's view. And the acts of sabotage continued, with the COS of UNTSO remaining aloof, thereby implying that Jordan was guiltless.[19]

General Bull wrote in his memoirs: 'The Jordanian authorities gave no support to the guerrilla activities but the border between Israel and Jordan was a long one and many of the villagers on the Jordanian side sympathized with the Palestinians.'[20] Thus the attacks could continue with both Jordan and the UN apparently rejecting any thought that they might be expected to do something to stop them. Nevertheless, General Bull did report that violations of the armistice agreements were being committed – not by Jordanians or others operating from Jordanian territory, to be sure, as the Jordanian government had rejected Israel's allegation in the matter. However, when Israel acted against those who continued to sow death and destruction in its territory while Jordan and the UN stood watching, it brought upon itself the condemnation of the MAC, naturally, as if it was Israel which had its soldiers masquerading as civilians, or allowed underground or open militias on its territory. All this meant that Arab saboteurs based in neighboring countries were able to pursue their campaign of murder and destruction inside Israel, and General Bull was aware of this; yet from his point of view the country from which they operated could be absolved of any responsibility. Thus the saboteurs were assured of sympathy for taking revenge for lost property during Israeli raids of reprisal, and Israel could be certain of being condemned should she dare retaliate in order to deter further attacks from across the armistice lines. In these circumstances the armistice was bound to degenerate.

In May 1965, gun-fire from the Jerusalem Old City wall at a particularly bad moment killed and wounded innocent Israeli civilians. There was a great outcry in the country, and General Bull was apprised by the Israeli Foreign Minister of the gravity of the situation. The MAC duly met and censured Jordan. A Jordanian 'straw' counter-complaint was heard but no action was taken on it; the Israeli representative cast a negative vote and the chairman of the MAC abstained for 'lack of evidence.' General Bull wrote in his memoirs that on 17 May 1965, shortly after that incident, Israeli Prime Minister Levy Eshkol proposed direct negotiations aimed at converting all the armistice agreements into peace treaties.[21] This proposal was rejected out of hand by the Arab authorities concerned because – according to General Bull – 'the Arabs had always rejected the idea of direct negotiations, on the grounds that this would imply recognition of Israel, which would throw away one of their strongest bargaining cards.'[22] The Jordanian answer was more predictable: 'The Palestinian problem was one of belief and principle. It is not a problem of interests or resources.'[23] Had the Arabs in general and the Jordanians in particular heeded Israel's call, they would probably have been rewarded by an Israeli recognition of the armistice lines as permanent frontiers, and Jordan's king would have kept both the West Bank and East Jerusalem. However, it was not surprising that the Arabs should have stuck to a negative position, as they wanted the whole of Palestine under Jordanian rule. King Abdallah at one point had felt that he was close to fulfilling this old dream of his, and his heir Hussain kept asserting for some time that 'Palestine is Jordan and Jordan is Palestine.'[24]

The Arabs were consistent in rejecting the idea that the people of the Bible were entitled to revive their statehood in the land of the Bible; but the UN acquiesced *post factum* in the reality of the Jewish state, and its mediator – Ralph Bunche – expected peace to follow the armistice. It seemed at times that the UN representatives who followed him into the area did not necessarily adopt his line. Some Israelis suspected that UN representatives were guided by their interest in keeping their prestigious functions which would end once peace replaced the armistice. Be that as it may, neither General Bull nor any of his staff did anything to win Arab hearts for the idea that it was time to move on from a crumbling armistice to solid peace. The general himself, it will be recalled, felt that the Arabs had no reason to 'throw away their strongest cards.' None of them stopped to think that perhaps there were no cards at all in the armistice game, and that negativism was not a good bargaining position in any game.

In December 1965, another serious incident on Mount Scopus resulted in loss of life. General Bull acknowledged that it resulted from an UNTSO failure to transmit accurately a map reference for an agreed location where olive picking was to take place. The Jordanians were also at fault in hastening to open fire, and General Bull confirmed this. Against this background the Secretary-General of the UN dispatched a Special Representative – Mr P. Spinelli – to Jerusalem for talks with both parties. The Jordanian rejection of Israeli peace proposals was followed by a tough Jordanian stand on the armistice, expressed in various border incidents, in difficulties for the Mount Scopus convoys, and in pushing the 'unfortunate villagers of Isawiyya' – as General Bull used to refer to them – to resist Israeli security arrangements.[25]

In the discussions with Mr Spinelli, Israel agreed to reduce its patrols which were designed to ensure observance of limits on land cultivation by Arabs on Mount Scopus, and this concession produced a more relaxed situation. Not for long. Since April 1965, Yasser Arafat's Fatah organization had launched armed raids into Israeli-controlled territory, to which Israel responded by retributory raids on the West Bank and the Hebron area. In March 1966, following the discussions with Mr Spinelli, Israel proposed that all military installations between the demarcation lines in the Jerusalem area be destroyed. General Bull acknowledged that 'there was some logic to that,'[26] but the Jordanians argued that the installations in question had been part of the *status quo* in Jerusalem since 1948, and that they gave Jordan a local advantage which would be lost if Israel's proposal were accepted. The UN gave up and had no proposals of its own for defusing a tense situation which was approaching boiling point.

The aging Ralph Bunche himself toured Jerusalem in 1966 and took up the matter of the Fatah activities with the Jordanian authorities – in vain. Acts of murder continued in the Jerusalem area and elsewhere within Israel, committed by PLO assassins from across the Jordanian border, and prompting Israeli Prime Minister Levi Eshkol to make his famous statement in which he warned that 'the ledger is open and the hand is recording in it,' meaning that a day of reckoning would come. The situation became more and more dangerous, justifying the phrase 'Countdown for War' which General Bull used in his memoirs.[27]

It must have been sad for him to end his book on such an unhappy note which implied an admission of failure – a painful failure to maintain a peaceful armistice. In the light of acknowledged UN errors, and other errors committed but not acknowledged or not reported to General Bull, one may rightly ask whether the organization and its representatives did all they could to avert the war that exploded in June 1967. One could go further and argue that the UN missed a golden opportunity in 1965, when the PLO launched its campaign of terror from Jordanian territory, to press hard for reining in the terrorists and negotiating a permanent peace settlement to replace the shaky armistice.

It was easier for the UN to 'understand' the Jordanian rejection of Israel's proposal to remove all military installations between the Israel–Jordan demarcation lines, and to conclude that nothing could be done to stop bloody PLO raids into Israel from Jordanian territory. Perhaps it was only human to satisfy one's sense of duty by dealing with formal or technical matters, rather than by taking a raging bull by the horns. It was cruelly ironic that early in June 1967, with the launching of the combined Arab assault on Israel led by Egypt's President Nasser, General Odd Bull was removed from his headquarters by the Jordanians who had other plans for the Hill of Evil Counsel. But the Israeli government soon invited him back to Government House, after defeating the attacking Arab armies in six days of fighting.

NOTES

1. Collins and Lapierre, *O Jerusalem*, pp. 187–8, 195, 321, 364, 386 and 496.

2. For a detailed account of his mission, see Bernadotte, *To Jerusalem*.
3. Ibid., p. 113.
4. See Chapter 2 above, Notes 11 and 12.
5. This in spite of the serious incident at Scorpion Pass in southern Israel where a passenger bus was attacked occasioning the death of nine passengers and the injury of others. As a result of the MAC's refusal to condemn Jordan 'for lack of conclusive evidence', Israel withdrew from the MAC. See the report of the UNTSO COS to the Security Council on 19 June 1954 (UN Document No. S/3252, 25 June 1954).
6. Bull, *War and Peace*, pp. 63–98.
7. Ibid., pp. 63–4.
8. Ibid., p. 64.
9. Ibid.
10. Ibid., p. 65
11. Ibid.
12. Ibid., pp. 66–7.
13. Ibid.
14. Ibid., p. 70.
15. Ibid., p. 72.
16. Ibid., pp. 78–83.
17. Ibid., p. 83.
18. Ibid., pp. 84–6.
19. Ibid.
20. Ibid., p. 85
21. Ibid., p. 86
22. Ibid.
23. Ibid.
24. Raphael Israeli, *Palestinians Between Israel and Jordan* (New York: Praeger, 1991), especially Chs 4 and 5.
25. Bull, *War and Peace*, pp. 88–92.
26. Ibid., p. 94.
27. Ibid., this is the title of his Ch. 6. See also, p. 99.

11. The International Repercussions of the Armistice

Like many other international agreements, the Armistice Regime was not merely a bilateral arrangement between the belligerent parties. From a legal standpoint, the UN was directly involved as the mediator and guarantor of the agreement, dragging in by extension all the complications of Cold War geopolitics and Great Power rivalries. Beyond that, the special religious and historical character of the armistice territory attracted the attention of many outside actors, including states with no apparent strategic interest in the region and religious bodies such as the Vatican. This was all the more pronounced with regards to Jerusalem. Aside from the city's religious significance, the UN Partition Plan had called for the city to be ruled by an international regime, spurring all interested powers which were jostling for position in advance in case the plan was ever implemented. For all these reasons, even local and otherwise insignificant incidents in Jerusalem could, and often did, become international issues.

Consequently, whenever a serious disruption of the armistice occurred in Jerusalem, UNTSO and the MAC were not the only organizations to take action. Often the Secretary General of the UN became involved, and on numerous occasions the Security Council was called on to help. In general, Security Council member states expected their Middle East envoys to devote special attention to developments affecting Jerusalem. The effect was to widen the circle of involvement in the question of Jerusalem, broadening the scope for rivalries and deals. Every delicate issue became more complex than it needed to be due to the multiplicity of parties seeking satisfaction.

Since the various international parties were rarely able to investigate events on the ground, they had to rely on the accounts of the governments involved, or, more often, accept the reports of UNTSO's official observers. All this inevitably strengthened the hand of UNTSO as the ultimate arbiter of truth and justice in matters touching peace and security in the holy city. Consequently, when Israeli policies relating to Jerusalem were out of line with those of UNTSO, Israel usually faced pressures and threats even from friendly countries, as it was not popular for democratic governments to go 'against the UN.' A case in point was in October 1952, when the French Ambassador in Tel Aviv made representations to the Israeli Foreign Ministry regarding the removal of an observation post that had been built by Israel on Mount Scopus. General Riley had himself demanded the dismantling of that position, and in order to gain leverage on the Israelis and prevail upon them, he asked the powers to interfere diplomatically. This is what the Director General of the Israeli Foreign Ministry wrote to the Israeli Ambassador in Paris:

> The French Ambassador came to see me today, following his government's directives, and asked for our consent to remove the observation point that was allegedly built in violation of the 7 July 1948 Agreement.[1] He emphasized that regardless of the question of who is right, the French Government was in full agreement with the American Administration that UN judgement cannot be overruled … The British Ambassador has already come to see me about the same affair, and the American Ambassador will follow today, therefore this *démarche* has to be seen as a tri-partite policy on the part of the Powers.[2]

Typically, acts of terrorism carried out inside Israel by infiltrators from Jordan led to Israeli reprisals which led to international censure of Israel. The logic underlying these inequitable cycles stemmed from the fundamental difference between democratic and authoritarian regimes. While no one in undemocratic Jordan wished or dared to challenge official Jordanian claims of innocence and total dedication to fighting terrorism from national territory, no government in democratic Israel could possibly hope to keep secret any cross-border operations by its armed forces.

On 23 January 1952, the American ambassador in Tel Aviv, M.B. Davis, requested an urgent meeting with Israeli Foreign Minister Moshe Sharett, to discuss the 'great concern' caused to the State

Department by a series of Israeli reprisal raids across the border. He read from his slip of paper the following:

- On 6 January, in the village of Beit Jallah south of Jerusalem, one house was blown up and one damaged. A man and his wife were killed in the house, and a pregnant woman was shot. 'Retaliation notes' were left.
- In Mar Elias, near Bethlehem, a hand grenade was thrown into a house, killing one woman and three young children. Two other children were wounded.
- On 18 January, near the village of Battir south of Jerusalem, a local resident working across the demarcation line was seized with his two sons by Israelis, and machine-gunned.

The senior American diplomat went into considerable detail regarding other incidents of this kind which had occurred in the Gaza area, emphasizing that reports about these have been received in Washington from US missions all over the Middle East, particularly the American legation in Amman and the American consulate in eastern Jerusalem, which had compiled the facts from reports of the MAC. He pointed out that the attacks had been particularly embarrassing because they came at the very time when the American government, at Israel's request, was using its good offices in an attempt to save two Jewish youths sentenced to death in Iraq. He suggested that these incidents may have been an Israeli reprisal for the provocative manner in which the Iraqis had carried out the executions. Sharett denied this. Davis pointed out the harm done to Israel by the policy of reprisals, although he said that the State Department understood the gravity of the infiltration problem. Since his government cared, as he said, about Israeli interests, it could not be indifferent to the fact that Israel was wrecking her own international image.[3]

Davis also made the point that he did not want to impute the Israeli reprisal attacks directly to the Israeli government, but judging from the way they were organized and carried out, they left the impression that these were not sporadic acts of irresponsible people. He was particularly worried that if these acts had been carried out by elements in Israel who did what they pleased – although what was done might not have reflected official Israeli policy – those deeds still spoke louder than words. His cable of instructions from Washington read as follows:

Without doubt the lack of progress in improving Israeli–Arab relations is the major obstacle in the way of stability and security of the Middle East and closer cooperation between the Arab world and the Western countries. The deterioration in the relations between the Arabs and the Western Powers definitely increases difficulties in the way of any effective collective defence arrangement in the Near East. It is hoped that the Israeli government will consider seriously the issues involved, and weigh carefully the wisdom of permitting its armed forces to employ terror tactics as opposed to making a genuine effort at all levels to conciliate its Arab neighbors ... The official Israeli policy involving military forays into neighboring states resulting in the death of Arab men, women and children, and destruction of their property, cannot but have its effect on the Arab attitude towards Jewish minorities [in their midst].[4]

Sharett, in his response, pointed out that the incidents in question were links in a chain of events triggered by constant attacks and outrages across the Jordanian border. Israel had manifested great patience and restraint over a long period of time, but in view of the further deterioration in the security conditions along the borders, notably in the Jerusalem area where people felt helpless and exposed, Israel was compelled to react. Ambassador Davis said that he fully understood the gravity of these violent acts of infiltration from neighboring countries. He himself had reacted in that spirit to the dispatches he received from the American diplomatic missions in the Arab countries; he called their attention to the provocations which had occasioned the Israeli reprisals. But he maintained that violence should not be met with violence, for armed forays involved serious violations of the armistice. Sharett responded that from his personal experience with Arabs since Turkish times, retaliation was the only way to stem their attacks. He also said that contrary to the view that violence breeds violence, one could also say that violence and reprisals might ultimately make both parties realize the instability inherent in their courses of action and encourage them to desist from violence.[5]

Interference from the Great Powers in armistice affairs in Jerusalem – and elsewhere for that matter – found yet another indirect channel: the Security Council of the UN. For, as permanent members of the Council, they demanded and received firsthand reports from the highest echelons of this organization – the COS of UNTSO, via the Secretary General. Then, based on those reports that were taken as impartial, hence undisputable, they made their representations to the parties and maneuvered to ascertain that their particular interests in the region were not harmed. For example, the serious shooting incident in Jerusalem in July 1954, was investigated in detail by the MAC, picked up by the COS of UNTSO in person, reported to the Secretary General, and then submitted to the members of the Security Council in all its detail,[6] as if that were an incident in the heart of the Super Power struggle and likely to produce a world-scale conflagration. In that particular case, a heavy exchange of fire took place along the demarcation lines, the origin of which could not be determined by the UN Observers. All the attempts of the MAC to arrange a cease-fire were at first frustrated by a renewed burst of gun-fire, which lasted intermittently for a few days, with each party accusing the other of triggering the incident. Nine people perished in the incident and some 52 were wounded. Since during the first day of shooting (30 June) eight of those casualties were hit in Israel and none in Jordan, that was evidence enough for the Israelis that the Jordanians had engineered the entire incident, a belief which was supported by Israeli eye-witnesses who saw Jordanian troops reinforcing their positions just prior to the outbreak of fire.

According to the Israeli complaint, five more of its people were wounded on the second day of firing (1 July) during the first half-hour, while none were hurt on the Jordanian side; something that was implicitly supported by a UN witness.[7] The Jordanian Delegation at the MAC also expectedly provided its own witnesses to counter the Israeli allegations. By 2 July, according to the Israeli draft resolution brought before the MAC, Israel had sustained 30 casualties, of whom four were dead. Of the dead one was a woman, two were male civilians and one a soldier. Of the wounded, seven were women, three children under 14, ten male civilians, one priest, one soldier and four policemen. The Jordanians claimed, on the other hand, that the Israeli fire affected 31 Jordanian victims, two of whom were killed – one woman and one man – and 29 injured, including two young children and nine women. Israel was also accused of having both used holy places as shooting positions and hitting other holy places in Jordanian territory during the exchange of fire.[8]

Caught between the claims and counter-claims of the parties, the Chairman of the MAC, the COS of UNTSO in person, refused to vote for either party or to condemn either party, for lack of conclusive evidence. Judging from the outrage of contemporary Israeli newspapers, and from skimpy inside information gleaned from eye witnesses and internal military and police reports, there is no doubt that the Israeli delegation to the MAC was absolutely convinced of the veracity of the findings and of the evidence that was presented. The same cannot be said with certainty for the Jordanian side, where inside reports were much harder to come by. But, judging from the vested interest of Israel to maintain the calm in Jerusalem on the one hand – something that could not always be said of the Jordanians at that time – and from the numbers of casualties sustained on the Israeli side upon the outbreak of violence, one has the clear impression that Israel was not at fault on that particular occasion. It is also evident, however, that once the shooting began, Israel reacted vigorously and was responsible for a number of victims on the other side. In any case, the incident was violent enough, and threatening enough to the peace in Jerusalem, that the Powers found it necessary to intervene through UN channels and use Security Council authority to put in motion the UN mechanism in the region at its highest level.

This was only one of many instances of international involvement in armistice problems with a view to preserving the Armistice Regime as the only road to stability. It was quite evident that expediency directed their efforts towards democratic, lonely and vulnerable Israel, which was likely to yield to pressure, rather than to the group of Arab states whose many millions of people, autocratic regimes, and vast oil reserves made them immune to sermonizing and fairly indifferent to public opinion.

UNTSO personnel, in private conversations with Israeli officers, took a somewhat different line based on the fact that the numerous Arabs had been defeated by a handful of Israelis, and therefore were thought to be angry and less open to reasoned persuasion: 'You are the strong party, they are the weak and the losers, you are not like them,' one would often hear them proclaim. It became apparent that the international community did not consider it politically acceptable to confront the Arab nations and their Moslem backers outside the Middle East.

For these various reasons the grave incidents in the Jerusalem area described in previous chapters hardly if ever ended in the settlement of fundamental problems. They were usually swept under the rug, for fear of stirring Arab discontent, and were readily rationalized in terms of 'understandable' outbursts of a 'poor villager' from Issawiyya on Mount Scopus, or an infiltration into Israel by a 'miserable refugee' to retrieve some movable property or to avenge its loss, or an 'angry' or 'mad' Legionnaire who could not bear the sight of his land being held by the Jews.

The international attention devoted to the armistice in Jerusalem was also turned to the tension between the city's religious significance and the military conflict which divided it. Not only were innumerable churches, convents, mosques, synagogues, monasteries, cemeteries, historical sites and places of pilgrimage directly hit during the 1948 war; some were even converted into military positions. Religious life was affected not only during the fighting but also under the often violated armistice. Foreign clergy, pilgrims and other visitors who belonged to neither side in the conflict but lived in Jerusalem or visited it occasionally, looked to their home governments to protect their safety and well-being as dwellers in the troubled Holy Land. Moreover, most of the resident Christians of various denominations in Jerusalem were Arabs, who could not be expected to see themselves as neutrals between the parties to the armistice; they naturally took their case to foreign diplomats in Jerusalem in an attempt to secure their own interests as victims of the vagaries of life under armistice.

When Pope Paul VI visited Jerusalem in January 1964, the Armistice Regime was put to the test in various contexts. Overall arrangements were the responsibility of the Israeli and Jordanian Governments, but UNTSO was also involved. The Pope was to come first to the Old City, entering through the Damascus Gate situated a few yards from the demarcation line. He needed to cross twice: first on his way to Nazareth and then back to Jerusalem. It had been suggested by Israel, for reasons of security and prestige, that the Pope should cross at the Mandelbaum Gate and that UN Observers be posted on the Israeli side of Mount Zion and in Abu Tor on the Jordanian side. General Odd Bull reported that the Secretary General of the UN had misgivings about the program and made it clear that the UN would take no responsibility for its implementation.[9] Taking advantage of a rare manifestation of Jordanian benevolence, Israel paved a special road for the occasion (which then came to be known as the Pope's Road), leading down from Mount Zion along the demarcation line. At the Mandelbaum Gate a ceremonial welcome by the President of Israel awaited the Pope, in the presence of UNTSO officials, many Christian dignitaries and representatives of foreign countries which maintained consular missions in West Jerusalem. On the Jordanian side of the gate a similar ceremony was held with the participation of the same dignitaries and foreign representatives from East Jerusalem. The Pope received General Bull in audience together with his French Political Adviser, Henri Vigier. The visit was deemed a success.[10]

The international interest in the armistice was due in part to the proposed internationalization of Jerusalem suggested as part of the ignored UN Partition Plan of 1947. That plan proposed an international regime in Jerusalem for an interim period of ten years, following which a referendum would help determine the permanent status of the city.[11] The Jews of Palestine saw the exclusion of Jerusalem from their prospective state as an affront to their historic ties to Judaism's holiest city, but they accepted it out of a desperate need to achieve statehood without delay and so provide a haven for the stateless Jewish refugees who had survived the Holocaust. Perhaps the Jewish leadership in Palestine hoped that the Jewish majority in Jerusalem ultimately would determine the future of the city.[12] Transjordanian occupation of eastern Jerusalem by force simply was not foreseen.

Similarly, the Arabs rejected the internationalization of Jerusalem as part of their total rejection of the Partition Plan. Foremost among them was King Abdallah who hoped to annex the whole of Palestine to his kingdom. Also opposed to strengthening the Jewish presence in Palestine was Amin al-Husseini, the Mufti of Jerusalem, who had signed a pact with Hitler committing the Muslim leader to promote Arab and Islamic support for the Nazis, in return for extending Hitler's extermination of Jews to the Middle East in due course. Despite his heinous crimes, the Mufti managed to escape trial by the War Crimes Tribunal at Nuremberg, and made it back to the Middle East to head the Palestinian war effort against nascent Israel.[13]

The British Government, though opposed to the Partition Plan, still expected to participate in the governance of an internationalized Jerusalem. Already in 1936, Britain's Peel Commission had recommended a permanent British mandatory power in the holy cities of Jerusalem, Bethlehem and Nazareth. Other nations, especially those influenced by the Holy See, supported internationalization of Jerusalem as a price the Jews had to pay for a majority UN vote in favor of Jewish statehood in a partitioned Palestine.

Ironically, a UN Working Committee on Jerusalem was busy detailing the structure and functioning of an international regime in Jerusalem when the 1948 Arab invasion of Palestine made the Partition Plan obsolete. The Working Committee had proposed to extend the limits of the city to include Bethlehem and three other Arab settlements in order to obtain a demographic balance between Jews and Arabs in the internationalized area. The committee also resolved to divide the city into three boroughs: one Arab, one Jewish, and one to include the walled part of Jerusalem, the Old City, which would be open to the whole world. It was also decided that the city would be demilitarized, and would be administered by a governor appointed by the UN and aided by an elected legislative council. Justice was to be dispensed by a complex court system. The city was to fly a flag of its own, sporting the UN emblem and a city seal. The formal, legal status of internationalized Jerusalem was to be defined as *corpus separatum*.[14]

As already noted, the Arab countries were adamantly opposed to internationalization, while Israel's position shifted with the fortunes of war. Before the Truce of June 1948, when it seemed that the Jewish population of Jerusalem was about to be destroyed by an effective Arab siege, the new State of Israel made representations to the Powers which had supported partition and internationalization, requesting them to dispatch an international police force to Jerusalem to help save the besieged Jewish population from starvation and to prevent the fall of the entire city. Thirty more days of fighting throughout the country elapsed before the UN Security Council finally ordered a month's truce. By then the military balance had shifted, and when fighting was renewed Israel gained the initiative. But Transjordan's grip on eastern Jerusalem remained firm and Israel made no further attempts to dislodge the Arab Legion from there. At the same time, the internationalization plan for Jerusalem began to recede from center stage, and in due course it became the principal casualty of the 1948–49 Arab war on Israel.

The Armistice now became the *de facto* framework for coexistence between the warring parties, and hopefully the first step towards peace. However, the Jerusalem question could not remain quiescent for long, as the outside world remained actively interested in the Holy City for quite a long time. Most countries were not prepared to recognize any part of Jerusalem as Israel's capital, which created many diplomatic and protocol difficulties for

Israel. When, on 12 July 1953, the Foreign Ministry of Israel was transferred to Jerusalem, along with most other Ministries, six governments lodged protests: the US, Britain, France, Italy, Turkey and Australia, all insisting that in line with UN desire, the city ought to acquire some form of international status. That meant that they rejected Israel's plea for international recognition of her capital city, and for many months they boycotted the official Israeli ceremonies that were conducted in Jerusalem. Moreover, when Cuba decided to move its legation to Jerusalem in 1957, it was pressed by the US to move back to Tel Aviv.[15]

Jordan did not face the same difficulties, as it kept its capital in Amman. This was due to its location in the heart of Transjordan – the King's bastion and source of support from his Bedouin-dominated Arab Legion – and also to the desire not to lend prominence to the Palestinians who were subversive to the King's rule, which would happen if the King shifted his seat of government to Jerusalem. That left eastern Jerusalem a quaint backwater and under-developed border town, the focus of tourism and Christian pilgrimage, but of no real political significance. The internationalization project was left to die quietly; but as soon as Israel moved their Foreign Ministry offices to the city, Jordan retaliated by declaring the eastern section as 'the alternative capital of the Hashemite Kingdom.'[16] This turned out to be an empty statement, because for all intents and purposes the city remained as remote and as marginal as before. As in the times of the Crusades, when Jerusalem acquired importance in the eyes of Islam only after it fell to the rule of the Unbelievers – until it was rescued by Saladin – and then slipped again into oblivion, so in modern times it did not attract much attention until it was taken over by Israel in 1967. There might have been another emotional reason for King Hussein to keep Jerusalem on the margin of his kingdom: he had never recovered from the trauma, when he was barely 16 years old, of watching his adored grandfather, King Abdallah, slaughtered there, before his eyes in 1951.

For the duration of his rule, right down to 1967, King Hussein had, then, every interest not to stir the question of Jerusalem, and not only for fear that the specter of internationalization might be revived. But Israel had, on the contrary, her eye set on drumming up the city as her capital. Not only issues of prestige, history and heritage were at stake, but also two major concrete interests:

1. *Demography* – At the inception of the State of Israel, about one-sixth of its population lived in its capital city. In those early days, with an overall population of about 600,000 Jews, the country was anxious to integrate into its society all available manpower, for obvious reasons. The fledgling state would need strong defence forces, an efficient public service, expanding agriculture, a scientific establishment, a skilled labor force, a center of intellectual activity, etc. Internationalization of Jerusalem would have deprived the country of this immensely important center of human resources which constituted one-sixth of the total population. Even if this Jewish population were allowed to act as part of Israeli economy and culture, it is certain that its special status under a separate rule would have drained much of its energy elsewhere, something Israel could ill-afford in those days.

2. *Strategy* – An internationalized Jerusalem under the Partition Plan would have become an enclave within essentially Arab territory, while the Jewish state would have been confined mainly to the coastal plain with scarcely a reliable link with the mountainous hinterland. Conversely, once Jerusalem became Israel's capital, a firm Israeli foothold in the Judean Highlands became a possibility. It was necessary only to develop safe land communications between Jerusalem and the coastal plain to the west. To the east, Jerusalem's eastern reaches, particularly the towering position of Mount Scopus, could dominate the mountain slopes leading towards the Dead Sea. Hence the tremendous attention devoted to Jerusalem, even by those who favored or merely accepted internationalization but realized that Israel and Jordan between them left little prospect, if any, of seeing it implemented. The more each part of the now-divided city went its separate way, the more unlikely their reunion became, and hardly anyone seemed to support the use of force and to accept its horrible price even if that was the only means of achieving a reunion of the holy city.

However, for the UN internationalization remained a formal goal, since the General Assembly had not abrogated its partition/internationalization resolution of 1947, the new realities notwithstanding. An effort by Count Folke Bernadotte in his capacity as UN Mediator to promote a formula that would place

Jerusalem as a whole in Jordanian hands, did not materialise. Next, the matter was discussed by the General Assembly and the UN Trusteeship Council, but no action was taken and there the matter rested. Officially, the proposed internationalization of Jerusalem remains current, but in fact it is obsolete.

For a long time the community of states, with few exceptions, consistently refused not only to recognize western Jerusalem as Israel's capital, but also to act in a manner implying such recognition, for instance by allowing their ambassadors to meet with Israeli officials in the Foreign Ministry offices in Jerusalem. As to the territory known as the West Bank, which Jordan occupied in 1948, only Britain and Pakistan recognized the Jordanian annexation, but most other states accepted the *de facto* situation. Eastern Jerusalem was seen as part of the West Bank and, in any case, it did not present a problem in the context of internationalization because, unlike western Jerusalem, it had not become the seat of a national government.

The world community took a different approach to the religious and historical aspects of Jerusalem, which were held to be the reasons for international interest in the city and the wish to place it under international control. Forty sites within the Jerusalem area were listed by the UN as 'holy' to the three monotheistic religions. The annexation of eastern Jerusalem by Jordan left only three of them in Israeli-held West Jerusalem. Nevertheless, international interest in the holy city remained focused on West Jerusalem, leaving East Jerusalem virtually overlooked.[17]

Since the defeat of the Crusaders in the Middle Ages the Christian world had come to accept Muslim rule over Christian holy places. That acceptance was enshrined in the universally recognized *status quo* under the Ottoman Empire which defined in careful detail the respective rights of the various Christian church communities in the Christian holy sites in Bethlehem and Jerusalem. This state of affairs guided the British administration in Palestine in resolving the conflicting claims concerning ownership and guardianship of holy places and the traditional rituals and ceremonies held in them, and even the rights to clean and maintain parts of them. This arrangement was highly discriminatory against Jewish interests but, as could be expected at the time, the Christian world registered no protest against this. Less understandable was Christian acquiescence in the 1948 Bernadotte Plan which proposed placing Jerusalem as a whole under Jordanian rule.

Jewish rule over any part of Jerusalem was out of the question. Against this background, it was no great surprise to see both Christians and Muslims opposing Israel's decision to renew Jerusalem's role as the Jewish capital – no matter that it was the Jewish people who had brought Jerusalem into world history as the capital of the ancient Israelite Kingdom and the fountainhead of monotheism.

When Israel was established in 1948, Jerusalem had been under siege, and therefore it was impractical to make it the seat of government, which was therefore temporarily situated in Tel Aviv. It followed that the first foreign diplomatic missions in Israel were also based in Tel Aviv, except for those of Holland and Greece, which simply upgraded their consulates in Jerusalem to the level of missions. When the Israeli government offices began to move to Jerusalem in 1949 – the Foreign Ministry moved in 1953 – the anomaly of foreign embassies residing outside the capital became a strident political statement, not simply a matter of convenience.[18] However, many new embassies which were established after 1953 located their offices in Jerusalem, not because they recognized Jerusalem as the Israeli capital but for the practical reason that it was the seat of government. Israel became the sole example of a sovereign country whose capital city was not recognized by foreign powers, although legally it was her exclusive business to determine where her capital was to be.[19] Israel never asked for Jerusalem to be recognized as her capital, for she thought it was no one's affair but her own. The fact that most embassies were located in Tel Aviv, or were transferred there after 1980 when the Israeli Knesset passed a Basic Law reaffirming its permanent hold on the city,[20] did not alter the practice of asserting Jerusalem as the capital.

NOTES

1. This was the agreement signed between the Israeli and Jordanian local commanders regarding the supplies to the Israeli enclave on Mount Scopus.
2. Coded Dispatch No. 130.09/2345/1, dated 16 October 1952, from Director General Walter Eytan to the Israeli Embassy in Paris (ISA).
3. Report No. 130.02/2415/1, regarding the Sharett–Davis talks in Tel Aviv, dated 23 January 1952 (ISA).
4. Ibid.
5. Ibid., pp. 46–7.
6. See UN Document No. S/3278, dated 6 August 1954, especially its eight-page Appendix which describes the details of the MAC meeting chaired by the COS himself, General V. Bennike on 11 May 1954.
7. Ibid., p. 7.

8. Ibid., pp. 9–13.
9. General Odd Bull dwelt at length on the Pope's visit and on the role he tried to play there (see *War and Peace*).
10. Ibid.
11. See Martin Gilbert, *Jerusalem in the Twentieth Century* (London: Pimlico, 1996), pp. 171–85; also, Collins and Lapierre, *O Jerusalem*, pp. 4–5, 78, 132, 234, 298–9, 359, 422–3 and 525.
12. Collins and Lapierre, *O Jerusalem*, pp. 96 and 567–8.
13. Ibid. pp. 79–81.
14. Gilbert, *Jerusalem in the Twentieth Century*, pp. 171–4.
15. Ibid., p. 253.
16. Ibid., p. 254.
17. For documents relating to the international aspects of the Holy Places in Jerusalem, see Meiron Medzini's monumental collection, *Israel's Foreign Relations: Selected Documents*, Vol. 1, p. 215ff.
18. It has been suggested that a parallel situation exists in Holland, where foreign diplomatic missions are based in Amsterdam rather than in the Hague, which is the Dutch capital city and seat of government.
19. See Walter Eytan's article, 'The Struggle for the Political Status of Jerusalem', *Monthly Survey*, 10 (October 1984), pp. 15–21.
20. Earlier, right after the 1967 war, the Israeli Knesset adopted a law declaring the applicability of the Israeli legal and administrative system on Jerusalem, which meant in effect its annexation to Israel.

12. The End of Armistice

We have already discussed the Jordanian policy towards the armistice which, like the policy of other Arab states, in effect refused to recognize the demarcation lines as a basis for permanent boundaries. In fact, in spite of the sweet talk at the informal meetings between Israeli and Jordanian officials in the King's Palace at Shuneh, it was clear through the year of 1951 that Amman would only abide by the armistice as long as it suited her purposes, and would refuse to implement the problematic Article VIII discussed above which might have given some similitude of permanence to the relations between the two countries.[1] One year later, an embarrassing incident at the UN revealed that the Jordanians could not even utter the word 'Israel'. Israeli Ambassador to the UN, Abba Eban, in a letter to the President of the Security Council, reacted to the message sent by Jordanian Prime Minister abu al-Huda to the Secretary General[2] where he had referred to alleged violations of the armistice agreement by 'the Jews' instead of 'by Israel.'[3]

At the height of Nasser's Pan-Arabism in the 1960s, it was widely believed that the new Saladin would throw the new Crusaders out of the land of Palestine. For that purpose – and as an addition to the mammoth growth of the Arab armies which had undertaken to fulfill that dream – the PLO was created in 1964–65, as a ready-made entity to take over the liberated land. This unison in Arab purpose involved the Kingdom of Jordan in a series of contradictions:

- The Hashemite Crown had been ruling the West Bank of Palestine since the inception of Jordan, yet it had insisted on its Jordanian identity. Eighty per cent of the population of Jordan was Palestinian, yet they were made to carry Jordanian passports.

- The country was Palestinian not only with regard to its population, but also in its culture, language, society and tradition; yet all these domains were claimed to derive from, and pertain to, the Jordan entity.
- Palestinians had their own political culture, institutions and leadership, and even their own armed forces, yet they were asked to submit to the Jordanian Crown.

During the 1948 war, the Palestinians had appealed for help to King Abdallah in rescuing Ramleh, Lydda and, especially, Jerusalem from the Jewish grip. The former had fallen to the new State of Israel because the Arab Legion had refused to intervene, and the King was accused by the Palestinians of betrayal.[4] But, in Jerusalem, it was the forces of Abdallah Tal who overwhelmed the Jewish Quarter and enabled the Arab forces to hold their own in that bitterly disputed city.[5] However, the Old City did not submit to Palestinian independent rule, and it was integrated, together with the entire West Bank into the Jordanian kingdom. In 1953, Hussein inherited not only his grandfather's throne, but also Palestinian suspicions and recriminations against his dynasty. In fact, he could argue that if it were not for the Arab Legion, all Western Palestine would have been lost; and that during all the years since 1948 Western Palestine has been the product of Jordan's defence and devotion to the Palestinian cause. In any case, the King felt compelled to explain that he did care for the Palestinians and was not simply pursuing his own interests. Nevertheless, he systematically objected to the creation of a Palestinian entity, arguing that Palestine was Jordan as Jordan was Palestine, which was certainly true on the historical, geographical, and, most importantly, demographic levels.[6]

Caught in these contradictions, the Hashemite public stand on Palestine began to erode during the early 1960s when Nasserism put the Palestinian issue at the top of the Arab agenda as a rallying point which was agreeable to all. When the first Arab Summit of 1964 decided to establish a Palestinian entity, Hussein had to pay lipservice to that resolution so as not to be labelled a 'traitor' to the Palestinian cause. At the same time, however, the King still hoped that the union of both banks of the Jordan would not be prejudiced by his upholding that resolution. How he thought he could sustain this contradictory stand in the long run, he never explained. Thus, when the PLO was founded in 1964–65, Jordan gave its support on the declaratory level while insisting that some limitations be put on its activity, such as: placing the PLO under joint Arab command; restricting its scope of action so that it did not interfere in the internal affairs of Arab states; and forbidding it to claim sovereignty over the West Bank. In other words, the Hashemite House, while submitting to the Arab demand for a Palestinian entity, adopted all measures to deprive it of any effective manifestations of peoplehood and statehood. Thus, the PLO, instead of finding satisfaction by achieving feasible goals within the population of the West Bank and of Jordan, found itself pushed to achieve the hopeless task of dismantling Israel and replacing it.

King Hussein perceived very clearly the either–or dilemma hanging over his rule. Either he asserted, in no uncertain terms, that he was the ruler, or the PLO would quickly move in. Thus, he had no choice but to continue to advocate his country's 'sacred unity,' and he vowed that he would resist any attempt to disrupt that unity as fiercely as he was fighting Zionism and Israel. Hussein also calculated that giving in to Palestinian demands would result in Israel's intervention, as he knew that Israel violently opposed any independent Palestinian entity. For that reason, the King could not allow significant PLO acts of terrorism to be mounted against Israel from his territory. He knew that – as in the 1950s – Israel would launch reprisal attacks against the West Bank or Jordan proper, which would only expose him as unable to fend off either, and make the PLO alternative more attractive. It might also lead to his losing his country altogether to Israel.

The PLO, and the Fatah faction in particular, was interested in launching guerrilla attacks against Israel in order to precipitate an all-out Arab–Israeli confrontation that, they believed, the Arabs could win. So, despite Hussein's policy and his attempts to inhibit the PLO, he could not totally prevent PLO attacks against Israel in 1966–67. Tension rose between Hussein, who feared for his throne, and the PLO leader, Ahmed Shukeiry, who was afraid of losing his leadership if he seemed to be lagging behind the more energetic Fatah group which was led by Yasser Arafat. Recriminations between the two ensued leading, in April 1966, to the arrest of most of the staff of the PLO in Amman, and to the closure of the PLO office in June. Jordan's authorities saw the subversive elements of the Palestinians openly attempting to lead the overthrow of the monarchy – so much so, that the PLO was publicly accused by the King of having come under the influence of communism and of having lost its character as a movement of liberation.

From the King's perspective, he faced yet another dilemma: his commitment to Arab solidarity and unity of action was absolute, for he needed the Arab umbrella to provide a refuge for his politically and geographically vulnerable country in case of a confrontation with Israel; but at the same time, by playing the inter-Arab game under the delirious Nasserite pan-Arabism, he was precipitating that dreaded confrontation he sought to avoid. The end result was, that after many hesitations and trepidations, he usually elected to toe the Arab line of consensus politics even to the detriment of his own interest. In 1965, for example, when the Federal Republic of Germany established full diplomatic relations with Israel, he was pressured by Nasser's call to all Arabs to sever their relations with Bonn in retaliation. He finally yielded, even though he and his advisers felt it was an empty and insignificant gesture.[7]

King Hussein was dragged into the 1967 war against Israel, hoping that the victorious armies of Nasser would neutralize the best of Israel's forces while he would be able to claim some of the spoils of the war and further enlarge his hold on Palestine. But then things went wrong, and the entire West Bank, with Jerusalem at its center, fell to Israel. This demonstrated not only that Jordan could not defend the Palestinians – paralleling King Abdallah's failure in Ramleh and Lydda in 1948 – but that the King had even failed to avert the tragedy of more Palestinian territory being lost and more refugees streaming into Jordan. The King's miscalculation was of catatrophic proportions, leading him to long for the uneasy armistice he had done so much to weaken. As usual, he hesitated too long in the face of the domestic PLO threat and was carried away by the fever of victory which infected the Arab world and brought about the end of the Armistice Regime between them and Israel.

Events started with the disintegration of security on all Israeli fronts – especially, and most dramatically, with Syria. But incidents also began to escalate *vis-à-vis* Jordan – most instigated by Fatah – which created a sense of insecurity in Israel. In May and September 1965, Israeli units crossed into Jordan to retaliate for such raids, and in November 1966, a large operation against the Samu village south of Hebron brought those incidents to boiling point. This reprisal had been planned as a limited punitive action against a local terrorist base, but it developed into a full-scale battle with the Arab Legion. There was no evidence that Jordan assisted the Fatah terrorist activities, but Israel took the attitude that under the

Armistice Regime Jordan was obligated to prevent irregulars from acting from within its territory. The Samu' raid provoked violent demonstrations against King Hussein, under the auspices of the PLO, even though the King had originally permitted the organization to establish its headquarters in East Jerusalem. The King reacted by arresting many PLO militants and closing down PLO offices throughout the kingdom, and made himself the declared enemy of the Palestinians in his realm. So much so, that the Fatah sent small terrorist groups into Jordan to commit acts of sabotage there.

A close aide of the King during those years, Samir Mutawi, testified in his book[8] that the King and his close associates were convinced that Israel had designs on the West Bank regardless of what Jordan did or refrained from doing. Therefore, he interpreted the Samu' incident as an act of aggression by Israel, without mentioning the underlying reasons for Israel's reprisal.[9] That interpretation would provide a *post factum* explanation why Jordan was unwisely dragged into the war, supposedly for self-defense, but it does not explain why the King joined the Nasser bandwagon when he hoped to gain a piece of Israel as a result of her demise. Moreover, if it was Israel who had aggressive designs on Jordan, then why did the latter not respond positively to Israel's calls, via the UN, to refrain from hostilities while battles were raging on the southern front with Egypt in June 1967? Had the King heeded those pleas, and not been carried away by the feverish rhetoric of Nasser and other Arabs, he might have emerged unscathed from that conflict, and his self-deluding concepts of Israel's 'aggressive designs' would have collapsed before his eyes.

However, history unfolded differently. Between May 1966 and May 1967, the crisis between Israel and her neighbors reached its peak along the border with Syria; and the Arab states were certain that a war was going to flare up on that troubled armistice line. On 15 May 1967, Israel again held its Independence Day military parade in Jerusalem, although this time reduced in size and not including heavy weapons which had been prohibited by the Armistice Agreement. This was interpreted by some Arab commentators as 'proof' that Israel had concentrated her best armaments on the front with Syria, in preparation for her attack. While Israel's Prime Minister was reviewing the parade, he received a note that the Egyptians were advancing their troops into Sinai; the next days saw a dramatic escalation towards war: Egypt asked for the UN forces, posted in the Sinai since the 1956 Suez War, to leave; then Egypt closed the Tiran Straits. At the beginning of June, King Hussein embarked on the road to war and agreed that his armed forces should be put under joint Arab command, a clear signal that he was determined to participate in the momentous event that by now had become inevitable, and of whose spoils he wished to partake. Not surprisingly then, when the war broke out on the Egyptian front on 5 June 1967, King Hussein saw an opportunity to redeem the lost prestige of his ancestor for his failure in 1948 to 'rescue' Palestine in general, and Jerusalem in particular, from the Zionist grip. Just as in Abdallah Tal's days, the Jordanians began their offensive in Jerusalem.

After the Arab failure in that war, the Jordanians began finding pretexts, rumors and theories in an attempt to rationalize what had happened during the days and weeks preceding the outbreak of hostilities. First, they said that Jordan, far from encouraging Egypt in the conflict with Israel, had in fact accused Nasser of not coming to Syria's aid when the latter's air force was battered by Israel[10] in April 1967, just two months prior to the war; and mocked him for not closing the Tiran Straits, which were Egyptian territory, to Israeli navigation, which added to the Zionist enemy's economic strength and aided their international relations. Another rumor imputed the failure of Jordan in the war to the Americans, who pushed them into allying themselves with Nasser. There was more finger-pointing by Prime Minister Wasfi Tal at his successor Sa'ad Jum'a, whom he accused of succumbing to the Nasserite fervor in order to gain popularity and advance his political career.[11] But the fundamental questions were not asked. For example, why did the Jordanians need to scold Nasser and humiliate him if they wanted to avoid war, rather than push him and themselves to the brink of war? Why did the King finally yield to the follies of the Unified Arab Command and let his army be decimated, if he truly wanted to remain out of the conflict?

The Israeli military chief who captured Jerusalem in 1967 was ironically General Uzi Narkiss, commander of Israel's Central Command. Narkiss had been a junior commander in the war for Jerusalem in 1948,[12] which had ended with substantial gains for the Arab Legion. In 1967, he redeemed himself by capturing all of the city. As in 1948, it was the Jordanians who started the offensive. Indeed, the first and major battles of the 1967 war were between Israelis and Egyptians, while the Israeli deployments on the

Jordanian and Syrian fronts were defensive. Moreover, Israel conveyed to King Hussein, via both the UNTSO COS General Bull and other channels, that it had no designs against the Hashemite rule on the West Bank, and would keep the armistice border with Jordan peaceful if the King reciprocated. Hussein, certain of the Arab victory and boosted by his dramatic embrace with Nasser in Cairo on 30 May, was not about to let this opportunity pass him by. He responded to the Israeli message with two large-scale operations, both in Jerusalem:

- He began bombing and shelling western Jerusalem with heavy mortar and artillery, reminiscent of the pounding the city had taken in the 1948 war; only this time there was vigorous return fire from Israeli troops.
- The Arab Legion realized the strategic importance of the Government House area and expected to conquer it with ease, due to the absence of enemy forces there. They immediately launched an assault, expelled the UN personnel, and triggered fighting in and around Jerusalem.

General Narkiss, for his part, was concerned right from the beginning (when the chances of Jordanian participation in the war were heightened), for the fate of Mount Scopus as an enclave in the heart of Jordanian territory at a time when the armistice had been torn to pieces and the arrangements to ensure the UN-sponsored survival of that enclave were no longer valid. Even though over the years the Israelis had found ways to smuggle means of help to the garrison so that it could hold its own in times of emergency, the available manpower there would have been overextended if it tried to defend the entire perimeter of the compound against the substantial troops that the Arab Legion would be able to commit to that crucial combat. A few days before the outbreak of hostilities the Jordanians had asked the UN to postpone the fortnightly Israeli convoy for fear, they said, that due to escalating tension in the area, they might be unable to control a mob attack against the Israeli vehicles. Israel agreed, due to its traumatic memories of the Arab attack against the Hadassah convoy in 1948 which had eliminated the top Jewish medical hierarchy in Palestine while British colonial troops refrained from interfering.[13] Israel's atypical yielding to the Jordanian request may also have stemmed from its desire not to provoke Amman unnecessarily as it was preparing to concentrate its forces on the Egyptian front. But Jordan's unusual request, which in normal times would have belied its lack of self-confidence in dealing with an otherwise routine matter, raises the suspicion that the Arab Legion wished to deprive the Israeli garrison on the Mount of fresh relief and supply before its anticipated attack against it.[14]

Besides the Mount Scopus problem, and the requisite state of alert lest the Jordanians attempted to take over Government House, Narkiss had also to avert any Jordanian move to besiege West Jerusalem or cut off the road leading to it. Once again, the lessons of the 1948 war had been learned, and as explained in a previous chapter, precautions had been taken by Israel in the intervening years to ensure that new settlements had been built on the ruins of old Arab villages in order to secure a wide corridor linking Jerusalem and the coastal plain. Therefore, when the inevitability of war became clear, Narkiss' war plan consisted primarily of breaking through with infantry to Mount Scopus and then moving his troops up to the high ground between Jerusalem and Ramallah, from which position he could dominate all of Jerusalem. As a preliminary to this move, Narkiss asked for a paratrooper brigade to enable him to conquer the Police School in northern Jerusalem in order to gain a foothold on Sheikh Jarrah and the road to Scopus. In conjunction with this, Narkiss planned to pit his infantry against the southern village of Sur Bahir, in the Government House area, in order to cut the enemy's route between Jerusalem and Bethlehem. The line-up of the Jordanian forces around Jerusalem constituted a significant threat to both Mount Scopus and the Government House area.

On the Jordanian side of the armistice line, the mirror image of the Israeli plan had been elaborated by the Arab Legion command, precisely in order to encircle Jerusalem and cut it off from the rest of Israel, to eliminate the threat of the Israeli enclave on Mount Scopus, and to capture the high ground in both the Mount Scopus area in the north and the Government House zone in the south. This would give the Legion a strategic launching pad for the conquest of West Jerusalem and the roads leading thereto. This plan, known as Operation Tariq, had been central to the planning, training and preparations of the Arab Legion since 1965.[15]

In the days preceding the war, an Iraqi division crossed the Jordan River onto the West Bank, thus posing an imminent danger of invasion. On the morning of 5 June 1967, Jordanian shelling and bombing occurred all along the border between Israel and Jordan, despite the plea sent by the Israeli Prime Minister to King Hussein to stay out of the conflict. The King thought that the 'hour of revenge had come,' and there was no turning back from the war. Narkiss swiftly grouped his forces for the counter-offensive all along the Jordanian front, determined to seize the opportunity and correct the deficiencies of the armistice lines. The Israeli commander of the Jerusalem area was immediately alerted and brought his tanks, which were in the hinterland due to armistice restrictions, into the city and prepared to intervene in the Government House area.[16] Narkiss was also prepared to attack Latrun – that key post on the road to Jerusalem which Israel had failed dismally to take in the 1948 war – as well as the other positions which dominated the approaches to the city from the north. As a precautionary measure, he ordered the trains from Tel Aviv to Jerusalem – which ran a mere 200 m from the armistice line on the southern border of Jerusalem – to continue to operate but to only run empty, without passengers.

On the Jordanian side, the Arab Legion command was rather optimistic. In spite of the litany of post-war apologetic pretexts – for example, that Jordan knew it was no match for Israel and therefore it deployed its forces defensively[17] – they were well prepared to absorb the spoils of war. This is what a firsthand witness, Mutawi, says:

> In Cairo it was agreed that in the initial stages of the war on the Egyptian front, Jordan's role would be to maintain a defence posture and to *open hostilities* [emphasis added] on a limited front with the aim of neutralizing a portion of Israel's forces which otherwise would be deployed on the Egyptian and Syrian fronts. This limited engagement was only to be expanded after the fulfilment of two conditions: the arrival of Iraqi and other Arab forces at the front and positive information that events on the Egyptian front were proceeding as planned ... Only when these two conditions had been fulfilled were the Jordanians to extend operations along the front and enter into the *offensive phase* [emphasis added] of the operation.[18]

Of course, after their failure in the war, both Hussein and his COS admitted that the term 'offensive' was exaggerated, because it only meant limited operations behind enemy lines.[19] However, one should not forget that while on the eve of the war the general feeling in Israel was one of anxiety, born out of a reluctance to be dragged into an unwanted and uncertain conflict, amongst the Jordanian military and political élite elation and optimism prevailed. Again, to quote Mutawi:

> Although they realized that Israel's military capability was far more powerful, they had been impressed by the Egyptians' display of confidence. They did not believe that they could regain the land Israel had seized in 1948, other than the territories assigned in the Partition Plan, but they did believe that with their capabilities enhanced by support from their Arab allies they could engage their enemy in combat, prevent it from seizing their land and perhaps gain a political victory.[20]

A measure of the reluctance of the Israeli authorities to open a second front with Jordan as the battles were raging against the Egyptians, despite Narkiss' eagerness to proceed with his plan, can be gauged from the repeated rejections Narkiss encountered from his superiors to his requests, even as the Jordanian shelling of Mount Scopus in the north and Ramat Rachel in the south gathered momentum during the morning of 5 June. By noon, when it became evident that the shelling had not diminished, Narkiss ordered the trains to the capital to be discontinued, and put an armored brigade on alert to join the Mount Scopus garrison in case an all-out attack was launched against it. At that point, Narkiss still believed that the Jordanians were just putting up a show of force in order to pay lip service to their allies' cause, and therefore he agreed to the cease-fire suggested by the UN. But soon, all these hopeful illusions were to be dispelled: Jordanian aircraft penetrated Israeli defences and bombed Tel Aviv, while Radio Amman announced the capture of Mount Scopus by the Jordanian forces. Earlier, Radio Cairo had announced the same regarding Government House, and both announcements had been taken as mere boasting. But, in retrospect, it appears that these two key positions were on the agenda of the Jordanian General Staff and of the Joint Arab Command, and these premature announcements assumed that both targets had been taken.

While the entire morning of 5 June was marked by heavy Jordanian shelling and bombing all around the city and its environment followed by Israeli reprisals in kind, noon brought the beginning of the Jordanian land offensive which triggered the battle for Jerusalem that was to wipe out the armistice (lines, regime, anomaly and all the rest). Mutawi tells us that, in spite of Jordanian objections, Egyptian General Riad, the Supreme Commander of the Arab Unified Command, gave the order to the Jordanian troops to occupy Government House.[21] However, shortly thereafter they were dislodged and badly depleted by the counter-attacking Israeli troops, and the swift takeover of the city began to unfold inexorably. Mutawi does not say what form the 'Jordanian objections' took, nor whether the King also objected and whether he tried to overrule General Riad and give his troops different orders. One can only assume that he could have done so, if he had wanted to avoid the war, judging from the way he ignored the Egyptian COS's 'advice' to evacuate the West Bank following the collapse of the Jordanian Army and decided to hold on.[22]

It transpired that three of the Israeli commanders who were responsible for Jerusalem had been born in that city; had fought for it in 1948 but failed; had experienced the vagaries of the Armistice Regime in and around it; and were now poised to redeem themselves through the redemption of Jerusalem. They were:

- General Yitzhak Rabin, the Israeli COS, who in 1948 commanded the Harel Brigade which had fought for the road to Jerusalem.
- General Uzi Narkiss, now the OC Central Commander, in charge of the entire Jordanian front, who had commanded one of the units of Harel in 1948 and taken part in the battles for the Old City which had all ended in disaster.
- Colonel Uri Ben-Ari, who had also fought in the Jerusalem area in 1948 and was now, on reserve duty, the commander of the armored brigade that had been instructed to break through northern Jerusalem and join with the besieged Mount Scopus.

At 14.00 hours, Ben-Ari was ordered to attack in the direction of Mount Scopus. At the same time, Narkiss was informed that the Government House had been occupied by the Jordanians. What had started as a defensive posture in the morning, an attempt to preserve the armistice, now turned into a full-scale offensive to dislodge the Jordanians from their new positions and bring relief to Mount Scopus, despite the new proposals for cease-fire coming from the dispossessed COS of UNTSO.

Another player entered the scene as of the afternoon when, due to the grave turn of events in Jerusalem, Colonel Motta Gur, commander of a reserve paratroop brigade, was rushed from his assigned duty on the Egyptian front. He arrived with his troops and carefully studied the Jordanian positions in Sheikh Jarrah – in particular the Police School – in preparation for the breakthrough into eastern Jerusalem to ensure the immediate link to Mount Scopus and to position his battalions for the take-over of the Old City. At the same time, Ben-Ari was to attempt to link up with Mount Scopus from northern Jerusalem. Simultaneously, Israel counter-attacked at Government House, and before 16.00 hours it was in Israeli hands, together with the Jordanian fortified positions around it. However, even at that point, the Israeli General Staff refused to allow Narkiss to attack Latrun. Ben-Ari's advance was rapid and by sunset, at the end of the first day of fighting, many Jordanian positions in northern Jerusalem were in Israeli hands. Once Israeli troops had captured Jordanian sectors of the city and the Israeli flag was flying over Government House, no more signs were needed that the Armistice Regime had foundered.

The Israeli ring continued to close on the city. At nightfall, Sur Baher, in the vicinity of Government House also fell into Israeli hands, thus securing an important outpost on the Bethlehem road. Gur's troops were ready for their mission after midnight, despite the General Staff's preference for attack the next morning with air and artillery support; however, Narkiss insisted upon sparing the city heavy bombardment, and he had his way.[23] The western part of Jerusalem had been subjected to a continuous pounding of shells from Jordan, and it was essential to silence that artillery by ground attack without waiting for the morning. Israeli tanks opened fire point blank on Jordanian positions in Sheikh Jarrah, to which the Arab Legion responded vigorously all along the metropolitan armistice line, which by now had no meaning. Five rows of thick barbed wire, which had accumulated over 19 years of armistice, now had to be cut by the paratroopers before they engaged in fierce hand-to-hand fighting with the Legionnaires in the Police School and Ammunition Hill trenches in the Sheikh Jarrah sector. After an all-night battle, the Jordanian positions fell to Israel: the Police School, Sheikh Jarrah and the American Colony were under Israeli control. The famous Mandelbaum Gate, and the adjoining office of the Israel–Jordan MAC, found themselves removed from the armistice border which no longer existed.[24]

Early in the morning of the second day of fighting, Ben-Ari's forces had also reached the Ramallah–Jerusalem road. In the eastern section of the city, Narkiss wanted his successful troops to march through the walls of the Old City, but the General Staff advised waiting. In the meantime, one of Ben-Ari's units took Latrun and reopened the old road to Jerusalem, where their commander had already joined forces with Gur's paratroopers in the monstrous stronghold on French Hill, which was also overwhelmed after heavy fighting and casualties. The Legionnaires kept their positions on the city wall, and they continuously sniped at, and caused casualties to, Gur's forces; however, access to Mount Scopus was opened, and Narkiss could savor his victory by accompanying Defence Minister Dayan there on 6 June 1967. The Mount Scopus Agreement too had come to an end. Gur's forces proceeded next to take over the eastern hills dominating Jerusalem, while Ben-Ari set off northwards towards Ramallah.[25]

Now, it was essential for Israel to hasten the pace, lest a Security Council resolution ordering cease-fire might freeze the situation in place before the Old City came under Israeli control. On 7 June, an attack was launched against the Old City, after the Augusta Victoria compound – namely, the Jordanian part of the Mount Scopus Demilitarized Zone – had been overpowered and suffered heavy casualties. The paratroopers, supported from the air and by heavy artillery fire, assaulted the Old City, the big prize of the war. Despite the very heavy fire, care was taken – successfully – not to hit any holy shrine of any religion.[26] So, finally, Article VIII of the defunct armistice could be enforced: there was free access to all the holy places as well as access to the humanitarian institutions on Mount Scopus, which had been provided for in that unfortunate clause.

With all Jerusalem under control, as was the rest of the West Bank, the Armistice Agreement between Israel and Jordan was no longer of any significance; it was declared 'dead and buried' by the Prime Minister of Israel. The Jordanians did not distance themselves from the Agreement so easily. At first, they hoped it could be maintained or restored, as they licked their wounds and tried to gloss over their mammoth miscalculation.[27] Many years after the 1967 debacle, they would attempt, with money, cajoling, threats and alliances with Palestinian groups among their supporters, to maintain a foothold in Jerusalem and on the West Bank, in the hope that some future settlement would recognize, once again, the primacy of the Hashemites in that area. The Federation Plan, spelled out by King Hussein in 1972, which provided for Palestinian autonomy under the Jordanian Crown, was one of these aborted attempts.

When the Intifadah broke out on the West Bank and in Jerusalem in late 1987, the King was forced to recognize the strength of Palestinian nationalism and that the prospects of his recovering the lost territories were unrealistic. He responded in August 1988 by renouncing his claim to the West Bank and was content with the new reality which returned him to the *status quo ante* that existed prior to 1948 when the Hashemite Kingdom was no more than 'Transjordan.' Moreover, while in the past the Hashemite House had had to accept the Palestinization of Jordan (80 per cent of the total population were Palestinians) as the cost of the annexation of the West Bank and Jerusalem,[28] since August 1988 the King had had to accept the *de facto* continuation of the Palestinization (60 per cent of the population being Palestinian) without the benefits of the West Bank and Jerusalem. Nevertheless, the King maintained his relationship with Jerusalem through generous grants to the Waqf personnel, who oversaw the Islamic Holy Shrines, and his claim to the title of Guardian of the Aqsa Mosque – a cornerstone to the problematic legitimacy of his rule. However, by signing the 1994 peace treaty with Israel, he appeared to have finally recognized that the dream of a Jordanian Jerusalem was gone forever and that he had no choice but to be content with a symbolic 'special role' in the Islamic places in Jerusalem, which was accorded him by the Israelis but much disputed by the Palestinians.

Jerusalem had come full circle. First, the UN Partition Plan had advised its internationalization, a program reluctantly accepted by Israel but rejected by King Abdallah. Then, the King offered the Jews autonomy under his realm, which they rejected. He then tried to occupy all Jerusalem by force during the 1948 war after the Bernadotte Plan, which would have accorded him the same by agreement was also rejected, but failed. The King was then forced to accept an armistice which guaranteed the Jews free access to their holy places and other institutions, but he never intended to implement it, as has been shown above. He never even agreed to consider a permanent boundary between Israel and Jordan based on armistice. In 1967, his grandson, King Hussein, attempted to achieve by force, once again, what his grandfather had failed to attain in 1948. Not only did he blunder but, at the end of the process, he found himself accepting Israeli rule over all of

Jerusalem while he was begging for some *ex-gratia* symbolic status in it. The supposedly 'moderate and smart King' had committed all the possible errors and miscalculations, before he wrecked the heritage that his truly moderate and wise grandfather had unwisely left to him.

NOTES

1. See for example, the report of the meeting between Israel's Reuven Shiloah of the Foreign Ministry and Prime Minister Samir a Rifa'i of Jordan, which took place on 23 February 1951 (Document No. 130.02/2408/13, dated 12 March 1951; ISA).
2. UN Document No. S/2485, dated 22 January 1952.
3. Eban to the President of the Security Council, 29 January 1952; Report No. 130.02/2433/10 (ISA).
4. Israeli, *Palestinians Between Israel and Jordan*, p. 72.
5. See, Collins and Lapierre, *O Jerusalem*; especially Chs 28–30.
6. Israeli, *Palestinians Between Israel and Jordan*; especially Chs 3, 4 and 6.
7. For the details of this story, see Samir Mutawi, *Jordan in the 1967 War* (Cambridge: Cambridge University Press, 1987), pp. 21–2.
8. Ibid., pp. 69–70.
9. Ibid., pp. 76–80.
10. Ibid., p. 85.
11. Ibid., pp. 85–6.
12. See Collins and Lapierre, *O Jerusalem*, p. 672. See also, Narkiss, *Liberation of Jerusalem* [Hebrew edn, Tel Aviv, 1975].
13. Collins and Lapierre, *O Jerusalem*, Ch. 23.
14. For a description of the escalation to war, and the main strokes of the swift Israeli moves in and around Jerusalem, see W. Laqueur, *The Road to War* (Harmondsworth: Penguin, 1968), especially Ch. 2; W. Churchill, *The Six Day War* (London: Heineman / Penguin, 1967), especially the chapter regarding Jerusalem and the West Bank; also, Narkiss, *Liberation of Jerusalem* [Hebrew edn].
15. Mutawi, *Jordan in the 1967 War*, p. 114ff.
16. Narkiss, *Liberation of Jerusalem* [Hebrew edn], p. 95ff.
17. Mutawi, *Jordan in the 1967 War*, pp. 112–21.
18. Ibid., p. 119.
19. Ibid.
20. Ibid., p. 121.
21. Ibid., p. 132.
22. Ibid., p. 139.
23. Narkiss, *Liberation of Jerusalem* [Hebrew edn]; especially pp. 154–95.
24. Ibid.
25. Ibid.
26. Ibid., p. 196ff.
27. Mutawi, *Jordan in the 1967 War*, pp. 141–62.
28. Israeli, *Palestinians Between Israel and Jordan*, Chs 4 and 6.

13. What Next?

After the 1967 war and the reunification of Jerusalem, though the city changed rapidly and considerably, one has a lingering sense of the legacy of the bygone Armistice Regime. New Israeli neighborhoods have grown into satellite towns all around the core of the city beyond the old demarcation line; development has dramatically altered the network of services throughout the city; Mount Scopus, now connected to the city by a major network of highways, has been rebuilt into a mammoth fortress-campus which accommodates the Hebrew University and the Hadassah Hospital; new roads and highways have been paved to criss-cross the city and link its new neighborhoods; what was a formidable array of military positions and fortifications has turned into sprawling housing projects; free access to the holy places of all faiths has been made available to all; new museums, shopping malls, entertainment centers and places of worship have sprouted everywhere; tourism has picked up considerably; and a general feeling of content springing from an improved standard of living is perceptible, in spite of the fact that the population doubled between 1967 and 1987 (from just under 300,00 in both parts of the divided city to about 600,000 within the unified municipal boundaries).

There is, however, a sense of unease stemming from the atmosphere of impermanence which still hovers over the city, as things do not appear to have been settled and to have attained the finality one finds in Amsterdam or in Stockholm. There are still far too many security personnel patrolling the streets or peeking into your bag when you enter a public establishment, as if to remind you that disputes are far from settled, there are still two separate and very different cities, coexisting side by side, rather than one unified municipal and socio-cultural system. Where the demarcation line used to run through the heart of the city, a north–south highway was built which, rather than unifying by transporting people rapidly from one end of the city to another, ironically exposes the divide, like a scar which refuses to heal. The populations and lifestyles do not mix: western Jerusalem has remained predominantly Jewish and Western, while eastern Jerusalem has remained prevailingly Arabic, Muslim and Oriental. Tensions, prejudices, suspicions and fears, which are at times translated into violence, are still rampant and necessitate special measures of caution and scrutiny, which in turn increase the level of unease.

The memories of armistice are also present by virtue of the many buildings and other physical features that are still there: no one over 40 can pass by the city wall on the one hand, or the towering and renovated Notre Dame, on the other, without reminiscing of the formidable military positions which had spurted out gun-fire and death during the years of the armistice. Many open spaces still exist; like the legendary Ammunition and French Hills in the north, or Government House in the south, which were no man's land or military positions – now turned into parks or roads, or new neighborhoods or war memorials – which cannot but remind the onlooker of the dramas that unfolded there during the many incidents which eroded the armistice and then finally destroyed it. One cannot pass through what was the Mandelbaum Gate without noticing the MAC House, and the Turdjman Post (now turned into a museum), and feel a chill down his back in remembrance of the many incidents of gun-fire, the MAC meetings, the daily crossings through the Gate, or the fortnightly convoys to Mount Scopus.

And then, there are the daily reminders of the unsettled problem of Jerusalem: political declarations; diplomatic meetings; demonstrations of one faction or another; and academic symposia, learned articles and newspaper reports, which express various views about what happened in the past and what needs to be done now and in the future, and expose the deepest strata of conflicting convictions, of contradictory narratives, of clashing hopes and of the most diverse remedies. No other world capital has seen its past, present and future so disputed and dipped in conflict, its history and fate so emotionally controversial. In other words, even though at the pinnacle of a temporarily unresolved conflict – the armistice is no more – the reigning doubts and disagreements still feed the spirit of uncertainty as if the armistice were still in place, refusing to die.

However, in view of the dismal failure of the armistice experience along Israeli–Arab boundaries in general and through the Jerusalem area in particular, some conclusions present themselves which merit consideration:

• Interim arrangements like the Israel–Jordan armistice are useless unless they lead to an agreed, gradual and clear timetable of steps towards a final accord. Leaving important clauses open for further negotiation, such as Article VIII of the Armistice Agreement, is a recipe for future trouble.

• Agreements must be hammered out by the parties concerned without outside interference. Experience has shown that intermediaries are inclined to develop interests of their own and, instead of facilitating agreement, they may at times aggravate existing disagreements.

• 'Constructive ambiguity' in agreements may be disastrous in the final analysis. For the problem is not finding the right wording for an agreement, but avoiding double meanings and multiple interpretations which generate crises of expectations when the parties end up with something different from what they understood from assurances given to them or from what they honestly expected. No matter how agreeable the wording of clauses may sound initially, the day of reckoning comes when formulae adopted at the negotiating table come to be applied in the real world, and the parties discover or suspect that they were misled.

• Divided cities are not viable in the long run, because the open wounds cutting through roads, communications, water and electricity grids and the very landscape of the city, remain as a negative reminder that things could be different and more normal. Naturally, in other settings, such as Berlin or Belfast, the scar in the middle of the city which partitioned the same people and culture, and possibly families, into two halves, was more cruel on the human level. In divided Jerusalem, except for small groups that had been evacuated during the 1948 war, the partition also followed along national, religious, ethnic and linguistic divides, which made the alienation between its halves less cruel, but present all the same.

• Where borders are drawn or defined, great care must be taken to avoid any vagueness, misinterpretation or faulty marking. To be respected, borders must be clearly delineated and policed. Authority to police borders and supervise peace along them must be delegated to local commanders who know each other, meet with each other, and are accessible to each other. When minor incidents are reported to higher authority, they tend to get distorted and exaggerated, and by the time the top leadership begins to deal with them, they acquire an importance of their own and become much more difficult to settle.

- Under Arab/Islamic rule, free access to the holy places in Jerusalem cannot be guaranteed. While local Muslims under the armistice generally enjoyed freedom of worship in the Aqsa Mosque and its adjoining shrines, the Muslims of Israel were denied entry to those holy places throughout the armistice period. Israeli Christians were allowed into Bethlehem on Christmas, but Jews were totally excluded from their shrines on the Temple Mount and in other parts of Jordanian-controlled Jerusalem, in spite of Article VIII of the Armistice Agreement which had provided differently. The issue is one of tolerance on a basis of equality and sharing, instead of exclusion and arrogance of power. In the view of Muslims, Jews have no rights on the Temple Mount and therefore they have no claim nor right of entry to any part of the entire complex, and this view was always enforced when Muslims were in control of Jerusalem.

- During the period of the armistice neither the UN nor any of the Powers sought to facilitate daily life in Jerusalem except for their own nationals. They interested themselves in the functioning of the Armistice Regime only to the extent that it served their interests. In no case did they seek permanent arrangements to replace the armistice, nor did they call Jordan to task for disrupting the functioning of the Armistice Regime by paralyzing the main provisions of the vital Article VIII.

- Jerusalem under armistice seemed everybody's concern and everybody knew better than the Israelis and the Jordanians what should be done there, what the parties' interests in it were, and what their Jerusalem policy ought to be. Seldom in the history of international relations have so many proffered so much gratuitous advice on so many issues in so limited a territory and with so little effect as the Powers did in relation to Jerusalem. Never before has the capital city of any sovereign country been the subject of such blatant intervention on the part of just about everybody, and never before has the sovereign government of any nation been so attentive and so sensitive about what others had to say with regard to its affairs.

The shortcomings of the armistice are evident. But is there another basis on which to seek a resolution to the Jerusalem problem, which has remained the most thorny in the Arab–Israeli dispute? Short of redividing the city and exposing it once again to the agonies of the armistice period, are there other ways of solving this quandary? Does the solution of the Jerusalem issue hinge upon a resolution of all the pending Arab–Israeli bones of contention, as some people believe,[1] or is it as Pope John Paul II sees it – the starting point for negotiating a settlement of the entire conflict?

The Oslo Accords of 1993 have relegated the issue of Jerusalem – along with other difficult aspects of the conflict – to the final phase of the Oslo process. This assumes that confidence-building through settling minor issues will have generated enough goodwill to produce agreed solutions for this more difficult problem. Experience thus far has shown that every step in the implementation of the Oslo Accords has led to new tensions, generated new accusations, and produced new expectations likely to make negotiations over Jerusalem harder, not easier.

There is a wide convergence of opinion against the repartition of Jerusalem. Israel's unequivocal stand on this issue is backed not only by historical claims and the clear reality of Israeli predominance in the city, but also by the negative experiences that had accumulated over the armistice years. If Jerusalem were to be redivided, or eastern Jerusalem revert to Arab rule in a context of peace, one ought to be aware of the possible consequences:

- West Jerusalem under Israel will be prosperous, free, open and thriving; the Arab-controlled east would be backward, poor, oppressed, over-crowded and neglected (compare East and West Berlin). The deprived and unemployed population of the eastern section – just like that of Nablus, Hebron, Tul-Karem, Jenin, Qalqiliya, Ramallah and Bethlehem, already ceded to the Palestinian Authority – will infiltrate illegally into Israel with the connivance of the Palestinian Authority to seek work at best, to steal and commit crime at worst.
- Palestinian crime within western Jerusalem will increase dramatically due to the proximity of the two parties of the city and the great attraction of the more modern, affluent and larger Israeli part. Those who wish to commit car thefts, the burglary of houses and businesses, document counterfeiting, manslaughter, rape, smuggling and drug peddling, will flood

into western Jerusalem. This is already the situation to a great extent, but at least the Israeli police can investigate and lay their hands on the perpetrators. If the criminals were free – as in Ramallah and Nablus today – to turn East Jerusalem into a haven, there is no certainty the Palestinian police will be able or willing to curtail this influx, and in any case would have to loosen or tighten its control on crime according to the changing relations between the two parties.

- There might be a renewed threat to Jewish freedom of access to their holy places, especially the Wailing Wall. The Mount of Olives might again be desecrated once under Palestinian sovereignty and Jews might no longer be permitted to bury their dead there.
- The great archaeological excavations carried out during the past 30 years, which uncovered the ancient Jewish past of Jerusalem, will be obliterated as part of a complete Arabization and Islamization of that part of the city.
- The Hebrew University on Mount Scopus, and the Hadassah Hospital which has become the most important medical center in eastern Jerusalem, will have to close their gates once again. For even if their existence as an enclave in an Arab environment and free access there were guaranteed, their operation at the mercy of a foreign government would become untenable.
- East Jerusalem under Palestinian authority might become a permanent strategic and security threat to Israel's capital city. Indeed, one or two kilometers from the Israeli Knesset and government offices, Palestinian fighters would be allowed to take up positions from which they could threaten daily life in the city, as in the days of armistice.

It is hard to imagine that Israelis would accept a reversion to that kind of situation. To make sure that they would not have to face such a possibility Israel enacted a Basic Jerusalem Law in July 1980, mandating that undivided Jerusalem must remain the sovereign capital of Israel. This was a complementary law to the one of June 1967, which applied the Israeli legal and administrative system to East Jerusalem, thereby placing it under Israeli sovereignty as part and parcel of the rest of Israel. It was not an act of annexation, because Israel did not regard itself as an occupying power in any part of Jerusalem, nor had it ever recognized Transjordan's occupation of Palestinian territory in 1948 (East Jerusalem included) as a rightful expansion of sovereignty.[2] Of course, there are other points of view advanced by Arab and some Western – even Israeli – jurists,[3] but since the practical absorption of the city happened in a situation where only Israel could advance a lawful claim to Jerusalem at the time, it is important to understand the reasons behind this step which originated partly from lessons drawn from the armistice experience.

Israel's Minister of Justice who introduced the relevant legislation to the Knesset on 27 June 1967, explained that what needed to be stated for the purpose of the relevant bill was that:

> The Israeli Defence Forces have liberated from foreign yoke considerable areas of the Land of Israel … which have now been under the control of the Israeli Defence Forces for more than a fortnight … The position of the State of Israel was based from the start on the principle that the law, the jurisdiction and administration of the State apply to all those parts of the Land of Israel which are *de facto* under the State's control … It was the view of the government – and this view conformed with the requirements of international law – that in addition to the control by the Israeli Defence Forces of these territories, there is required also an open act of sovereignty on the part of Israel to make Israeli law applicable to them … It is for this reason that the government saw fit to introduce the bill which I now submit to the Knesset.[4]

Thus, in the same way as the armistice boundaries in 1949 were not determined by the UN – whose Partition Resolution was rejected by the Arabs – but rather by war, in Jerusalem the armistice lines also had no validity the moment the Jordanian forces revoked the armistice and went on the attack on 5 June 1967. Hence the new territorial division in Jerusalem and the introduction of Israeli law and administration into East Jerusalem were fully valid. Some further juridical analysis of the new position created by Israel's repulse of Jordan's aggression against it on 5 June 1967 may interest the reader. Western Jerusalem and its corridor to the coastal plain, as well as other parts of the country which fell outside the Partition boundaries of what was to be a Jewish state, automatically became Israeli territory as a result of the Arab rejection of Partition and subsequent attack on the Jewish areas of Palestine. In the same way the Jordanian attack on 5 June 1967 made legal the takeover by

Israel of Jordanian-held territories which were no part of recognized sovereign Jordanian land.[5] The entire international community, with the exception of Great Britain and Pakistan, had never recognized Jordanian sovereignty over those territories occupied by Jordan's army in the war of 1948–49 which were beyond Jordan's national territory.

In August 1988, King Hussein of Jordan announced publicly that he was renouncing his country's claims to territories west of the river Jordan. He did so, it is believed, out of fear that the Palestinian anti-Israel rioting and violence (the so-called Intifadah), which was then rife and well publicized in many countries, might spill over across the Jordan river into his country. Then, of the existing sovereign entities which might have claim to Jerusalem, only Israel remained. But the Oslo Accords signed between Israel and the Palestinians in 1993 opened new vistas for claims and counter-claims, inasmuch as Israel agreed to discuss the question of Jerusalem as part of the permanent status of territories lost by Jordan to Israel in the 1967 assault on Israel by combined Arab forces, best known as the Six Day War. The Palestinian position is clear: the Oslo Accords open the way for them to establish a Palestinian state with Jerusalem as its capital. Israel opposes these ambitions and has made it abundantly clear that Jerusalem will remain united under Israeli sovereignty. In due course the signatories of the Oslo Accords are to negotiate a final agreement concerning the conditions and modalities of their coexistence within the boundaries of Mandated Palestine as redefined after 1922, namely the territory lying between the Mediterranean Sea in the west, Jordan in the east, Syria and Lebanon to the north and Egypt to the south. As these lines are written it is too early to attempt any prediction as to the kind of arrangement that could be accepted by the parties concerned. The size of the territory available is very small indeed – 25,000 square kilometers. Its natural resources are very modest, to say the least. Its historic capital of Jerusalem, where Judaism matured and became the fountainhead of two other monotheistic faiths, has developed a political magnetism unappreciative of spiritual and historical seniority. It will take Solomonic wisdom to structure the compromises that will allow the tiny land of the Bible to be a warm and safe home for the people of the Bible as well as a focus of religious sentiments for all the believers in the one God.

What remains contentious, however, is whether the city could be redivided between two sovereignties, or whether it could stay under Israel's sole jurisdiction, while allowance is made for particular religious and political interests which often merge into one as far as Jerusalem is concerned. Israel, drawing from its past history, and in response to cultural, religious and domestic political urges, can maintain its firm position due to the practical reality which exists on the ground where no one seriously challenges her rule. The Palestinians, however, who claim to inherit Jordan's rights in eastern Jerusalem – as if Jordan had any valid rights there – can only voice their aspirations and press for a settlement acceptable to Israel. Having no wherewithal to implement their dreams, their leaders, notably Yasser Arafat, use the Arab–Islamic symbolism of Jerusalem to mobilize the masses behind their claims. They too are bound by historical memories, real or imagined, and especially by the religious fervor that has been drummed up by the Hamas Islamists in the ongoing game of Islamic oneupmanship between the Palestinian Authority and its most formidable opponents. Since Arafat created the Palestinian Authority, in almost all his public speeches he invokes Jerusalem as a powerful unifying and mobilizing symbol. On every possible occasion, he lists all the towns so far regained from Israel and vows to 'march into Jerusalem,' or to 'pray in Jerusalem' at the end of the process.

Arafat often refers to Jerusalem as *al-Quds a-Sharif* (Jerusalem the Noble), or *al-Quds al-'arabiyya* (Arab Jerusalem) – the former signifying the whole of Jerusalem in Arab and Arafat's parlance in general; the latter, normally meaning East Jerusalem, namely the part of the city claimed by the Palestinians as their capital. On Christmas Eve of 1995, when he went to Bethlehem on the occasion of its handover by Israel to the Palestinian Authority, he declared Christ to be Palestinian, implying a connection between Islam and Christianity, both under his protective wing, since they are both Palestinian. This renders Arafat the Curator of the Holy Places of both Christianity and Islam in Jerusalem, and makes the PLO the partner of world Christianity and not only of world Islam in Holy Jerusalem. This, in itself, makes him a better and more universally accepted ruler of the city than the Jewish Israelis. His intentions were picked up by the Greek Orthodox Patriarch of Jerusalem, who declared to a delighted Arafat on that occasion: 'Here is the successor of Sophronius welcoming the successor of Umar ibn-al-Khattab!'[6] No one present or watching the ceremony on television could miss the parallel – the reference was to the submission of the Byzantine Patriarch of Jerusalem in 638 AD to the second Caliph of

Islam, Umar ibn-al-Khattab (634–44), who conquered Jerusalem and put an end to many centuries of Christian rule. Until the Crusaders, who established the Christian Kingdom of Jerusalem in 1099, the city was to remain, uninterruptedly, part and parcel of *Dar-al-Islam*, the Pax Islamica. Arafat liked the Patriarch's comment so much that he ordered the Palestinian press to publish it in their headlines. This became known when one ill-advised and independent-minded journalist called Mahir al-'Alami, the night editor of the daily *Al-Quds*, who refused to conform, found himself arrested and interrogated in the dark basements of the security apparatus in Jericho. Arafat's eagerness to get the Patriarch's sycophancy widely publicized did not stem from his intention to humiliate him, and was not due to his flattering comparison of Arafat with Umar, but was mainly due to his newly acquired glamorous image as the prospective liberator of Jerusalem.

This makes Arafat the latest link in the apostolic chain of great liberators which, to date, have included Umar, followed by Saladin who recaptured Jerusalem in 1187 from the Crusaders. If one bears in mind the oft-made comparison in Arab and Islamic circles between the medieval Crusader state and contemporary Israel, one necessarily comes to the conclusion that just as Umar had occupied Jerusalem by peaceful means through the surrender of the Christians, and Saladin by force through the conquest of the city and the expulsion or massacre of its inhabitants, so will Arafat. He will repeat that feat either by accepting the surrender of East Jerusalem to him by the Israelis, or by pressing his call for *Jihad* in order to capture all of it. Umar and Saladin had been celebrated as the legitimate rulers of the city following the oath of allegiance (*bai'a*) accorded them by the crowd. In Bethlehem, when the loudspeakers were enjoining the masses to deliver the *bai'a* to Arafat, the parallel became neat, complete, inescapable. History had come a full circle.

A mere six months after the fanfare surrounding the signature of the Oslo Accords in 1993, Arafat was on a visit to Johannesburg for the inauguration of President Mandela. Quite incidentally, and convinced that he enjoyed the privacy and the intimacy required to confide to his local fellow Muslims, gathered in the largest mosque of the city, his thinking about the peace process that he had initiated with Israel, he enjoined them to join *Jihad* in order to recover Jerusalem. He also compared the Oslo Agreement to the Hudaybiyya Treaty concluded by Mohammed, and he mentioned Umar ibn-al-Khattab and the Byzantine Patriarch Sophronius, the two heroes invoked two years later when Arafat entered Bethlehem. When Arafat's Johannesburg address became known in the spring of 1994, as a result of the release of a tape recorded by a reporter who attended that meeting, it raised a major storm in Israel. Later speeches that Arafat gave within the Autonomy and elsewhere, further fanned the idea of *Jihad* to liberate Jerusalem and the comparison of Oslo with Hudaybiyya, something which augured ill for its validity and ability to survive.

Following the Oslo Accords came the Israel–Jordan Peace Accord of 1994, which has complicated the matter of Jerusalem somewhat further. This accord recognizes the 'special historical role' of Jordan in the Islamic holy places in Jerusalem, which means that after Jordan had been severed from Jerusalem as a result of its aggression in 1967, and after Hussein himself had finally renounced his occupation of the West Bank (including Jerusalem) in 1988, Israel has reintroduced Hussein through the back-window. That the King needed the title of Curator of al-Aqsa, just like his much wiser grandfather, to legitimize his rule, is clear; it is difficult to see, however, how this measure will serve any of Israel's interests unless the idea was to displace Arafat's grip on the city. However, since the 'Jordanian Option' for resolving the Palestinian problem has collapsed at Oslo, the competition between Jordan and the PLO in the city will only add to the existing problems.

The death of armistice as a viable option to govern the relations between Israel and the Arabs, necessitates new and creative formulae for accommodation between the parties concerned. However, the future is seen differently, not only by Palestinians and Israelis, but by other nations across the world. The only comprehensive and unequivocal stand which is asserted with a credibility backed by concrete reality, is the one taken by Israel: namely, that undivided Jerusalem must remain Israel's sovereign capital. But will that continue to be accepted by all the other participants? Interesting variants to this option have also been elaborated by Israelis[7] and others.[8] Be that as it may, acceptance will certainly hinge on the proposed solution to two major issues: the method of rule over the Arabs who live in Jerusalem; and the regime that will govern universal access to all religious holy places, of all faiths, in the united city (King Hussein, for example, has spoken about an 'open city').[9]

On the municipal government level, many ideas have been floated which suggest the division of Greater Jerusalem into boroughs like London, or arrondissements like Paris, which would enable neighborhood administrations, whether Arab or Jewish, to manage their daily affairs; while an elected umbrella municipality would continue to govern the metropolitan services common to all: transportation, water, sewerage, etc. Others suggest that the present situation of one unified administration would satisfy all needs if only the Arabs would vote in the elections and send their representatives to the city council. However, due to Palestinian refusal to acquiesce in the present state of affairs – namely of a united city under Israeli rule – the likelihood that they would consent to either of the above suggestions looks minimal, pending a comprehensive solution of the political issue in the context of a permanent and mutually acceptable peace accord between Israel and the Palestinians, who are regarded by many international jurists as the sovereign over East Jerusalem.

Pending the permanent settlement, however, one needs to tackle the question of the holy places which must be regarded as separate from the issue of sovereignty. For, just as the Ministry of Education in Israel has decided not to enforce Israeli curricula on the Arab schools of East Jerusalem, but to allow them to pursue Jordanian curricula, it can do the same with holy places without renouncing one iota of Israel's sovereignty. The problem for the Israeli authorities will be to maintain the famous *status quo* from Ottoman times,[10] but at the same time also maintain equality between the various communities when their religious traditions are in conflict, and allow all disagreements to be settled by courts of law. Israel's law of 1967, which guaranteed the protection of, and free access to, the holy places, is the expression of the firm intent of the Israeli government to ensure that this remains the case. Territorial sovereignty, incidentally, does not necessarily mean that the State of Israel also must exert its jurisdiction over all spheres of life of the inhabitants of East Jerusalem. Education and religious worship are two such spheres; nationality may be another.

Coming back to the Armistice Regime, which was the main focus of this study, does it bear any relevance, residual or otherwise, to the permanent settlement of the question of Jerusalem now under discussion? The most likely point of departure for such an inquiry would seem to be Article XII of the Armistice Agreement between Israel and Jordan, whose second paragraph stated simply that the 'Agreement shall remain in force until a peaceful settlement between the parties is achieved.' The peace treaty concluded between Israel and Jordan in 1994 was certainly a peaceful settlement, and it included a paragraph on the special status accorded to the Hashemites in Jerusalem's Muslim Holy Places. On the other hand, as the Jordanians have renounced their territorial claim to the West Bank and Jerusalem in favor of the Palestinians, does the peace between Jordan and Israel still satisfy the requirement envisaged in the Armistice Agreement?

This question had already been raised during the negotiations between Israel and Egypt at Camp David in 1978. These agreements had encompassed not only the Egyptian–Israeli bilateral peace arrangement, but also a second framework for peace geared to resolve the Palestinian issue at what had come to be known as the 'Autonomy Talks' between Egyptian and Israeli officials (without Palestinian participation). Egypt insisted, in a letter, that Jerusalem was part and parcel of the West Bank, namely the area bound on the west, north and south by the respective portions of the armistice demarcation lines. Israel, in a parallel letter, held its ground, and there the matter rested, since the Autonomy Talks had been stalled in any case. An Israeli international lawyer, Y. Blum, analyzed the question in light of established treaty law whereby 'a material breach of an accord on the part of one side entitles the other side to regard the entire agreement as null and void.' Israel, he maintained, had acted formally in conformity with this rule, inasmuch as it had responded to the Jordanian abrogation of the Armistice Agreement when it launched its onslaught on West Jerusalem, and along the entire demarcation line, on 5 June 1967.[11]

After the Six Day War, the Security Council of the UN, which supervised the armistice agreements between Israel and the Arabs, adopted a new resolution (No. 242) which – while freezing on the ground new cease-fire lines to replace the defunct armistice lines – also made it clear that the new situation was temporary pending the outcome of peace negotiations. This not only rendered the Armistice Regime redundant because inoperative, but created a substitute for it which was to lead back not to the *status quo* of before the war, but to new peace arrangements. This was in effect the signature on the death writ for the Armistice Regime by the very international institution which had devised it in the first place, even though it was never explicitly invalidated. Therefore, subsequent Security Council resolutions regarding Israeli measures affecting Jerusalem do not have to be seen as attempts to revive the armistice but rather as expressions of displeasure at the changes effected by Israel to the status of Jerusalem (Jewish versus Islamic character, Jewish versus Arab demography, and changes in the administration of the city, the state of the holy places and archaeological excavations, etc.)[12]

One also has to remember that the UN components of the armistic bureaucracy have remained in being, notably UNTSO (although not the MACs). One may ask, what does this organization have to do beyond perpetuating its independent status in a place where its primary function is no longer needed? But this will not be the first time that the UN has wasted its limited resources on financing sinecures. Another constant element inherited from the armistice era is the 'Green Line,' which is the former demarcation line between Israel and Jordan and has become the only accepted reference point both within and outside Israel. In Israel there are towns, cities and villages, but beyond the Green Line they are 'settlements' and for some European media they are 'colonies;' west of the former armistice line you are in Israel, and east of it you are on the West Bank, Samaria and Judea – 'occupied territory,' 'liberated territory,' or 'administered area,' are among some of the phrases used.

With both the UN institution extant, and the line it was assumed to have supervised still living in the memories of those on all sides, one should not be surprised if among the arguments advanced against Israel in the context of a permanent solution to the Jerusalem problem, the spectre of the old armistice lines is raised once again. Already, the Palestinians, who insist that East Jerusalem should be their capital, have invoked the boundary that had divided the city during the years of armistice as a reference point for the reapportioning of the territory of the city, even if it is not physically redivided. For the old armistice line remains the sole agreed demarcation between Israel and any Arab authority in Jerusalem, even though it was, supposedly, traced at the start 'without prejudice to future territorial settlements or boundary lines or to claims of either party.'[13] This means that if the Palestinians conclude that they cannot otherwise extract what they want from Israel in permanent settlement negotiations, they are likely to revive the old notion of the demarcation line and demand that it be the basis for the negotiations.

To force the issue, the Palestinians may use measured and controlled violence within the urban area of Jerusalem in order to challenge Israel's firm stand on a united Jerusalem under its exclusive rule. By so doing, they would also seek to confront the Christian world and convince it that Israel is not capable of assuring peace and stability in Jerusalem – the prerequisite for the unhindered flow of Christian pilgrims to the Holy Land. The Palestinians can also invoke the paradox that while prior to 1967 there were occasional disturbances on the armistice demarcation line, peace was guaranteed for the Christians who flocked to their holy places, which were mostly located within Arab-controlled East Jerusalem. Now that the city is entirely under Israeli rule and no demarcation lines exist, the hazards for Christian pilgrims will increase due to Palestinian discontent. According to this logic, it would be better, from their point of view, to restore Arab control (this time Palestinian) of the city under the protective wing of Arafat, so that the new Sophroniuses might enjoy the favors of the new Umar. In this regard, Palestinian and Christian interests converge; did not Arafat himself declare Christ a Palestinian?

In these circumstances the challenge to Israel would be considerable. Patent, uncontrollable violence might attract sympathy for Israel, or at least understanding for its need to quell it; but measured and calculated disturbances, which could be construed by the world as legitimate manifestations of discontent against 'occupation,' would put Israel in an untenable situation. If she responded to the violence by force, she would surely be condemned for a 'disproportionate' reaction against peaceful citizens; if she did not, she would be blamed for her inability to ensure peace, stability and security in the Holy City. Since the outbreak of the Al-Asqa Intifadah in late September 2000 – in which widespread violence engulfed the entire West Bank and Gaza – East Jerusalem has been relatively spared, although it was, ironically, the trigger of the riots. But with no end to violence in sight, things may also get out of hand there.

The plight of Christians in the Muslim world has been well documented,[14] and the Christian world would certainly prefer to have its holy places protected by liberal and democratic Israeli laws than dependent on the whims of some tyrant. However, the matter is not one of cosy idealism but of expedient pragmatism: Christians around the world would rather have a practical arrangement that works, even if it approximates the Armistice Regime of yesteryear, than support the impracticality of Israeli democratic rule which cannot be enforced and cannot ensure the peace. The challenge for

Israel is to move effectively beyond the 1967 Law for the Protection of Holy Places – in coordination with various Christian organizations (including the Vatican)[15] – to develop a broad common denominator for the preventative measures to be adopted to guarantee peace in the holy places, and also to reach an agreement about the necessary measures to restore it, should it be disrupted. Only under such conditions might the Armistice Regime be finally buried and never invoked again.

NOTES

1. See Walter Eytan – the man who negotiated the Armistice Agreement – 'Struggle for Political Status of Jerusalem', p. 20.
2. See Ora Ahimeir (ed.), *Jerusalem: Aspects of Law* (Jerusalem, 1980) [in English and Hebrew]; especially the articles by Y. Bar-Sela and Y. Englard ('The Status of Holy Places in Jerusalem', pp. 4–24).
3. Sarah Kaminker, 'Building Restrictions in East Jerusalem', *Journal of Palestine Studies*, 26, 4 (Summer 1997); also, Kate Maguire, 'The Israelisation of Jerusalem', in *Arab Papers* (London: The Arab Research Centre, 1989).
4. *Israel's Parliamentary Records*, Vol. 49, p. 2420 [Hebrew]; cited by Yehuda Blum, 'The Juridical Status of East Jerusalem', in Ahimeir (ed.), *Aspects of Law*, p. 24.
5. Ruth Lapidoth and Moshe Hirsch, *Jerusalem: Political and Legal Aspects* (Jerusalem: The Jerusalem Institute for Israeli Studies, 1994), p. 5.
6. The story was widely covered and reported by both the Palestinian and Israeli media, written and electronic.
7. See, for example, Moshe Hirsch and Debra Housen-Couriel, *The Jerusalem Problem: Proposals for its Resolution* (Jerusalem: The Jerusalem Institute for Israeli Studies, 1994) [Hebrew]; also, Menachem Klein, *Jerusalem in the Peace Negotiations* (Jerusalem: The Jerusalem Institute for Israeli Studies, 1995) [Hebrew].
8. See, for example, *Jerusalem: City of Universal Peace* [reprinted from *SIDC*, 4, 2 (1971)].
9. Sh. Meir, 'United Jerusalem in Jordanian Eyes', *Intenational Problems*, 19, 3–4 (Autumn 1980), p. 7 [Hebrew].
10. See Englard, 'Holy Places in Jerusalem', p. 4.
11. See Blum, 'The Juridical Status of East Jerusalem', pp. 25–8; also, Y. Blum, 'The Juridical Status of Jerusalem', *Jerusalem Papers on Peace Problems*, 2 (Feb. 1974), pp. 6–32.
12. See Resolution No. 465, dated 1 March 1980; and Resolution No. 467, dated 30 June 1980.
13. Article II of the Armistice Agreement.
14. See Bat Ye'or, *The Dhimmi: Jews and Christians under Islam* (Madison, WI: Fairleigh Dickinson University Press, 1987) and *The Decline of Eastern Christianity under Islam: From Jihad to Dhimmitude* (Madison, WI: Fairleigh Dickinson University Press, 1996).
15. See Aharon Lopez, 'Israel's Relations with the Vatican', *Jerusalem Letter*, 401 (March 1999), pp. 1–28.
16. See Hirsche and Housen-Couriel, *The Jerusalem Question*; also, Klein, *Jerusalem in the Peace Negotiations*.

Appendix 1. Text of the Hashemite Kingdom of Jordan–Israel Armistice Agreement

(Signed in Rhodes, 4 April 1949)

PREAMBLE

The parties to the present agreement:

Responding to the Security Council Resolution on 16 November 1948, calling upon them, as a further provisional measure under Article 40 of the Charter of the United Nations and in order to facilitate the transition from the present truce to permanent peace in Palestine, to negotiate an armistice.

Having decided to enter into negotiations under United Nations' chairmanship concerning the implementation of the Security Council resolution of 16 November 1948: and having appointed representatives empowered to negotiate and conclude an armistice agreement. The undersigned representatives of their respective governments, having exchanged their full powers found to be in good and proper form, have agreed upon the following provisions:

ARTICLE I

With a view to promoting the return of permanent peace in Palestine and in recognition of the importance in this regard of mutual assurances concerning the future military operations of the parties, the following principles which shall be fully observed by both parties during the armistice, are hereby affirmed:

1. The injunction of the Security Council against resort to military force in the settlement of the Palestine question shall henceforth be scrupulously observed by both parties.
2. No aggressive action by the armed forces – land, sea or air – of either party shall be undertaken, planned or threatened against the people or the armed forces of the other; it being understood that the use of the term 'planned' in this context has no bearing on normal staff planning as generally practiced in military organizations.
3. The right of each party to its security and freedom from fear of attack by the armed forces of the other shall be fully respected.
4. The establishment of an armistice between the armed forces of the two parties is accepted as an indispensable step toward the liquidation of armed conflict in Palestine.

ARTICLE II

With a specific view to the implementation of the resolution of the 16 November 1948, the following principles and purposes are affirmed:

1. The principle that no military or political advantage should be gained under the truce ordered by the Security Council is recognized.
2. It is also recognized that no provision of the Agreement shall in any way prejudice the rights, claims and positions of either party hereto in the ultimate peaceful settlement of the Palestine Question. The provisions of this Agreement being dictated exclusively by military considerations.

ARTICLE III

In the pursuance of the foregoing principles and of the resolution of the Security Council of 16 November 1948, a general armistice between the armed forces of the two parties – land, sea and air – is hereby established.

2. No element of the land, sea or air military or paramilitary forces of either party, including non-regular forces, shall commit any warlike or hostile act against the military or paramilitary forces of the other party, or against civilians in territory under the control of that party; shall advance beyond or pass over for any purpose whatsoever the armistice demarcation lines set forth in Articles V and VI of this Agreement; or enter into or pass through the air space of the other party.
3. No warlike act or act of hostility shall be conducted from territory controlled by one of the parties to this agreement against the other party.

ARTICLE IV

1. The lines described in Articles V and VI of this Agreement shall be designated as the Armistice Demarcation Lines and are delineated in pursuance of the purpose and intent of the resolution of the Security Council resolution of 16 November 1948.
2. The basic purpose of the Armistice Demarcation Lines is to delineate the lines beyond which the armed forces of the respective parties shall not move.
3. Rules and regulations of the armed forces of the parties, which prohibit civilians from crossing the fighting lines or entering the area between the lines, shall remain in effect after the signing of this Agreement with application to the Armistice Demarcation Lines defined in Articles V and VI.

ARTICLE V

The Armistice Demarcation Lines for all sectors other than the sector now held by Iraqi forces, shall be as delineated on the Maps in Annex I to this Agreement, and shall be defined as follows:

1. In the sector Kh Deir Arab (MR 1510–1574) to the northern terminus of the lines defined in the 30 November 1948 cease-fire agreement for the Jerusalem area. The Armistice Demarcation Lines shall follow the truce lines as certified by the United Nations Truce Supervision Organization.

2. In the Jerusalem sector, the Armistice Demarcation Lines shall correspond to the lines defined in the 30 November 1948 cease-fire agreement for the Jerusalem area.
3. In the Hebron–Dead Sea sector, the Armistice Demarcation Lines shall be delineated on Map 1 and marked (B) in Annex I to this Agreement.
4. In the sector from a point on the Dead Sea (MR 1925–0958) to the southernmost tip of Palestine, the Armistice Demarcation Line shall be determined by existing military positions as surveyed in March 1949 by United Nations observers, and shall run from north to south as delineated on Map 1 in Annex I to this Agreement.

ARTICLE VI

1. It is agreed that the forces of the Hashemite Jordan Kingdom shall replace the forces of Iraq in the sector now held by the latter forces. The intention of the government of Iraq in this regard having been communicated to the acting mediator in the message of 20 March from the Foreign Minister of Iraq authorizing the delegation of the Hashemite Jordan Kingdom to negotiate for the Iraqi forces and stating that those forces would be withdrawn.
2. The Armistice Demarcation Line for the sector now held by Iraqi forces shall be as delineated on Map 1 in Annex I to this Agreement and marked (A).
3. The Armistice Demarcation Line provided for in paragraph 2 of this Article shall be established in stages, as follows, pending which the existing military lines may be maintained:
    a. In the area west of the road from Baqa to Jaljulia and thence to the east of Kafr Qasim: within five weeks of the date on which the Armistice Agreement is signed.
    b. In the area of Wadi Ara north of the line from Baqa to Zubeiba: within seven weeks of the date on which this Armistice Agreement is signed.
    c. In all other areas of the Iraqi sector: within 15 weeks of the date on which this Armistice Agreement is signed.
4. The Armistice Demarcation Line in the Hebron–Dead Sea sector, referred to in paragraph 3 of Article V of this agreement and marked (B) on Map 1 of Annex I, which involves

substantial deviation from the existing military lines in favor of the forces of the Hashemite Jordan Kingdom, is designed to offset the modifications of the existing military lines in the Iraqi sector set forth in paragraph 3 of this Article.

5. In compensation for the road acquired between Tulkarem and Qalquliya, the government of Israel agrees to pay to the government of the Hashemite Kingdom of Jordan the cost of constructing 20 km of first class new road.

6. Wherever villages may be affected by the establishment of the Armistice Demarcation Line provided for in paragraph 2 of this article, the inhabitants of such villages shall be entitled to maintain, and shall be protected in, their full rights of residence, property and freedom. In the event any of the inhabitants should decide to leave their villages, they shall be entitled to take with them their livestock and other movable property, and to receive without delay full compensation for the land which they have left. It shall be prohibited for Israeli forces to enter or to be stationed in such villages, in which locally recruited Arab police shall be organized and stationed for internal security purposes.

7. The Hashemite Jordan Kingdom accepts responsibility for all Iraqi forces in Palestine.

8. The provisions of this Article shall not be interpreted as prejudicing, in any sense, an ultimate political settlement between the parties to this Agreement.

9. The Armistice Demarcation Lines defined in Articles V and VI of this Agreement are agreed upon by the parties without prejudice to future territorial settlements or boundary lines or to claims of either party relating thereto.

10. Except where otherwise provided, the Armistice Demarcation Lines shall be established, including such withdrawal of forces as may be deemed necessary for this purpose, within ten days from the date on which this Agreement is signed.

11. The Armistice Demarcation Lines defined in this Article and in Article V shall be subject to such rectifications as may be agreed upon by the parties to this Agreement, and all such rectifications shall have the same effect as if they had been incorporated in full in this general armistice agreement.

ARTICLE VII

1. The military forces of the parties to this Agreement shall be limited to defensive forces only in the areas extending ten kilometers from each side of the Armistice Demarction Lines, except where geographical considerations make this impractical, as at the southernmost tip of Palestine and the coastal strip. Defensive forces permissible in each sector shall be as defined in Annex II of this Agreement. In the sector now held by Iraqi forces, calculations in the reduction of forces shall include the number of Iraqi forces in this sector.
2. Reduction of forces to defensive strength in accordance with the preceding paragraph shall be completed within ten days of the establishment of the Armistice Demarcation Lines defined in this Agreement. In the same way the removal of mines from mined roads and areas evacuated by either party, and the transmission of plans showing the location of such minefields to the other party, shall be completed within the same period.
3. The strength of the forces which may be maintained by the parties on each side of the Armistice Lines shall be subject to periodical review with a view toward further reduction of such forces by mutual agreement of the parties.

ARTICLE VIII

1. A Special Committee, composed of two representatives of each party designated by the respective governments, shall be established for the purpose of formulating agreed plans and arrangements designed to enlarge the scope of this Agreement and to effect improvements in its application.
2. The Special Committee shall be organized immediately following the coming into effect of this Agreement and shall direct its attention to the formulation of agreed plans and arrangements for such matters as either party may submit to it, which, in any case, shall include the following, on which agreement in principle already exists: free movement of traffic on vital roads, including the Bethlehem and Latrun–Jerusalem roads; resumption of the normal functioning of the cultural and humanitarian institutions on Mount Scopus and free access thereto; free access to the holy places and cultural institutions,

and use of the cemetery on the Mount of Olives; resumption of operation of the Latrun pumping station; provision of electricity for the Old City; and resumption of operation of the railroad to Jerusalem.

3. The Special Committee shall have exclusive competence over such matters as may be referred to it. Agreed plans and arrangements formulated by it may provide for the exercise of supervisory functions by the Mixed Armistice Commission established in Article XI.

ARTICLE IX

Agreements reached between the parties subsequent to the signing of this Armistice Agreement relating to such matters as further reduction of forces as contemplated in paragraph 3 of Article VII. Future adjustments of the Armistice Demarcation Lines. And plans and agreements formulated by the Special Agreement established in Article VIII. Shall have the same force and effect as the provisions of this Agreement and shall be equally binding upon the parties.

ARTICLE X

An exchange of prisoners of war having been effected by special arrangement between the parties prior to the signing of this Agreement. No further arrangements on this matter are required, except that the Mixed Armistice Commission shall undertake to re-examine whether there may be prisoners of war belonging to either party which were not included in the previous exchange. In the event that prisoners of war shall be found to exist, the Mixed Armistice Commission shall arrange for an early exchange of such prisoners. The parties to this Agreement undertake to afford full cooperation to the Mixed Armistice Commission in its discharge of this responsibility.

ARTICLE XI

1. The execution of the provisions of this Agreement, with the exception of such matters as fall within the exclusive

competence of the Special Committee established in Article VIII, shall be supervised by a Mixed Armistice Commission composed of five members, of whom each party to this Agreement shall designate two, and whose chairman shall be the United Nations Chief of Staff of the Truce Supervision Organization or a senior officer from the observer personnel of that organization designated by him following consultation with both parties to this Agreement.

2. The Mixed Armistice Commission shall maintain its headquarters at Jerusalem and shall hold its meetings at such places and at such times as it may deem necessary for the effective conduct of its work.

3. The Mixed Armistice Commission shall be convened in its first meeting by the United Nations Chief of Staff of the Truce Supervision Organization not later than one week following the signing of this Agreement.

4. Decisions of the Mixed Armistice Commission, to the extent possible, shall be based on the principle of unanimity. In the absence of unanimity, decisions shall be taken by majority vote of the members of the commission present and voting.

5. The Mixed Armistice Commission shall formulate its own rules of procedure. Meetings shall be held only after due notice to the members by the chairman. The quorum for its meetings shall be a majority of its members.

6. The commission shall be empowered to employ observers, who may be from among the military organizations of the parties or from the military personnel of the United Nations, or from both, in such numbers as may be considered essential to the performance of its functions. In the event United Nations observers should be employed, they shall remain under the command of the United Nations Chief of Staff of the Truce Supervision Organization. Assignments of a general or special nature given to United Nations observers attached to the Mixed Armistice Commission shall be subject to approval by the United Nations Chief of Staff or his designated representative on the commission, whichever is serving as chairman.

7. Claims or complaints presented by either party relating to the application of this Agreement shall be referred immediately to the Mixed Armistice Commission through its chairman. The commission shall take such action on all such claims or

complaints by means of its observation and investigation machinery as it may deem appropriate, with a view to equitable and mutually satisfactory settlement.

8. Where interpretation of the meaning of a particular provision of this Agreement, other than the Preamble and Articles I and II, is at issue, the commission's interpretation shall prevail. The commission, in its discretion and as the need arises, may from time to time recommend to the parties modifications in the provisions of this Agreement.

9. The Mixed Armistice Commission shall submit to both parties reports on its activities as frequently as it may consider necessary. A copy of each such report shall be presented to the Security General of the United Nations for transmission to the appropriated organ or agency of the United Nations.

10. Members of the commission and its observers shall be accorded such freedom of movement and access in the area covered by this Agreement as the commission may deem to be necessary, provided that when such decisions of the commission are reached by a majority vote, United Nations observers only shall be employed.

11. The expenses of the commission, other than those relating to the United Nations observers, shall be apportioned to equal shares between the two parties to this Agreement.

ARTICLE XII

1. The present Agreement is not subject to ratification and shall come into force immediately upon being signed.

2. This Agreement, having been negotiated and concluded in pursuance of the resolution of the Security Council of 16 November 1948, calling for the establishment of an armistice in order to eliminate the threat to the peace in Palestine and to facilitate the transition from the present truce to permanent peace in Palestine, shall remain in force until a peaceful settlement between the parties is achieved, except as provided in paragraph 3 of this Article.

3. The parties to this Agreement may, by mutual consent, revise this Agreement or any of its provisions, or may suspend its application, other than Articles I and III, at any time. In the absence of mutual agreement and after this Agreement has been

in effect for one year from the date of its signature, either of the parties may call upon the Security General of the United Nations to convoke a conference of representatives of the two parties for the purpose of reviewing, revising, or suspending any of the provisions of this Agreement other than Articles I and III. Participation in such conference shall be obligatory upon the parties.

4. If the conference provided for in paragraph 3 of this Article does not result in agreed solution of a point in dispute, either party may bring the matter before the Security Council of the United Nations for the relief sought, on the grounds that this Agreement has been concluded in pursuance of Security Council action toward the end of achieving peace in Palestine.

5. This Agreement is signed in quintuplicate, of which one copy shall be retained by each party, two copies communicated to the Security General of the United Nations for transmission to the Security Council and to the Conciliation Commission on Palestine, and one copy to the United Nations Acting Mediator on Palestine.

Done at Rhodes, Island of Rhodes, Greece etc.

Appendix 2. Annex to 7 July 1948 Agreement on Mount Scopus

Pending the proposed negotiation of a new comprehensive agreement covering the demilitarized zone of Mount Scopus and at the specific direction of the Senior United Nations Observer in Jerusalem, it is agreed as an interim measure that the terms of the Agreement of 7 July 1948, regarding Mount Scopus shall be interpreted as follows:

1. The United Nations Observers shall arrange for the relief of 50 percent of the Jewish personnel on Mount Scopus during the first and third weeks of each month.
2. The United Nations Observers shall arrange a supply convoy to the Jewish personnel on Mount Scopus during both the first and third weeks of the month.

Signed in the presence of the United Nations Observer and the Security Council Truce Commission on this 30th day of November 1948.

Lt Colonel Moshe Dayan
Pierre Landy, French Consul
For the Chairman of the
Security Council
Truce Commission

Lt Colonel Abdullah el Tel
Colonel Roger T. Carleson,
USMC
Senior United Nations Military
Observer, Jerusalem

Appendix 3. Area Commanders' Arrangement: Jerusalem and Vicinity

(Jerusalem, February 1955)

1. The purpose of this arrangement is to prevent, if possible, or in any case to suppress immediately all outbreaks of firing and other hostile acts in the Jerusalem area.
2. The area covered by this arrangement is bounded by the grid lines NS 168, 175, EW 126, 135.
3. The Hashemite Kingdom of Jordan and Israel agree to the arrangement:
   a. That a senior military or police officer will be designated to have full control of all military, paramilitary or police personnel detailed to the defence of this area.
   b. That only well-trained and disciplined military or police personnel will be employed in the first line of the defensive organization in this area.
   c. That sentries, police guards, etc., will have strict orders not to fire unless by orders of an officer or if they are in danger of attack by superior numbers.
   d. That the designated senior officers will have direct telephone communication through which they may speak to each other to discuss and settle questions regarding the maintenance of peace in Jerusalem.
   e. That the Chief of Staff of the United Nations Truce Supervision Organization, or such other United Nations Military Observer as he may nominate to act on his behalf, may communicate with the designated officers and call for an informal meeting in case of firing or other disturbances.
   f. That the senior officers responsible, on receiving any report

of firing or other hostile acts or threat thereof, will take immediate action to stop the firing, or put an end to other disturbances.

g. That each senior officer, when absent from his command headquarters, will be represented by an officer having full authority to act on his behalf.

Bibliography

DOCUMENTS

The Hashemite Kingdom of Jordan–Israel Armistice Agreement (1949).
Report by COS UNTSO to Security Council (19 June 1954).
Security Council Official Records, Fourth Year (1949).
Security Council Official Records, Meeting No. 517 (30 October 1950).
Security Council Resolution (11 August 1949).
Security Council Resolution (November 1967).
Security Council Resolution 465 (1 March 1980).
Security Council Resolution 467 (30 June 1980).
UN Documents: S/714, S/727, S/773, S/801, S/902, S/1070, S/1357, S/1376, S/1794, S/1907, S/2048, S/2485, S/2833, S/3139, S/3180, S/3252, S/3278, S/3670.
UN General Assembly Recommendation (11 December 1948).

ISRAEL DEFENCE FORCES ARCHIVES

Ben-Gurion, David, *Diary*. [Hebrew]

ISRAEL STATE ARCHIVES

A Memorandum from the Director of Armistice Affairs to the Prime Minister (22 March 1965).
Coded dispatch from the Director General of the Foreign Ministry to the Israeli Embassy in Paris (16 October 1952).
Directives to the Delegation of Israel for Negotiations with Transjordan (undated).

Eban to the Foreign Ministry (29 January 1952).

Foreign Policy Documents, No. 15 (9 May 1949), No. 70 (10 June 1949), No. 83 (12 March 1951), No. 113 (1 July, 1949), No. 220 (17 August 1949), and No. 267 (3 April 1949).

Israel's Parliamentary Records, Vol. 49, p. 2420.

Israel's Press Office Release (25 January 1950).

Letter from General Odd Bull to the Chief of Armistice Affairs (18 January 1965).

Letter from General Burns to the Foreign Office (11 September 1956).

Memorandum by Shiloah to Shertok (4 March 1949), and the response thereto (5 March 1949).

Report by Colonel Caleff from the General Assembly (undated).

Report of a meeting between Foreign Ministry officials and the Prime Minister of Jordan (23 February 1951).

Report of meeting between the Director General of the Foreign Ministry and three representatives from the USA, Britain and France (2 July 1954).

Report of talk between Foreign Minister Sharett and Ambassador Davis (23 January 1952).

Report of the Israeli Representative to the Special Committee to the Foreign Ministry (9 January 1951).

NEWSPAPERS

The Jerusalem Post, 1950–66.
Ha'aretz, 1950–66

ARTICLES

Eytan, Walter, 'The Struggle for the Political Status of Jerusalem', in *Monthly Survey*, 10 (October 1984), pp. 15–21. [Hebrew]

Kaminker, Sarah, 'Building Restrictions in East Jerusalem', *Journal of Palestine Studies*, 26, 4 (Summer 1997), pp. 1–30.

Lopez, Aharon, 'Israel's Relations with the Vatican', *Jerusalem Letter*, 401, (1 March, 1999), pp. 1–28.

Meir, Sh. 'United Jerusalem in Jordanian Eyes', *International Problems*, 19 (Autumn 1980), pp. 1–28. [Hebrew]

BOOKS

Abdallah, King, *Memoirs* (London: Philip Groves, 1950). [Translated into Hebrew under the title *Soul Searching*, Amman, 1951]

Ahimeir, Ora (ed.), *Jerusalem: Aspects of Law* (Jerusalem: The Jerusalem Institute for Israeli Studies, 1980).

Bat Ye'or, *The Dhimmi: Jews and Christians under Islam* (Madison, WI: Fairleigh Dickinson University Press, 1987).

Bat Ye'or, *The Decline of Eastern Christianity under Islam: From Jihad to Dhimmitude* (Madison, WI: Fairleigh Dickinson University Press, 1996).

Bernadotte, Count Folke, *To Jerusalem* (London: Hodder and Stoughton, 1951).

Blum, Yehuda, 'The Juridical Status of Jerusalem', in Ahimeir (ed.) *Jerusalem Papers on Peace Problems* (1974), pp. 1–32.

Blum, Yehuda, 'The Juridical Status of East Jerusalem', in Ahimeir, *Jerusalem Papers on Peace*, pp. 24–8.

Brooks, David, *Preface to Peace* (Washington, DC: Public Affairs Press, 1964).

Bull, Odd, *War and Peace in the Middle East* (London: Leo Cooper, 1973).

Caplan, Neil, *Futile Diplomacy*, Vol. 2 (London: Frank Cass, 1986).

Churchill, Winston Jr, *The Six Day War* (London: Heinemann and Penguin, 1967).

Collins, Larry and Lapierre, Dominique, *O Jerusalem* (London: Grafton Books,1984).

Dayan, Moshe, *Milestones* (Tel Aviv: Dvir Publishers, 1976). [Hebrew]

Englard, Itzhak, 'The Status of the Holy Places in Jerusalem', in Ahimeir, *Jerusalem Papers on Peace*, pp. 4–7.

Gilbert, Martin, *Jerusalem in the Twentieth Century* (London: Pimlico, 1996).

Glubb, John Bagot, *A Soldier with Arabs* (London: Hodder and Stoughton, 1957).

Hirsch, Moshe and Housen-Couriel, Debra, *The Jerusalem Problem: Proposals for its Resolution* (Jerusalem: The Jerusalem Center for Israeli Studies, 1994). [Hebrew]

Israeli, Raphael, *Palestinians Between Israel and Jordan* (New York: Praeger, 1991).

Itzhaki, Aryeh, *Latrun: The Battle for the Road to Jerusalem* (Jerusalem: Cana Publishers, 1982). [Hebrew]

Klein, Menachem, *Jerusalem in the Peace Negotiations* (Jerusalem: The Jerusalem Institute for Israeli Studies, 1995). [Hebrew]

Lapidoth, Ruth and Hirsch, Moshe, *Jerusalem: Political and Legal Aspects* (Jerusalem: The Jerusalem Institute for Israeli Studies, 1994).

Laqueur, Walter, *The Road to War* (Harmondsworth: Penguin Books 1968).

Lie, Trygve, *In the Cause of Peace* (New York: Macmillan, 1954).

Lorch, Netan'el, *The Edge of the Sword* (London: Putnam and Co., 1961).

Maguire, Kate, 'The Israelisation of Jerusalem', in *Arab Papers* (London: The Arab Research Centre, 1989), pp. 1–30.

Medzini, Meiron (ed.), *Israel's Foreign Relations: Selected Documents*, 12 Vols (Jerusalem: The Israel State Archives).

Muatawi, Samir, *Jordan in the 1967 War* (Cambridge: Cambridge University Press, 1987).

Narkiss, Uzi, *The Liberation of Jerusalem* (London: Vallentine Mitchell, 1983). [Hebrew edn – Tel Aviv: Am Oved, 1975]

Narkiss, Uzi, *Soldier of Jerusalem* (Tel Aviv: Israel Ministry of Defense, 1991). [Hebrew]

Rabinovich, Itamar, *The Road not Taken* (Jerusalem: Keter Publishers, 1991). [Hebrew]

Rivlin, Benjamin (ed.) *Ralph Bunche: The Man and His Time* (New York: Holmes and Meir, 1990).

Rosenne, Shabtai, *Israel's Armistice Agreements with the Arab States* (Tel Aviv: Blumstein Bookstores, 1951).

Shlaim, Avi, *Collusion Across the Jordan* (Oxford: Clarendon Press, 1988).

Shueftan, Dan, *The Jordanian Option* (Tel Aviv: Yad Tabenkin, 1987) [Hebrew]

Vilna'y, Ze'ev, *Israel Guide* (Jerusalem: Central Press, 1960).

Index

119, 128, 148, 161, 174, 180, 183ff., 201,
204
Husseini Clan, 117, 122; Abd al-Qader,
117, 142; Haj Amin, 117, 138, 141, 172

immigrants, 1–3, 6, 59, 112, 114, 123,
138–40, 151
incidents, xi, 1ff., 12, 37, 54–6, 59ff. 72ff.,
77ff., 88ff., 116, 121, 128–30, 148, 155,
160–2, 164–5, 168–9, 182ff., 195, 201
infiltrators/marauders, 54, 66–7, 80, 83–4,
97, 112–13, 115
Intercontinental Hotel, 107, 118
internationalization/*corpus separatum*, xii,
16, 51, 81, 141–3, 149, 165, 172ff., 192
Intifadah, 65, 192, 201, 208
Iraq, 13, 15, 17, 31, 37–8, 137, 139, 167,
186–7, 212–15
Iraqi Revolution, 83
Irgun, 100
Isawiyya, 20, 66, 69, 71ff., 126ff., 129, 156,
162, 171
Israel, 28, 36, 38, 79, 110, 200 (*see also*
Jews); State Archives, xii, 59, 75, 87–8
Israeli, Defense Forces, xii, 19, 21, 25, 78,
82, 99–100, 115, 121, 146, 166, 168, 182,
184ff., 200; District Commissioner, 7;
festivals 159, 183 (*see also* holidays);
Government Offices, 113; President,
171; Prime Minister, 4, 52, 80, 83, 161,
183, 187, 191; Defense Ministry, 4, 111,
191; Foreign Ministry, xii, xiii, 32, 53, 87,
160–1 166, 174, 176–7; Provisional
Government, 17; representative to the
United Nations, 58, 84, 104
Israeli, Captain R., 63, 90, 93
Israeli, Abraham, 93
Israelites, 177
Italy, 174
Italian Hospice, 123

Jabal al Mukabbar, 64, 133
Jaffa, Gate, 3, 8, 129–30; Street /Road, 8,
124, 139
Jaljulya, 213
Jenin, 119, 198
Jericho, 119, 203; Conference, 26
Jerusalem, xii, 8, 16, 19, 21, 24, 52, 58, 72;
Archives, xii; Basic Law, 199ff.; battles,
5, 1–25, 179–93; Corridor, 18, 111, 146,
148, 200; divided, xii, 5–6, 8–9, 19, 47,
92, 96, 109, 150, 196, 201, 204; District
Commissioner, 7; East/Arab, 91–2, 95,
99,103, 107–8, 110, 113, 116ff., 122–3,
131, 133, 144–5, 161, 167, 172–4, 176,
183, 190ff., 194ff., 202; Greater, 204;
Jewish Quarter in, 16–17, 21, 24,
116–18, 120, 130; Kingdom of, 203;
Municipality of, 1, 3, 22, 110ff., 120, 124;

Old City, 1–3, 6–8, 16–17, 19–24, 40–1,
54, 57, 61, 80, 85, 95, 116–17, 120, 123ff.,
129ff., 130–1, 142, 146, 157, 161, 171, 173,
180, 189, 190ff., 216; unification of, xi,
xii, 22, 158, 175, 194ff.; united, xii, 150,
158, 194ff., 204, 208; Western/Jewish, 7,
16–17, 19, 21–4, 65, 80, 85–6, 91–2, 103,
107ff., 117–18, 123ff., 129–31, 134, 142,
144–5, 147–8, 150, 172, 176, 185ff., 194ff.
Jews, xii, 1, 7, 13, 23–4, 101, 111, 138, 167;
Iranian, 3
Jewish, Agency, 12, 15, 28, 140;
community, 15, 18, 117, 149; Forces, 19,
142–4; minorities, 168; National Home,
15, 138–9, 149; Quarter, 16-17, 21, 130,
142, 144, 180 (*see also* Jerusalem); State/
entity, 14, 26–7, 51, 119, 142–4, 149
Jezreel Valley, 14
Jihad, 203–4
Johannesburg, 203–4
John Paul II, Pope, 198
Jordan, xi, 1–3, 5–7, 9, 23–4, 31, 36, 42, 46,
50–1, 60, 80, 84, 128–9, 131, 136 143ff.,
159–60, 166, 179ff., 201 (*see also*
Hashemite Kingdom/House); Foreign
Ministry, 53; history, 11ff.; Legion, 2–3,
5, 12, 21, 23, 82, 84, 118, 121, 134, 184ff.
(*see also* Arab Legion); King of, 161, 174
(*see also* Hussein and Abdallah); Prime
Minister of, 159–60, 179; River, 12, 14,
26, 119, 138, 143, 147, 150, 186, 201
Joshua, 93
Judaism, 23, 201 (*see also* Jews)
Judea, 207
Judean desert, 126; highlands, 175
Jum'a, Sa'ad, 184
Justice, 51, 71

Kafr Qassem, 213
Katamon, 1, 5, 13, 24, 112
Katz, Yitzhak, 9
Kaukji, Fawzi, 142–4
Khalidi Clan, 117
Khan-al Ahmar, 119
Khirbat Deir Arab, 212
Khurva (Synagogue), 24
Kidron, 87
King David Hotel, 7, 21, 130; Street, 130;
Tower/Citadel, 8, 129–30
Kiryat Yovel, 113
Kishleh, 130
Knesset, 46, 111, 113, 177, 199, 200
Kollek, Teddy, 1–2

Landy, Pierre, 220
Last Supper, 7, 131
Latin America, 116
Latrun, 17, 19, 40, 92, 144–5, 187, 190–1,
215–16